Daily devotionals are wonderful aids, ensuring that we stay close to our God and deep in his word. What better guide to lead us to the throne of God each day than the Reformer, John Calvin. Mostly taken from his commentaries, Scott Manetsch (a world-renowned Calvin scholar) has picked selective passages that highlight the scripture passage and urge us on to 'run the race that is set before us'. Keep this book beside your favorite armchair and allow the sixteenth-century Reformer to guide and instruct you. I can promise that if you do, dipping in and out of this devotional as life's business allows, you will be greatly blessed.

DEREK W. H. THOMAS
Former Senior Minister, First Presbyterian Church,
Columbia, South Carolina.

John Calvin: Daily Readings is a superb collection of readings drawn from Calvin's commentaries, sermons, and treatises. Scott Manetsch's choices cover everything one could want to see: Calvin's thinking on God's provision, the church, prayer, the brevity of life, the resurrection, suffering, temptation, heaven, etc. Whether one knows Calvin well or not at all, they will be delighted with this volume. In particular, for the novice who might feel intimidated about the prospect of picking up something as daunting as Calvin's *Institutes of the Christian Religion*, Manetsch's volume is perfect. But also for someone who's been reading Calvin for decades, the book is such a pleasure to peruse. The readings do a fantastic job of showing why Calvin is regarded as such a blessing to the church. They are deeply thoughtful, accessible, crystal clear, and uplifting. Manetsch is to be commended for producing such a first-rate introduction to Calvin's theology and spirituality.

JON BALSERAK
Author, *Calvinism: A Very Short Introduction*.

JOHN CALVIN
DAILY READINGS

Edited by
Scott M. Manetsch

Scripture quotations are from *The Holy Bible, English Standard Version (ESV), Anglicised Version*, and used by kind permission of Crossway and Harper Collins. All rights reserved.

Copyright © Scott M. Manetsch 2025

Print ISBN: 978-1-5271-1257-5
E-book ISBN: 978-1-5271-1332-9

Published in 2025
in the
Christian Heritage Imprint
by
Christian Focus Publications,
Geanies House, Fearn, Tain, Ross-shire,
IV20 1TW, Scotland, UK
www.christianfocus.com

Cover design by Daniel van Straaten

Printed and bound by Imprint Press, India

INTRODUCTION

Interpreting and proclaiming God's Word was at the center of John Calvin's vocation as a Christian pastor and religious reformer. Calvin's commitment to the ministry of the Word was already on display in his preface to his cousin Pierre Olivétan's French Bible published in the summer of 1535. In his preface, Calvin acknowledged that Olivétan's Bible was illegal in that it lacked official approval from the Catholic king, Francis I; but even so, 'the King of Kings is the guarantor of the privilege [to publish it]!' Calvin went on to insist that all people, men and women alike, were invited to read and benefit from God's Word, no matter their social rank or training. After all, 'since the Lord has chosen prophets for himself from the ranks of shepherds [and] apostles from the boats of fisherman, why should he not even now condescend to choose similar disciples?' The importance of making God's Word accessible to everyone was thus central to Calvin's concerns: 'But I desire only this, that the faithful people be permitted to hear their God speaking and to learn from his teaching.' With this striking statement, Calvin articulated a vision for ministry that served as his lodestar for the next three decades.

John Calvin was born in the cathedral town of Noyon, France on July 10, 1509 to devout Catholic parents, Gérard and Jeanne Lefranc, who determined early on that their gifted son should prepare for the priesthood. In 1523, Calvin was sent to Paris to begin his formal education, first at the Collège de la Marche, and then at the more prestigious Collège de Montaigu, where he earned his arts degree in 1528. At that moment, a sudden change occurred in Calvin's life that altered the trajectory of his future plans: Gérard fell out of favor with the bishop of Noyon, and decided that his son should pursue a career in law rather than theology. Hence, in 1528, Calvin dutifully matriculated at the University of Orléans – and later moved on to the University of Bourges – where he received legal training from two of the great jurists of the age. More importantly, during this period Calvin became a partisan of French humanist culture that championed the study of the humane letters (*studia humanitatis*), the cultivation of eloquence, and the retrieval and mastery of classical texts in their original languages of Latin, Greek, and Hebrew. Central to the humanists' concern was to glean wisdom from these ancient sources for the purpose of fostering renewal in church and society in sixteenth-century Europe. Though Calvin earned his license in law in 1531, his devotion to the humane letters now took priority. He moved to Paris and associated with a group of reform-minded humanists as he read the church fathers, studied the Greek New Testament, began to learn Hebrew, and composed his first published work, a commentary on Seneca's *De Clementia* (1532). In his religious outlook, Calvin was becoming increasingly critical of the Catholic church and calling for evangelical reforms according to the Word of God.

Calvin's sympathies for religious reform became apparent on November 1, 1533 when his boyhood friend, the newly appointed university rector, Nicholas Cop, delivered an inaugural address that espoused controversial Protestant themes. Rumors circulated that Calvin himself had assisted Cop in writing the inflammatory speech. With the authorities in pursuit, Calvin was forced to flee Paris and seek safety in the south of France, under the protective wing of the reform-minded princess Marguerite d'Angoulême (the sister of Francis I). Later in the spring of 1534, he returned to Noyon, his boyhood home, and resigned the two church stipends (*benefices*) that he had held since childhood. Calvin was strategically severing ties of loyalty with the traditional church. Many years later, Calvin spoke cryptically of the 'sudden conversion' (*subita conversio*) to teachableness that he experienced during these formative years. Most likely, this growing teachableness emerged from the influence of French humanism, the writings of Protestant reformers like Martin Luther, and Calvin's own study of the biblical text. By 1535, Calvin had decisively broken from the Catholic church of his youth and found refuge in the Protestant city of Basel. It was there, in 1536, that he published the first edition of the theological text that would make him famous, the *Institutes of the Christian Religion* (1536; final Latin edition, 1559).

No one could have predicted that John Calvin's life story would become intertwined with the history of the Reformation in Geneva. The human agent responsible for this twist of providence was a fiery reformer named Guillaume Farel who, in July 1536, confronted John Calvin as he passed through Geneva on his way to Strasbourg. From Farel's perspective, Calvin was the perfect candidate to provide theological leadership for a fledgling church that had only recently escaped the tyranny of the papal religion. Calvin later described this famous encounter with unusual flare:

> Farel, who burned with an extraordinary zeal to advance the gospel, immediately strained every nerve to detain me. And after having learned that my heart was set upon devoting myself to private studies, and finding that he gained nothing by entreaties, he proceeded to utter an imprecation that God would curse my retirement, and the tranquility of the studies which I sought, if I should withdraw and refuse to give assistance, when the necessity was so urgent. By this imprecation I was so stricken with terror, that I desisted from the journey which I had undertaken; but sensible of my natural bashfulness and timidity, I would not bring myself under obligation to discharge any particular office.

Fearing God's judgment, a timid Calvin agreed to remain in Geneva – a second decisive change in his life circumstances. With the exception of a three-year hiatus in Strasbourg from 1538–41, John Calvin served the Genevan church as a refugee pastor, preacher, theologian, and founder of the Genevan Academy until his death in 1564. His theological precision and commitment to moral discipline transformed the Genevan church into a reformed bastion that attracted the praise of foreign visitors, including the Englishman William Whittingham, who in the early 1550s praised the republic as the 'mirror and model of true religion and true piety.' Though Calvin and his wife Idelette de Bure had no children who survived infancy, the Genevan reformer became the spiritual father of countless numbers of students and pastors throughout Europe who looked to him for religious guidance and theological inspiration.

John Calvin's ministry in Geneva was saturated in God's Word. More than thirty sermons were preached each week in Geneva's three urban churches, with three preaching services conducted on Sundays, and weekday sermons beginning as early as 4:00 a.m. (for servants and maids). As one of five or six ministers in the city, Calvin regularly preached twice on Sundays, and every day of the week on alternative weeks – totaling around 18–20 sermons each month. This sometimes involved very lengthy sermon series: between July 1556 and September 1559, for example, Calvin preached 343 sermons on Isaiah alone. In addition to these preaching services, Calvin and his colleagues also led a public Bible study (known as the *Congrégation*) intended for ministers, theological students, and interested lay persons every Friday morning. And, on top of it all, Calvin routinely delivered biblical lectures each week to theological students in the city and Academy. In time, many of these lectures were revised and published as full-length commentaries on Scripture. By the time of his death in 1564, Calvin had published commentaries on every book of the New Testament (except 2 and 3 John and Revelation), and roughly half of the Old Testament.

Clearly, interpreting and explaining God's Word was central to Calvin's vision of ministry. But why was this so? For the Genevan reformer, holy Scripture was the timeless, infallible voice of God speaking to His people. The proclamation of the Christian gospel, as announced in Scripture and illumined through the Holy Spirit, was the power of God for salvation, capable of tenderizing and transforming even the hardest of human hearts. Scripture also provided an authoritative guide for living the Christian life as well as a spiritual weapon to vanquish Satan and his minions. Calvin vividly described the power of God's Word in a memorable passage from the *Institutes*:

> Here, then, is the sovereign power with which the pastors of the church ... ought to be endowed. That is that they may dare boldly to do all things by God's Word; may compel all worldly power, glory, wisdom, and exaltation to yield to and obey his majesty; supported by his power, may command all from the highest even to the last; may build up Christ's household and cast down Satan's; may feed the sheep and drive away the wolves; may instruct and exhort the teachable; may accuse, rebuke, and subdue the rebellious and stubborn; may bind and loose; finally, if need be, may launch thunderbolts and lightnings; but do all things in God's Word.

Calvin's final years in Geneva were difficult ones, as he watched his beloved France descend into civil war and as he battled a variety of illnesses, including migraine headaches, kidney stones, gout, and tuberculosis. He preached his final sermon in early February 1564; thereafter he remained bedridden, corresponding with friends, seeing occasional visitors, praying and often groaning 'Lord, how long?' In his last will and testament, dated April 25, 1564, Calvin thanked God for rescuing him from the 'pit of idolatry' and for granting him salvation in 'the light of his gospel.' In this testament he also reaffirmed his unwavering commitment to his vocation as a gospel minister: 'I have sought, according to the measure of grace given to me, to teach his Word in all its purity, whether by sermons or in writings, and faithfully to expound Holy Scripture.' Calvin died a month later, on May 27, at the age of fifty-four. His colleague and friend Theodore Beza reported Calvin's death with this fitting tribute: '[A]t the very same moment that day, the sun set and the greatest light that was in this world for the good of the church of God was taken away to heaven. We can truly say that in this one man God has been pleased to demonstrate to us in our day the way to live well and to die well.' To the very end of his life, Calvin remained a faithful minister of the gospel and instructor of the Word of God.

* * * * * * * * *

This present devotional booklet offers a sample of the riches of John Calvin's interpretation of Scripture. The reader will find here choice selections from Calvin's commentaries, sermons, catechisms, prayers, and the *Institutes*, drawn from throughout his career as a pastor and reformer in Geneva. The majority of selections are drawn from Calvin's commentaries, as they appear in the nineteenth-century English translation provided by the Calvin Translation Society. The editor has taken the liberty to edit lightly these translations for clarity in accordance with modern usage. In addition, this devotional offers a number of selections from modern English editions of Calvin's *Institutes* (1536 and 1559) and his first *Catechism* (1538). Finally, the editor is responsible for the translations of Calvin's French prayers and sermons presented in this volume, based on *La forme des prières ecclésiastiques*, the *Calvini Opera* and the *Supplementa Calviniana*.

This devotional booklet has several features intended to enhance its use. First, the editor reproduces five prayers drawn from Calvin's liturgy, intended to be recited as the believer awakens in the morning, works during the day, dines at the table, and prepares to retire at night. Readers may want to incorporate these beautiful prayers into their devotional life from time to time. Second, given the variable dates of Easter, the editor has included seven undated devotions addressing Christ's passion and resurrection to be used during holy week. These Easter devotions are inserted between the readings for March 31 and April 1.

A host of people deserve my gratitude for their assistance with this project. First, thanks are in order to the editors of Christian Focus publishers for inviting me to create this booklet, and for their expertise in bringing it to publication. Second, I am deeply grateful to my research assistants, Michael Jones, Bridget Jefferies, and especially Carl Johnson for reading multiple drafts of this booklet and helping me locate devotionally rich material. My sincere thanks to each one of you. Finally, I would like to express my appreciation to several thousand students that I've had the privilege to know and teach, and who have enriched my life, over the past quarter-century that I have served on the faculty of Trinity Evangelical Divinity School. Their perceptive questions and rich insights over the years have significantly shaped my understanding of Christian history and the Reformation era. This small volume is dedicated to them with my deep affection.

SCOTT MANETSCH
July 2025

CALVIN'S DAILY PRAYERS

Morning Prayer: Our God, Father, and Savior, since you have been pleased to give us the grace to come through the night to this new day; please now also grant this favor, that we may employ it entirely in your service, that we may not think, say, or do anything except to please you and obey your good will; so that in this way all our efforts may be for the glory of your name and the edification of our neighbors. And as you have been pleased to make your sun shine upon the earth to give us physical light, be pleased also to grant the light of your Spirit to illumine our understanding and hearts to direct us in the right path of your righteousness. Thus, whatever we endeavor to do, may our chief purpose and intention always be to walk in the fear of you, to serve and honor you, resting all our good and prosperity only on your blessing, so as to do nothing except what is pleasing to you. Moreover, even as we are laboring so hard for our bodies and the present life, may we always keep our eyes fixed above, on the heavenly life, which you have promised your children. May it please you to be our protector in body and soul, strengthening us against all the temptations of the devil, and delivering us from all the dangers that could afflict us. And since it is nothing to begin well if one does not persevere, please receive us into your holy guidance, not only for this present day, but for our entire lives, daily continuing and increasing your grace toward us until you have brought us to full union with your Son Jesus Christ our Lord, who is the true light of our souls.... We pray for all these things in the name of your Son our Savior Jesus Christ. Amen. [La forme des prières ecclésiastiques (1561), 181-183]

Prayer for Daily Work: Our good God, Father and Savior, since you have been pleased to command us to work to provide for our needs, may you by your grace so bless our labor that your blessings may extend to us, without which we cannot continue to live. And may your favor serve as a witness to your goodness and help, that by this we may know the fatherly care you have for us. Moreover, O Lord, please empower us by your Holy Spirit, so that we may faithfully exercise our position and vocation, without any fraud or deception; may we devote ourselves to following your commands rather than satisfying our own lust for gain. And if it pleases you to prosper our labor, may you also give us the heart to help those who are in poverty, according to the ability that you have given us – but without wishing to set ourselves above those who have not received such generosity from you. And where you choose to give us greater poverty and destitution than our flesh would like, please O Lord give us the grace to recognize that you always nourish us by your goodness, so that we may not be tempted to defy you. But may we wait patiently for you to fill us with your spiritual gifts, so that we may always have greater reason and occasion to thank you, and to rest entirely in your goodness alone. Hear us, Father of all mercy, through Jesus Christ your Son, our Lord. Amen. [La forme des prières ecclésiastiques (1561), 54-56]

Prayer Before a Meal: 'The eyes of all look to you, Lord, and you give them food in due season. When you open your hand, they receive it and are satisfied with good things.' (Ps. 145:15-16). O Lord, in whom lies the abundance of all good things, extend your blessing to us, your poor servants, and sanctify to us the gifts which we receive from your bounty, that we may use them in a sober and holy manner according to your good will. By this means may we recognize you as the Father and Author of all goodness, always seeking primarily the spiritual bread of your word, with which our souls are eternally nourished by Jesus Christ, your Son, our Lord. Amen. [La forme des prières ecclésiastiques (1561), 183-184]

Prayer After a Meal: 'Let all the nations praise the Lord, let all the peoples sing praises to him' (Ps. 67:3). 'For great is his mercy toward us and his truth remains for eternity'

(Ps. 117:2). O Lord God, we give you thanks for all the benefits that we constantly receive from your hand, that you are pleased to sustain us in this bodily life, providing us with all our necessities. And we especially thank you for the fact that it was your pleasure to give us new birth in the hope of a better life, which you revealed to us through your holy gospel. We pray that you would not allow our affections to be rooted here in these corruptible things, but that we would always look higher, waiting for our Lord Jesus Christ, until He appears for our redemption. Amen. [La forme des prières ecclésiastiques (1561), 184-185]

Prayer at Day's End: O Lord God, since you were pleased to create the night for people to rest, even as you ordained the day for work, please give us the grace to so rest in the body this night that our soul may always be watching for you and our heart lifted up in your love, and may we so let go of all earthly cares that we may be comforted as our frailty requires. May we never forget you, but may the remembrance of your goodness and grace remain always imprinted on our memories, so that by this means our conscience also may have its spiritual repose even as our body takes its physical rest. Do not allow our sleep to be excessive, to gratify beyond measure the laxity of our flesh, but only to satisfy the weakness of our nature, so that we might be able to serve you. Also, please preserve us unpolluted, in body as well as spirit, and protect us from all dangers so that our sleep itself may bring glory to your name. And since there is not a day that passes by in which we do not offend you in many ways, for we are all poor sinners – as everything is now hidden in the darkness that you send on the earth – please also bury all our offenses by your mercy so that we may not be driven from your presence by them. Hear us, our God, our Father and our Savior, by our Lord Jesus Christ, in whose name we pray, saying 'Our Father...' [La forme des prières ecclésiastiques (1561), 186-187]

JANUARY 1

Christ Our Redeemer

For while we were still weak, at the right time Christ died for the ungodly ... God shows his love for us in that while we were still sinners, Christ died for us. ROMANS 5:6-8

The Mediator's task was to restore us to God's grace so as to make of the children of men, children of God; of the heirs of Gehenna, heirs of the heavenly Kingdom. Who could have done this had not the self-same Son of God become the Son of Man, and had He not so taken what was ours as to impart what was His to us, and to make what was His by nature ours by grace? ... God's natural Son fashioned for Himself a body from our body, flesh from our flesh, bones from our bones, that He might be one with us. Ungrudgingly He took our nature upon Himself to impart to us what was His, and to become both Son of God and Son of man in common with us. ...

For the same reason it was also imperative that He who was to become our Redeemer be true God and true man. It was His task to swallow up death. Who but the Life could do this? It was His task to conquer sin. Who but very Righteousness could do this? It was His task to rout the powers of the world and air. Who but a power higher than world and air could do this? Now where does life or righteousness, or lordship and authority of heaven lie but with God alone? Therefore, our most merciful God, when He willed that we be redeemed, made Himself our Redeemer in the person of His only-begotten Son. [Institutes (1559), II.xii.2]

JANUARY 2

Counting Our Days

So teach us to number our days that we may get a heart of wisdom.

PSALM 90:12

It indeed seems at first sight absurd to pray that we may know the number of our years. What? Since even the strongest persons scarcely reach the age of eighty years, is there any difficulty in reckoning up so small a sum? Children learn to count as soon as they begin to prattle; and we do not need a teacher in arithmetic to enable us to count up to a hundred upon our fingers. So much the fouler and more shameful is our stupidity in never comprehending the short term of our life. Even persons who are most skillful in arithmetic, and who can precisely and accurately understand and investigate millions of millions, are nevertheless unable to count eighty years in their own lives. It is surely a monstrous thing that people can measure all distances outside themselves, that they know how many feet the moon is distant from the center of the earth, what space there is between the different planets; and, in short, that they can measure all the dimensions both of heaven and earth; while yet they cannot number seventy years in their own case. ... We then truly apply our hearts to wisdom when we comprehend the shortness of human life. ... No one then can regulate their lives with a calm mind except those who, knowing the end of it (that is to say death itself), are led to consider the purpose of human existence in this world, that they may aspire after the prize of the heavenly calling. [Commentary on Psalm 90]

JANUARY 3

The Whole Gospel

The grass withers, the flower fades, but the word of our God will stand forever.

ISAIAH 40:8

After having learned how empty and destitute we are of all blessings, how transitory and fading is the glory of the flesh, the only consolation left for us … is that though we are frail and fading, the word of the Lord is durable and eternal. Thus, in a word, the life that we need is provided to us from another quarter.…

This passage captures the whole gospel in a few words; for it consists of an acknowledgment of our misery, poverty, and emptiness so that, being sincerely humbled, we may fly to God by whom alone we shall be perfectly restored. Therefore, let men and women not faint or be discouraged by the knowledge of their nakedness and emptiness; for the eternal word is exhibited to them by which they may be abundantly supported and upheld. We are likewise taught that we ought not to seek consolation from any other source than from eternity, which ought not to be sought anywhere else than in God; since nothing that is firm or durable will be found on the earth. Nothing is more foolish than to rest satisfied with the present state, which we see is fleeting; and everyone is mistaken who hopes to be able to obtain perfect happiness till they have ascended to God, whom the Scripture calls eternal, in order that we may know that life flows to us from Him. And, indeed, God adopts us to be His children on this condition, to make us partakers of His immortality. [Commentary on Isaiah]

JANUARY 4

Search the Scriptures!

You search the Scriptures because you think that in them you have eternal life; and it is they that bear witness about me.

JOHN 5:39

[W]e are taught by this passage that if we wish to obtain the knowledge of Christ, we must seek it from the Scriptures; for people who imagine whatever they choose concerning Christ will ultimately have nothing of Him but a shadowy phantom. First, then, we ought to believe that Christ cannot be properly known in any other way than from the Scriptures; and if that is the case, it follows that we ought to read the Scriptures with the express purpose of finding Christ in them. People who turn aside from this object, though they may weary themselves in learning throughout their whole life, will never attain the knowledge of the truth; for what wisdom can we have without the wisdom of God?

Next, as we are commanded to seek Christ in the Scriptures, so He declares in this passage that our labors shall not be fruitless; for the Father testifies in them concerning His Son in such a manner that He will reveal the Son to us beyond all doubt. But what hinders the greater part of men and women from profiting is that they invest to the subject nothing more than a superficial and cursory glance. By contrast, it requires the utmost attention, and, therefore, Christ enjoins us to search diligently for this hidden treasure. [Commentary on John]

JANUARY 5

Fruitfulness of Scripture

For whatever was written in former days was written for our instruction, that through endurance and through the encouragement of the Scriptures we might have hope.

ROMANS 15:4

This is an interesting passage, by which we understand that there is nothing vain and unprofitable contained in the oracles of God; and we are at the same time taught that it is by the reading of the Scripture that we make progress in piety and holiness of life. Whatever then is delivered in Scripture we ought to strive to learn; for it would be a reproach against the Holy Spirit to think that He has taught anything which is unnecessary for us to know. Let us also know that whatever is taught us also contributes to the advancement of religion. And though Paul speaks of the Old Testament, the same thing is true of the writings of the Apostles, for since the Spirit of Christ does not change, there is no doubt but that He has adapted His teaching by the Apostles, as formerly by the Prophets, for the edification of His people. Moreover, we find here a most striking condemnation of those fanatics who assert that the Old Testament is abolished, and that it belongs not in any degree to Christians. ...

But when Paul adds the statement 'through endurance and the encouragement of the Scriptures we might have hope,' he does not include all the benefits which are derived from God's word, but points out the main end, for the Scriptures are especially profitable for this purpose – to raise up those who are prepared by patience, and strengthened by consolation, to the hope of eternal life, and to keep them in the contemplation of it. [Commentary on Romans]

JANUARY 6

God's Blessed People

He is like a tree planted by streams of water that yields its fruit in its season, and its leaf does not wither. In all that he does, he prospers.

PSALM 1:3

The Psalmist here ... shows in what respect those who fear God are to be accounted happy, namely, not because they enjoy a fleeting and empty gladness, but because they are in a desirable condition. There is in the words an implied contrast between the vigor of a tree planted in a situation well-watered, and the decayed appearance of one which, although it may flourish beautifully for a time, yet soon withers on account of the barrenness of the soil in which it is placed. With respect to the ungodly ... they are sometimes like 'the cedars of Lebanon' (Ps. 37:35). They have such an overflowing abundance of wealth and honors, that nothing seems lacking to their present happiness. But however high they may grow, and however far and wide they may spread their branches, yet having no root in the ground, nor even a sufficiency of moisture from which they may derive nourishment, the whole of their beauty disappears in time and withers away. It is, therefore, the blessing of God alone which preserves anyone in a prosperous condition. ... [The children of God constantly flourish, and are always watered with the secret influences of divine grace, so that whatever may befall them is conducive to their salvation; while, on the other hand, the ungodly are carried away by the sudden tempest, or consumed by the scorching heat.] [Commentary on Psalms]

JANUARY 7

Sparks of God's Glory

[God's] invisible attributes, namely his eternal power and divine nature, have been clearly perceived, ever since the creation of the world, in the things that have been made.

ROMANS 1:20

The final goal of the blessed life, moreover, rests in the knowledge of God. Lest anyone, then, be excluded from access to happiness, He not only sowed in the minds of men and women the seed of religion ... but revealed Himself and daily discloses Himself in the whole workmanship of the universe. As a consequence, humans cannot open their eyes without being compelled to see Him. Indeed, His essence is incomprehensible; hence His divineness far escapes all human perception. But upon His individual works He has engraved unmistakable marks of His glory, so clear and so prominent that even unlettered and stupid folk cannot plead the excuse of ignorance. Therefore, the prophet very aptly exclaims that He is 'clad with light as with a garment' (Ps. 104:2). ... Likewise, the same prophet skillfully compares the heavens, as they are stretched out, to His royal tent and says that He has laid the beams of His chambers on the waters, has made the clouds His chariot, rides on the wings of the wind, and that the winds and lightning bolts are His swift messengers (Ps. 104:2-4). And since the glory of His power and wisdom shine more brightly above, heaven is often called His palace (Ps. 11:4). Yet, in the first place, wherever you cast your eyes, there is no spot in the universe wherein you cannot discern at least some sparks of His glory. You cannot in one glance survey this most vast and beautiful system of the universe, in its wide expanse, without being completely overwhelmed by the boundless force of its brightness. [Institutes (1559), I.v.1]

JANUARY 8

Brevity of Life

You return man to dust and say, 'Return, O children of man!' For a thousand years in your sight are but as yesterday when it is past, or as a watch in the night.

PSALM 90:3-4

This account of human life sets in a clearer light the gracious manner in which God deals with His servants, in adopting them to be His special people, that He may at length gather them together into His everlasting inheritance. Nor is it in vain that [Moses] adds by way of contrast that 'a thousand years in God's sight are but as yesterday.' Although we are convinced from experience that human beings, when they have completed their earthly journey, are abruptly taken out of the world, yet the knowledge of this frailty fails to make a deep impression upon our hearts, because we do not lift our eyes above the world. Whence proceeds the great stupidity of men and women who, bound tightly to their present existence, proceed in the affairs of life as if they were going to live two thousand years … In short, people are so dull as to think that thirty years, or even a smaller number, are, as it were, an eternity; nor are they impressed with the brevity of their life so long as their thoughts remain fixed on this world. This is the reason why Moses awakens us by elevating our minds to the eternity of God, which, if we ignore it, we will not recognize how speedily our life vanishes away.

Let us learn, then, not to judge according to the understanding of the flesh, but to depend upon the judgment of God; and let us elevate our minds by faith, even to His heavenly throne, from which He declares that this earthly life is nothing. [Commentary on Psalms]

JANUARY 9

An Inexhaustible Fountain

For from his fullness we have all received grace upon grace.

JOHN 1:16

[John] begins now to preach about the office of Christ, that it contains within itself an abundance of all blessings, so that no part of salvation must be sought anywhere else. True, indeed, the fountain of life, righteousness, virtue, and wisdom, is with God, but to us it is a hidden and inaccessible fountain. But an abundance of those things is exhibited to us in Christ, that we may be permitted to have recourse to Him; for He is ready to flow to us, provided that we open up a channel by faith. He declares in general that outside of Christ we ought not to seek anything good. ... First, he shows that we are all utterly destitute and empty of spiritual blessings; for the abundance which exists in Christ is intended to supply our deficiency, to relieve our poverty, to satisfy our hunger and thirst. Secondly, he warns us that, as soon as we have departed from Christ, it is in vain for us to seek a single drop of happiness, because God has determined that whatever is good shall reside in Him alone. Accordingly, we shall find angels and human beings to be dry, heaven to be empty, the earth to be unproductive, and, in short, all things to be of no value, if we wish to be partakers of the gifts of God in any other way than through Christ. Thirdly, he assures us that we shall have no reason to fear the lack of anything, provided that we draw from the fullness of Christ, which is in every respect so complete, that we shall experience it to be a truly inexhaustible fountain. [Commentary on John]

JANUARY 10

The Soul's Anchor

We have this as a sure and steadfast anchor of the soul, a hope that enters into the inner place behind the curtain, where Jesus has gone as a forerunner on our behalf...

HEBREWS 6:19-20

It is a striking comparison when he compares faith leaning on God's word to an anchor; for doubtless, as long as we sojourn in this world, we do not stand on firm ground, but are tossed here and there as it were in the midst of the sea – indeed, a very turbulent sea. For Satan is constantly stirring up innumerable storms, which would immediately upset and sink our vessel, were we not to cast our anchor fast in the deep. For our eyes perceive no safe-haven, but wherever we look water alone is in view; indeed, waves also rise up and threaten us. But as the anchor is cast through the waters into a dark and unseen place, and while it lies hidden there, it keeps the vessel beaten by the waves from being overwhelmed; so much our hope is fixed on the invisible God. ... Thus, when united to God, though we must struggle with continual storms, we are yet beyond the peril of shipwreck. ... It may indeed be that by the violence of the waves the anchor may be plucked off, or the cable broken, or the beaten ship be torn to pieces. This happens on the sea; but the power of God to sustain us is entirely different, and so also is the strength of hope and the firmness of His word. [Commentary on Hebrews]

JANUARY 11

Nature Declares God's Glory

The heavens declare the glory of God, and the sky above proclaims his handiwork. Day to day pours out speech, and night to night reveals knowledge.
                                        PSALM 19:1-2

David shows how it is that the heavens proclaim to us the glory of God, namely, by clearly testifying that they have not been put together by chance, but were wonderfully created by the supreme Architect. When we behold the heavens, we cannot but be elevated by the contemplation of them to Him who is their great Creator. And the beautiful arrangement and wonderful variety which distinguish the courses and station of the heavenly bodies, together with the beauty and splendor which are manifest in them, cannot but furnish us with evident proof of His providence. ... As soon as we acknowledge God to be the supreme Architect, who has created the beautiful fabric of the universe, our minds must necessarily be ravished with wonder at His infinite goodness, wisdom, and power. ... [And] when we see the sun and the moon performing their daily revolutions ... and when we see that by this means the length of the days and nights is regulated, and that the variation of their length is arranged according to a law so uniform, as invariably to recur at the same points of time in every successive year, we have in this a much brighter testimony to the glory of God. David, therefore, with the best of reasons, declares that although God should not speak a single word to human beings, yet the orderly and useful succession of days and nights eloquently proclaims the glory of God, and that there is now left to men and women no pretext for ignorance. [Commentary on Psalms]

JANUARY 12

God's Majesty in Creation

Lift up your eyes on high and see: who created these? He who brings out their host by number, calling them all by name, by the greatness of his might...

ISAIAH 40:26

Every day people look at the heavens and the stars; but who is there that thinks of their author? By nature, men and women are formed in such a way as to make it evident that they were born to contemplate the heavens, and thus to learn about their author. For while God formed other animals to look downward for pasture, He alone made humans erect, and commanded them to look [heavenward] at what may be regarded as His own habitation. ... The Prophet therefore points out the wickedness of those who do not acknowledge what is openly placed before their eyes concerning God, but, like cattle, bury their muzzles in the earth. For whenever we raise our eyes upwards, with any degree of attention, it is impossible for our senses not to be impressed with the majesty of God. ... By mentioning the stars, Isaiah states more clearly that the wonderful order which shines brightly in the heavens preaches loudly that there is one God and Creator of the world. And everyone who observes it will be forced to acknowledge that there is a regular order and path amidst the vast number and variety of the stars. For it is not by chance that each of the stars has had its place assigned to it ... so that they do not deviate a hairbreadth from the path which God has marked out for them. Thus, the wonderful arrangement of the stars shows that God is the author and sustainer, so that men and women cannot open their eyes without being forced to behold the majesty of God in His creation. [Commentary on Isaiah]

JANUARY 13

Contemplating God in Creation

In the beginning, God created the heavens and the earth.

GENESIS 1:1

Even though men and women maliciously try to obscure God's glory, it is certain that they cannot open their eyes to look here or there without seeing evidence that leads them to the knowledge of Him – which they would flee and choose to completely bury if they could. For God displays Himself everywhere and provides marks of His majesty, His power, His righteousness, His goodness, and everything that can lead us to Him. That is also why Saint Paul in Acts 14:17 says that 'he did not leave himself without witness,' for all things created demonstrate that they do not have their source in themselves. It's as if God were enlightening us to draw us to Himself and enable us to recognize that He is the source and origin of all things, that everything depends on Him and is founded upon and supported by His power. Hence, the world, from its heights to its depths, is like a mirror to make us contemplate God, who is by His nature and essence invisible. Paul says the same thing in Romans 1:20 that the things that our eyes perceive show us that there is one God, although He is incomprehensible in Himself unless we understand Him in His works. At least we are responsible and will be inexcusable if we remain stupid and in our ignorance. [Sermons on Genesis, SC 11:1]

JANUARY 14

Dignity and Frailty

Then God said, 'Let us make man in our image, after our likeness. And let them have dominion over the fish of the sea and over the birds of the heavens and over the livestock and over all the earth and over every creeping thing that creeps on the earth.'

GENESIS 1:26

Human beings are God's noblest creation. We now see two things in us. One is the dignity that God has put within us when He raised up our heads to behold, as in a theater, all the creatures being raised up in this world, so that we might give Him glory. He gave us the ability to discern between good and evil. He gave us mastery and superiority over all the animals and all other things, as we will see hereafter. But consider how frail we all are! We barely begin to live and already death is grasping at our heels! How many children die in their mothers' wombs, before they ever see the sun? It is clear that we are like the wind, or like grass which soon withers; our life is so fragile that in no time at all our strength becomes like smoke. Seeing that, are we not forced to acknowledge that whatever dignity we recognize in ourselves cannot exist without God's most excellent and admirable workmanship? And further, our weakness demonstrates that everything we have depends on something outside us? ... So let us note well this word 'create' and be armed against all diabolical fantasies, and let us remain steadfast in resisting them, for everything created has come from nothing because there is no existence except in God alone, and all that we have and are comes from Him alone. [Sermons on Genesis, SC 11:8]

JANUARY 15

Profitable for Teaching

All Scripture is breathed out by God and profitable for teaching, for reproof, for correction, and for training in righteousness, that the man of God may be complete, equipped for every good work.

2 TIMOTHY 3:16-17

First, Paul commends the Scripture on account of its authority; and secondly, on account of the utility which springs from it. In order to uphold the authority of Scripture, He declares that it is divinely inspired; for, if that is the case, it is beyond all controversy that men and women should receive it with reverence. This is a principle which distinguishes our religion from all others, that we know that God has spoken to us, and are fully convinced that the prophets did not speak at their own suggestions, but that, being organs of the Holy Spirit, they only uttered what they had been commissioned from heaven to declare. Whoever then wishes to profit in the Scriptures, let them first of all establish this as a settled point, that the Law and the Prophets are not a doctrine delivered according to the will and pleasure of human beings, but dictated by the Holy Spirit.

Now comes the second part of the commendation, that the Scripture contains a perfect rule of a good and happy life. When Paul says this, he means that Scripture is corrupted by sinful abuse when this usefulness is not sought. ... The Lord, when He gave us the Scriptures, did not intend either to gratify our curiosity, or to encourage ostentation, or to give reasons for chatting and talking, but to do us good; and, therefore, the right use of Scripture must always tend to what is profitable. [Commentary on 2 Timothy]

JANUARY 16

Coming to Christ

One of the two who heard John speak and followed Jesus was Andrew, Simon Peter's brother. He first found his own brother Simon and said to him, 'We have found the Messiah' (which means Christ).

JOHN 1:40-41

The purpose of John the Evangelist ... is to inform us how gradually the disciples were brought to Christ. Here he relates about Peter, and afterwards he will mention Philip and Nathanael. The circumstance of Andrew immediately bringing his brother expresses the nature of faith, which does not conceal or quench the light, but rather spreads it in every direction. Andrew has scarcely a spark [of faith], and yet, by means of it, he enlightens his brother. Woe to our laziness, therefore, if we do not, after having been fully enlightened, endeavor to make others partakers of the same grace.

We may observe in Andrew two things which Isaiah requires from the children of God; namely, that each should take his neighbor by the hand, and next, that they should say, 'Come, let us go up to the mountain of the Lord ... that he may teach us his ways' (Isa. 2:3). For Andrew stretches out the hand to his brother, but at the same time he has this object in view, that he may become a fellow disciple with him in the school of Christ. We ought also to observe God's purpose which determined that Peter, who was to be far more eminent, was brought to the knowledge of Christ by the agency and ministry of Andrew; that none of us, however excellent, may refuse to be taught by an inferior. For those people will be severely punished for their peevishness, or rather for their pride, who, through their contempt of others, will not humble themselves to come to Christ. [Commentary on John]

JANUARY 17

God's Abundance in Creation

And God said, 'Behold, I have given you every plant yielding seed that is on the face of all the earth, and every tree with seed in its fruit. You shall have them for food.'

GENESIS 1:29

Why then does God speak here only about plants and fruits? It is to show His generosity toward them, as if He were saying: 'Consider the good things that the earth produces. What variety there is, and with such abundance! In time you will recognize that I have spared nothing and have not been stingy toward you.' For we see how many plants are given for people to enjoy; we see what an abundance of fruits there are, so good and excellent, and in such great diversity. All this bounty is given to nourish men and women – indeed, not simply to provide for their basic needs, for necessity does not require much: water and bread will always be adequate. When a person says, 'I cannot live without drinking and eating,' they have water and bread for their provisions. But now God adds wine to gladden the heart (as Psalm 104:15 says). He adds so many excellent fruits, from which one can make beverages, especially in the countries of the Orient. And even if we do not have fruits in equal abundance, it is nevertheless the case that even where there are not vineyards, as in colder regions, there are pears and apples, from which one can make beverages. In brief, there is such a variety that it's as if God were lavishing our tables with infinite gifts. ... When we see that our Lord is not satisfied to provide only what we need, but that He gives to us a superabundant supply, we must realize how greatly indebted we are to Him. [Sermons on Genesis, SC 11:71]

JANUARY 18

Tree of Life

The tree of life was in the midst of the garden, and the tree of the knowledge of good and evil.

GENESIS 2:9

God gave the tree of life its name, not because it could confer on human beings that life with which they had been previously endued, but in order that it might be a symbol and memorial of the life which they had received from God. ... He intended, therefore, that men and women, as often as they tasted the fruit of the tree, should remember whence they received their life, in order that they might acknowledge that they live not by their own power, but by the kindness of God alone; and that life is not ... an intrinsic good, but proceeds from God. Finally, in that tree there was a visible testimony to the declaration, that in God 'we live, and move, and have our being' (Acts 17:28). But if Adam, hitherto innocent, and of an upright nature, needed a warning sign to lead him to the knowledge of divine grace, how much more necessary are such signs now, in this great weakness of our nature, since we have fallen from the true light? ... [Yet] that tree of life was a figure of Christ, inasmuch as He is the Eternal Word of God. ... For we must maintain what is declared in the first chapter of John, that the life of all things was included in the Word, but especially the life of human beings, which is conjoined with reason and intelligence. Wherefore, by this sign, Adam was admonished, that he could claim nothing for himself as if it were his own, in order that he might depend wholly upon the Son of God. [Commentary on Genesis]

JANUARY 19

God's Righteousness

Enter not into judgment with your servant, for no one living is righteous before you.

PSALM 143:2

When overtaken by adversity, we are always to conclude that it is a rod of correction sent by God to stir us up to pray. Although God is far from taking pleasure in our trials, it is certain that our sins are the cause of His dealing toward us with this severity. While those by whom David was oppressed were wicked men, and he was perfectly conscious of the justice of his cause as regarded them, he freely acknowledged his sin before God as a condemned beggar. We are to hold this as a general rule as we seek to reconcile ourselves to God, that we must pray for the pardon of our sins. If David found refuge nowhere else than in prayers for pardon, who is there among us who would presume to come before God trusting in their own righteousness and integrity? Nor does David here merely set an example before God's people how they ought to pray, but he declares that there is no human being who could be just before God were they called to plead their cause.

This passage ... teaches us that as we approach God, He can only show favor to us by setting aside His role as judge, and reconciling us to Himself in a gracious remission of our sins. Accordingly, all forms of human righteousness count for nothing when we come to His tribunal. ... The passage before us clearly proves that the man or woman who is justified, is the one who is judged and reckoned as just before God, or whom the heavenly Judge Himself acquits as innocent. [Commentary on Psalms]

JANUARY 20

Knowledge of God

Yet [God] is actually not far from each one of us, for 'In him we live and move and have our being'; as even some of your own poets have said.
ACTS 17 27-28

Nearly all the wisdom we possess, that is today, true and sound wisdom, consists of two parts: the knowledge of God and of ourselves. But, while joined by many bonds, which one precedes and brings forth the other is not easy to discern. In the first place, no one can look upon himself without immediately turning his thoughts to the contemplation of God, in whom he 'lives and moves.' For, quite clearly, the mighty gifts with which we are endowed are hardly from ourselves; indeed, our very being is nothing but subsistence in the one God. Then, by these benefits shed like dew from heaven upon us, we are led as by rivulets to the spring itself. Indeed, our very poverty better discloses the infinitude of benefits reposing in God. The miserable ruin, into which the rebellion of the first man cast us, especially compels us to look upward. ... Thus, from the feeling of our own ignorance, vanity, poverty, infirmity, and – what is more – depravity and corruption, we recognize that the true light of wisdom, sound virtue, full abundance of every good, and purity of righteousness rest in the Lord alone. To this extent we are prompted by our own ills to contemplate the good things of God; and we cannot seriously aspire to Him before we begin to become displeased with ourselves. [Institutes (1559), I.i.1]

JANUARY 21

Christ's Satisfaction for Sinners

Grace to you and peace from God our Father and the Lord Jesus Christ, who gave himself for our sins to deliver us from the present evil age, according to the will of our God and Father, to whom be the glory forever and ever. Amen.

GALATIANS 1:3-5

The person who knows Christ in a proper manner beholds Him earnestly, embraces Him with the warmest affection, is absorbed in the contemplation of Him, and desires no other object. The best remedy for purifying our minds from any kind of errors or superstitions, is to remember our relation to Christ and the benefits which He has conferred upon us.

The words 'who gave himself for our sins' were intended to convey to the Galatians a doctrine of vast importance: that no other satisfactions can lawfully be provided in comparison with the sacrifice of Himself, which Christ offered to the Father; that in Christ, therefore, and in Him alone, atonement for sin, and perfect righteousness, must be sought; and all of this should excite our highest admiration. What Paul here ascribes to Christ is, with equal propriety, ascribed in other parts of Scripture to God the Father; for, on the one hand, the Father decreed this atonement by His eternal purpose, and gave this proof of His love to us, that He 'who did not spare his own Son but gave him up for us all' (Rom. 8:32); and Christ, on the other hand, offered Himself as a sacrifice in order to reconcile us to God. Hence it follows, that His death is the satisfaction for sins. [Commentary on Galatians]

JANUARY 22

Ministry of Angels

And to which of the angels has he ever said, 'Sit at my right hand until I make your enemies a footstool for your feet'? Are they not all ministering spirits sent out to serve for the sake of those who are to inherit salvation?

HEBREWS 1:13-14

From this passage the faithful receive no small consolation; for they learn that heavenly hosts are assigned to them as ministers, in order to secure their salvation. It is indeed no ordinary promise of God's love toward us, that they are continually engaged on our behalf. From this also comes a singular confirmation to our faith, that our salvation being defended by such guardians, is beyond the reach of danger. God has provided abundantly for our infirmities by giving us such assistants to oppose Satan and to expend their power in every way to defend us!

But this benefit He grants especially to His chosen people; thus, if we wish angels to minister to us, we must be the members of Christ. Yet some testimonies of Scripture may, on the other hand, be adduced to show that angels are sometimes sent forth for the sake of the reprobate; for mention is made by Daniel of the angels of the Persians and the Greeks (Dan. 10:20). But to this I answer that they were assisted by angels in such a way that the Lord might thus promote the salvation of His own people; for their success and their victories always had reference to the benefit of the Church. This is certain, that … we can have no communion with angels except through the reconciliation made by Christ. [Commentary on Hebrews]

JANUARY 23

God's Gift of Dominion

You have given him dominion over the works of your hands; you have put all things under his feet, all sheep and oxen, and also the beasts of the field.

PSALM 8:6-7

[I]t is by the wonderful providence of God that horses and oxen yield their service to human beings, that sheep produce wool to clothe them, and that all sorts of animals supply them with food for their nourishment and support, even in giving their own flesh. And the more that this dominion is apparent, the more ought we to be affected with a sense of the goodness and grace of our God as often as we either eat food, or enjoy any of the other comforts of life. ... [David] brings this forward as an example, and as a mirror in which we may view and contemplate the dominion over the works of His hands, with which God has honored human beings. The sum is this: God, in creating man and woman, gave a demonstration of His infinite grace and more than fatherly love toward them, which should truly amaze us; and although, by the fall of humankind, that happy condition has been almost entirely ruined, yet there is still in them some remains of the generosity which God then displayed toward them. ... David here confines his attention to God's temporal benefits, but it is our duty to rise higher, and to contemplate the invaluable treasures of the kingdom of heaven which He has unfolded in Christ, and all the gifts which belong to the spiritual life, that by reflecting upon these things our hearts may be inflamed with love for God, that we may be stirred up to the practice of godliness, and that we may not allow ourselves to become slothful and negligent in celebrating His praises. [Commentary on Psalms]

JANUARY 24

Sincere Prayer

I say to the LORD, you are my God; give ear to the voice of my pleas for mercy, O LORD! O LORD, my Lord, the strength of my salvation, you have covered my head in the day of battle.
PSALM 140:6-7

In these words [David] shows that his prayers were not merely those of his lips, as hypocrites will make loud appeals to God for mere appearance sake, but that he prayed with earnestness, and from a hidden principle of faith. Until we are persuaded of being saved through the grace of God there can be no sincere prayer. We have here an excellent illustration of the nature of faith, in the fact that the Psalmist turns himself away from humans' view, that he may address God apart – thereby excluding hypocrisy in this internal exercise of the heart. This is true prayer – not the mere idle lifting up of the voice, but the presentation of our petitions from an inward principle of faith. So as to beget within himself the conviction that he will obtain his present requests from God, David recalls to mind the deliverances that God had already extended to him. He speaks of the fact that God has been to him like a shield in every time of danger. Some interpreters read the words in the future tense: 'You will cover my head in the day of battle.' But it is clear that David here speaks of protection previously experienced from the hand of God, and from this he derives comfort to his faith. He emerges, not as a raw and undisciplined recruit, but as a soldier well-tested in previous engagements. [Commentary on Psalms]

JANUARY 25

Adam's Rib

So, the LORD God caused a deep sleep to fall upon the man, and while he slept took one of his ribs and closed up its place with flesh. And the rib that the LORD God had taken from the man he made into a woman ...

GENESIS 2:21-22

Although to profane persons this method of forming woman may seem ridiculous, and some of these persons may say that Moses is dealing in fables, yet to us the wonderful providence of God here shines forth; for, to the end that the conjunction of the human race might be the more sacred, He purposed that both males and females should spring from one and the same origin. Therefore, He created human nature in the person of Adam, and thence formed Eve, that the woman should be only a portion of the whole human race. ... In this manner Adam was taught to recognize himself in his wife, as in a mirror; and Eve, in her turn, to submit herself willingly to her husband, as being taken out of him. But if the two sexes had proceeded from different sources, there would have been occasion either of mutual contempt, or envy, or contentions. ... [S]omething was taken from Adam in order that he might embrace, with greater benevolence, a part of himself. He lost, therefore, one of his ribs; but, instead of it, a far richer reward was granted him, since he obtained a faithful associate of life; for he now saw himself, who had before been imperfect, rendered complete in his wife. And in this we see a true resemblance of our union with the Son of God; for he became weak that he might have members of his body endued with strength. [Commentary on Genesis]

JANUARY 26

Created with Purpose

The Lord God took the man and put him in the garden of Eden to work it and keep it.

GENESIS 2:15

Since God has given us feet and hands, our natural senses, and reason to understand various trades, each of us should think, 'I was not created here for drinking and eating. I must serve some purpose.' ... Now it is true that all people are not in the same condition. There are some who are quite robust, who can endure more painful work, and others who cannot endure much. ... Thus, our Lord has carefully distinguished between the abilities He has distributed to various people. Certainly, God has created everyone in His image – that we have in common – but that image does not shine in equal proportion to everyone, and our Lord, in His generosity, distributes due measure to each person according to their need. ... There are a diversity of gifts that are distributed to everyone throughout the world. ... Some will be in the mechanical trades; others in various sciences; others will be fit for public office; others for trading and moving merchandise; still others to serve human needs. ... So we must remember what Moses teaches us here, that we have not been created to be do-nothings, but must employ ourselves in some good service, and if our responsibility is to cultivate the land, each person should put the hand to the work. Why? Because God has assigned us to this particular occupation. [Sermons on Genesis, SC 11:107-108]

JANUARY 27

The Believer's Race

[B]ut they who wait for the LORD shall renew their strength; they shall mount up with wings like eagles; they shall run and not be weary; they shall walk and not faint.

ISAIAH 40:31

The prophet Isaiah shows that godly people, who hope in God, will not lack for strength; and he confirms what he formerly stated, 'In quietness and in trust shall be your strength' (Isa. 30:15). ... 'They shall run and not be weary.' It is as if the prophet had said that the Lord will assist them, so that they shall run their race without being disturbed. This is a figurative expression by which Isaiah intimates that believers will always be ready to perform their duty with cheerfulness. But someone might say, 'There are so many troubles which we must endure in this life; why then does he say that we shall be exempt from exhaustion?' I reply, believers are indeed distressed and wearied, but they are in due time delivered from their distresses, and feel that they have been restored by the power of God. For they experience what Paul states: 'We are afflicted in every way, but not crushed; perplexed, but not driven to despair; persecuted, but not forsaken; struck down, but not destroyed' (2 Cor. 4:8-9). Let us therefore learn to flee to the Lord, who, after we have encountered many storms, will at length bring us to the harbor. For He who has opened up a path, and has commanded us to advance in that course in which He has placed us, does not intend to assist us only after a single day, and then to forsake us in the middle of our race, but will conduct us safely to the goal. [Commentary on Isaiah]

JANUARY 28

Election to Holiness

Blessed be the God and Father of our Lord Jesus Christ, who ... chose us in him before the foundation of the world, that we should be holy and blameless before him.

EPHESIANS 1:3-4

[H]oliness, purity, and every excellence that is found among human beings are the fruit of election; so that once more Paul expressly puts aside every consideration of merit. If God had foreseen in us anything worthy of election, it would have been stated in language the very opposite of what is employed here, and which plainly means that all our holiness and purity of life flow from the election of God. How is it that some people are religious, and live in the fear of God, while others give themselves up without reserve to all manner of wickedness? If Paul is believed, the only reason is because the latter retain their natural disposition, and the former have been chosen to holiness. ... We learn also from these words, that election gives no occasion to wickedness or to the blasphemy of wicked people who say, 'Let us live in any manner we please; for if we have been elected, we cannot perish.' Paul tells them plainly that they have no right to separate holiness of life from the grace of election; for 'those whom he predestined he also called, and those whom he called he also justified' (Rom. 8:30) ... This is the goal to which the whole course of our life must be directed, and we shall not reach it till we have finished our course. Where are the people who dread and avoid the doctrine of predestination as an inextricable labyrinth, who believe that it is useless and almost dangerous? No doctrine is more useful provided it be handled in the proper and cautious manner. [Commentary on Ephesians]

JANUARY 29

New Birth

'Truly, truly, I say to you, unless one is born again he cannot see the kingdom of God.'

JOHN 3:3

Christ saw that the mind of Nicodemus was filled with many thorns, choked by many noxious herbs, so that there was scarcely any room for spiritual doctrine. This exhortation, therefore, resembled a plowing to purify him, that nothing might prevent him from profiting by his teaching. Let us, therefore, remember that this was spoken to one individual, in such a manner that the Son of God addresses all of us daily in the same language. ...

To 'see the kingdom of God' means to enter into the kingdom of God. ... But they are mistaken who suppose that the kingdom of God means Heaven; for it rather means the spiritual life, which is begun by faith in this world, and gradually increases every day according to the continued progress of faith. So, the meaning is, that no one can be truly united to the Church, so as to be counted among God's children, until they have been previously renewed. This expression shows briefly what is the beginning of Christianity, and at the same time teaches us, that we are born exiles and utterly alienated from the kingdom of God, and that there is a perpetual state of variance between God and us, until He makes us altogether different by our being born again. ... By the phrase 'born again' Jesus means not the correction of one part, but the renovation of the whole nature. Hence it follows, that there is nothing in us that is not sinful; for if reformation is necessary in the whole and in each part, corruption must have been spread throughout. [Commentary on John]

JANUARY 30

Faith Amidst Wickedness

Save, O LORD, for the godly one is gone; for the faithful have vanished from among the children of man.

PSALM 12:1

In the beginning [of this passage], David complains that the land was so overspread with the wicked ... that none was found to defend the cause of the good; in short, that there remained no longer either humanity or faithfulness. It is probable that the Psalmist here is speaking of the time when Saul persecuted him, because then everyone, from the highest to the lowest, had conspired to destroy an innocent and afflicted man. ... David does not here accuse strangers or foreigners, but informs us that this deluge of wickedness prevailed in the Church of God. Let the faithful in our day, therefore, not be unduly discouraged at the sad sight of the very corrupt and confused state of the world; but let them consider that they ought to bear it patiently, seeing their condition is just like that of David in time past. And it is to be observed that, when David calls upon God for assistance, he encourages himself in the hope of obtaining it from this, that there was no uprightness among the people; so that from his example we may learn to commit ourselves to God when we see nothing around us but black despair. We ought to be fully persuaded of this, that the greater the confusion of things in the world, God is so much the readier to aid and support His people, and that it is then the most proper season for Him to extend His assistance. [Commentary on Psalms]

JANUARY 31

Glad Obedience

Teach me to do your will, for you are my God! Let your good Spirit lead me on level ground!

PSALM 143:10

[David] now rises to something higher, praying not merely for deliverance from outward troubles, but (what is of still greater importance) for the guidance of God's Spirit, that he might not stray to the right hand or to the left, but be kept in the path of righteousness. This is a request that we should never forget when we are severely assailed by temptations, as it is especially difficult to submit to God without resorting to inappropriate methods of relief. As anxiety, fear, disease, languor, or pain often tempt us to take particular steps, David's example should lead us to pray for divine restraint, that we may not allow our strong emotions to rush us into unjustifiable paths. We should mark carefully the way that David expresses himself, for what he asks for is not simply to be taught what the will of God is, but to be taught and understand it, and then to do it. ... God therefore must be master and teacher to us not only in the dead letter, but by the inward motions of His Spirit. Indeed, there are three ways in which He acts the part of our teacher, instructing us by His word, enlightening our minds by the Spirit, and engraving instruction upon our hearts, so as to bring us to observe it with a true and glad consent. The mere hearing of the word would serve no purpose, nor is it enough that we understand it; we must also possess the willing obedience of the heart. [Commentary on Psalms]

FEBRUARY 1

Sin's Curse

And to Adam he said, 'Because you have listened to the voice of your wife and have eaten of the tree of which I commanded you, "You shall not eat of it," cursed is the ground because of you ...'
GENESIS 3:17-19

During the time that Eve and Adam continued to obey God – before Adam had lost his integrity – the world remained whole and the earth completely satisfied our desires. Thus, if we had persevered in honoring God for the good things that He had bestowed on the entire human race, there is no doubt that, today, it would not be a painful task to cultivate the earth. Moreover, the land would never fail to provide in abundance; all our hopes would be satisfied with pleasure; and we would lack nothing. Why is the earth in rebellion (in a manner of speaking) and why are our hopes often frustrated, when we have toiled at plowing and planting, yet the harvest does not produce what we expected? Our rebellion against God fully deserves that the creation should rise up and be armed against us. Nevertheless, we must also note that God has overcome our evil, inasmuch as the earth is still subject to us, at least in part.

Thus, because we have been despoiled of so many blessings by our audacity, we have an opportunity to humble ourselves and acknowledge our offenses before God. ... Yet God still shows Himself to be our Father ... and continues to give us a taste of His goodness and love so that we might be able to trust ourselves to Him. ... Our souls are still very precious to Him and, if we seek in Him our eternal salvation, we will find it there. [Sermons on Genesis, SC 11:69-70]

FEBRUARY 2

Temporary Exile

[T]herefore the LORD GOD sent Adam out from the garden of Eden to work the ground from which he was taken. He drove out the man, and at the east of the garden of Eden he placed the cherubim and a flaming sword, that turned every way to guard the way to the tree of life.

GENESIS 3:23-24

God mercifully softens the exile of Adam, by still providing for him a remaining home on earth, and by assigning to him a livelihood from the earth – although the difficult culture of the ground; for Adam thence infers that the Lord has some care for him, which is a proof of paternal love. Moses, however, again speaks of punishment, when he relates that the man and woman were expelled, and that cherubim were opposed with the blade of a burning sword, which would prevent their entrance into the garden. … Therefore, God having granted life to Adam, and having supplied him with food, yet restricts the benefit, by causing some tokens of divine wrath to be always before his eyes, in order that he might frequently reflect that he must pass through innumerable miseries, through temporal exile, and through death itself to the life from which he had fallen; for what we have said must be remembered, that Adam was not so dejected as to be left without hope of pardon. He was banished from that royal palace of which he had been the lord, but he obtained elsewhere a place in which he might dwell; he was bereft of his former delicacies, yet he was still supplied with some kind of food; he was excommunicated from the tree of life, but a new remedy was offered him in sacrifices. [Commentary on Genesis]

FEBRUARY 3

Pervasiveness of Sin

'That which is born of the flesh is flesh, and that which is born of the Spirit is spirit.'

JOHN 3:6

Here another question arises; for it is certain that in this degenerate and corrupted nature some remnant of the gifts of God still lingers; and hence it follows that we are not in every respect corrupted. The reply is easy. The gifts which God has left to us since the fall, if they are judged by themselves, are indeed worthy of praise; but as the contagion of wickedness is spread through every part, there will be found in us nothing that is pure and free from every defilement. That we naturally possess some knowledge of God, that some distinction between good and evil is engraved on our conscience, that our faculties are sufficient for the maintenance of the present life, that – in short – we are in so many ways superior to the brute beasts, that is excellent in itself, so far as it proceeds from God; but in us all these things are completely polluted, in the same manner as the wine, which has been wholly infected and corrupted by the offensive taste of the vessel, loses the pleasantness of its good flavor, and acquires a bitter and pernicious taste. For such knowledge of God as now remains in human beings is nothing else than a frightful source of idolatry and of all superstitions ... and the will itself, with furious impetuosity, rushes headlong to what is evil. Thus, in the whole of our nature there remains not a drop of uprightness. Hence it is evident that we must be formed by the second birth, that we may be fitted for the kingdom of God. [Commentary on John]

FEBRUARY 4

The Joy of Faith

And when they came up out of the water, the Spirit of the Lord carried Philip away, and the [Ethiopian] eunuch saw him no more, and went on his way rejoicing.

ACTS 8:39

Faith and knowledge of God always brings forth this fruit of rejoicing. For what purer form of joy can be invented than when the Lord not only sets upon us the treasures of His mercy, but also pours His heart into us (in a manner of speaking), and gives us Himself in His Son, that we may lack nothing of perfect happiness? Then, the heavens begin to look clear and the earth begins to be quiet. The conscience is then delivered from the sorrowful and horrible feelings of God's wrath, and, having been freed from Satan's tyranny and escaping out of the darkness of death, it beholds the light of life. Therefore, it is a solemn thing among the prophets to exhort us to be joyful and to triumph as often as they are about to speak of the kingdom of Christ. But because those whose minds are possessed with the vain joys of this world cannot lift themselves up to experience this spiritual joy, let us learn to despise the world and all the vain delights it contains, so that Christ may make us merry indeed. [Commentary on Acts]

FEBRUARY 5

The Lord's Prayer

'Pray then like this, "Our Father in heaven, hallowed be your name."'

MATTHEW 6:9

Whenever we engage in prayer, there are two things to be considered so that we may have access to God, and may rely on Him with full and unshaken confidence: His fatherly love toward us and His boundless power. Let us therefore have no doubts that God is willing to receive us graciously and that He is ready to listen to our prayers – in a word, that He is disposed to help us. 'Father' is the title given to Him; and under this title Christ supplies us with sufficient and abundant reasons for confidence. But, since only half of our reliance is founded on God's goodness, in the next clause He gives us a lofty vision of the power of God when He states 'who art in heaven.' When the Scripture says that God is 'in heaven,' the meaning is that all things are subject to His dominion: that the world, and everything in it, is held by His hand; that His power is everywhere diffused; that all things are arranged by His providence. David says, 'He who sits in the heavens laughs' (Ps. 2:4), and again, 'Our God is in the heavens; he does all that he pleases' (Ps. 115:3). When God is said to be 'in heaven,' we must not imagine that He dwells only there; but, on the contrary, we must hold what is said in another passage, that 'even the highest heaven cannot contain him' (2 Chron. 2:6). This mode of expression … reminds us that, when we think of Him, we ought not to form any low or earthly conceptions; for He is higher than the whole world. [Commentary on the Harmony of the Gospels]

FEBRUARY 6

Praying in Christ's Name

'Truly, truly, I say to you, whatever you ask of the Father in my name, he will give it to you. Until now you have asked nothing in my name. Ask, and you will receive, that your joy may be full.'

JOHN 16:23-24

Now we know that the [Old Testament] patriarchs were not accustomed to pray without a Mediator; for God had trained them, by so many exercises, to such a form of prayer. They saw the high priest enter into the holy place in the name of the whole people, and they saw sacrifices offered every day, that the prayers of the Church might be acceptable before God. It was, therefore, one of the principles of faith, that prayers offered to God, when there was no Mediator, were rash and useless. Christ had already testified to His disciples plainly enough that He was the Mediator, but their knowledge was so obscure, that they were not yet able to form their prayers 'in His name' in a proper manner. ...

[W]e ought to pay attention to the frequent repetition of this clause, that we must pray 'in the name' of Christ. This teaches us that it is a wicked profanation of the name of God, when people, leaving Christ out of view, venture to present themselves before the judgment-seat of God. And if this conviction is deeply impressed on our minds, that God will willingly and abundantly give to us 'whatever we ask in the name' of His Son, we will not run here and there to call to our aid various advocates, but will be satisfied with having this single Advocate, who so frequently and so kindly offers to us his labors on our behalf. [Commentary on John]

FEBRUARY 7

Contentment in God Alone

The LORD is my chosen portion and my cup; you hold my lot. The lines have fallen for me in pleasant places; indeed, I have a beautiful inheritance.

PSALM 16:5-6

This passage teaches us that none are taught aright in true godliness except those who recognize God alone sufficient for their happiness. David, by calling God his 'chosen portion,' and 'his inheritance,' and 'his cup,' insists that he is so fully satisfied with Him alone that he neither covets anything besides Him nor is excited by any depraved desires. Let us therefore learn, when God offers Himself to us, to embrace Him with the whole heart, and to seek in Him only all the ingredients and the fullness of our happiness. All the superstitions that have ever prevailed in this world have undoubtedly proceeded from this source, that superstitious people have not been content with possessing God alone. But we do not actually possess Him unless He is our 'chosen portion,' in other words, unless we are wholly devoted to Him, so as no longer to have any unfaithful desire to depart from Him. ... This doctrine may be profitable to us in many ways. It ought to draw us away not only from all perverse inventions of superstitions, but also from all the allurements of the flesh and the world. Whenever, therefore, those things present themselves to us which would lead us away from resting in God alone, let us make use of the sentiment as an antidote against them, that we have sufficient cause for being contented, since He who has in Himself an absolute fullness of all good has given Himself to be enjoyed by us. ... [H]e who has God as his portion is destitute of nothing which is required to constitute a happy life. [Commentary on Psalms]

FEBRUARY 8

First Petition

'Pray then like this: "Our Father in heaven, hallowed be your name."

MATTHEW 6:9

In the first three petitions [of the Lord's Prayer] we ought to lose sight of ourselves and seek the glory of God; not that it is separated from our salvation, but that the majesty of God ought to be greatly preferred by us to every other object of concern. It is of unspeakable advantage to us that God reigns, and that he receives the honor which is due him; but no one has a sufficiently earnest desire to promote God's glory, unless they forget themselves and raise their minds to seek God's exalted greatness ...

To sanctify the name of God means nothing else than to give to the Lord the glory due to His name, so that men and women may never think or speak of Him except with the deepest veneration. The opposite of this is the profanation of the name of God, which takes place when people either speak disrespectfully of the divine majesty, or at least without that reverence which they ought to feel. Now the glory by which God's name is sanctified flows and results from the confession that people make as to the wisdom, goodness, righteousness, power and all the other attributes of God. ... [Thus,] the substance of this petition is that the glory of God may shine throughout the world, and may be rightfully acknowledged by men and women. Religion is in its highest purity and vigor when people believe that whatever proceeds from God is right and proper, full of righteousness and wisdom, and – as a result – embrace His word with the obedience of faith and approve all of His commands and works. [Commentary on the Harmony of the Gospels]

FEBRUARY 9

Second Petition

'Your kingdom come, your will be done, on earth as it is in heaven.'
MATTHEW 6:10

We must first examine the definition of the kingdom of God. He is said to reign among men and women when they voluntarily devote and submit themselves to be governed by Him, placing their bodies under the yoke, and renouncing their desires. Such is the corruption of our nature that all our affections are so many soldiers of Satan, who oppose the justice of God and consequently obstruct or disturb His reign. By this petition we ask that God may remove all hindrances, and may bring all men and women under His dominion, and may lead them to meditate on the heavenly life.

This is done partly by the preaching of the word, and partly by the secret power of the Spirit. It is His will to govern men and women by His word. But if the inward power of the Spirit is not added, the bare voice [of the preacher] does not pierce the human heart – both must be joined together in order that the kingdom of God may be established. We therefore pray that God would exert His power, both by the Word and by the Spirit, so that the whole world may willingly submit to Him. ...

Since the kingdom of God is continually growing and advancing to the end of the world, we must pray every day that it may come: for to whatever extent wickedness abounds in the world, to that extent the kingdom of God – which brings along with it perfect righteousness – is not yet come. [Commentary on the Harmony of the Gospels]

FEBRUARY 10

Prosperity of the Wicked

All of them are put to shame and confounded; the makers of idols go in confusion together. But Israel is saved by the LORD with everlasting salvation… ISAIAH 45:16-17

Isaiah exhorts [the Jews] not to judge the power of God from the present condition of things, nor to have their minds fixed on temporary happiness, but to raise them to eternal salvation, and, when struck by the hand of God, to bear patiently their condition, and, on the other hand, not to envy the prosperity of the wicked, which shall be followed by a mournful reversal, as it is excellently described by the Psalmist (Ps. 37:1-2). … [W]hoever shall know that God, when He is a savior, is 'hidden,' will not be surprised that wicked men and women enjoy prosperity, and that good men and women are poor, and despised, and tested by various afflictions. Thus, the Lord makes trial of our faith and patience, and yet no part of our eternal salvation is lost; but they who now appear to be a thousand times safe and happy shall in due time perish, and all the wealth which they possess shall plunge them in deeper ruin; because they abuse God's benefits, and, like robbers, seize on what belongs to other people…. Whenever, therefore, this thought arises to our minds – 'Wicked people are at ease, and therefore God must favor them, and the promises on which we rely are unworthy of credit' – let us remind ourselves of this declaration of the prophet as the surest anchor, and let us fortify ourselves by it [by saying], 'The Lord will not disappoint our expectation, but we shall at length be delivered, even though we are now exposed to the reproaches, slanders, mocking, and cruelty of the wicked.' [Commentary on Isaiah]

FEBRUARY 11

Eyes Fixed on Christ

... according to the working of his great might, that he worked in Christ when he raised him from the dead and seated him at the right hand in the heavenly places.

EPHESIANS 1:19-20

Our blessedness which lies in hope, is not perceived by the world. ... A thousand distresses, to which we are daily liable, render us more despised than other people. Christ alone, therefore, is the mirror in which we can contemplate that which the weakness of the cross hinders from being clearly seen in ourselves. When our minds rise to a confident anticipation of righteousness, salvation, and glory, let us learn to turn them to Christ. We still lie under the power of death; but He, raised from the dead by heavenly power, has the dominion of life. We labor under the bondage of sin, and, surrounded by endless troubles, are engaged in a hard warfare (1 Tim. 1:8); but He, sitting at the right hand of the Father, exercises the highest government in heaven and earth, and triumphs gloriously over the enemies whom He has subdued and vanquished. We lie here disregarded and despised; but to Him has been 'given a name' (Phil. 2:9) which angels and human beings look upon with reverence, and devils and the wicked with dread. We are pressed down here by the scantiness of all our comforts; but He has been appointed by the Father to be the sole dispenser of all blessings. For these reasons, we shall find our advantage in directing our vision to Christ, that in Him, as in a mirror, we may see the glorious treasures of divine grace, and the unmeasurable greatness of that power, which has not yet been manifested in ourselves. [Commentary on Ephesians]

FEBRUARY 12

Few Disciples

*'Truly, truly, I say to you, we speak of what we know, and
bear witness to what we have seen, but you do not receive
our testimony.'*

JOHN 3:11

Now though the meaning of the words is simple and clear,
still we must draw from this passage a twofold doctrine. The
first is, that our faith in the gospel may not be weakened if
it has few disciples on earth; as if Christ had said, 'Though
you do not receive my doctrine, it remains nevertheless certain
and durable; for the unbelief of men and women will never
prevent God from remaining always true.' The other [doctrine]
is, that those people who, in the present day, disbelieve the
gospel, will not escape with impunity, since the truth of God
is holy and sacred. We ought to be fortified with this shield,
that we may persevere in obedience to the gospel in opposition
to the obstinacy of other people. True indeed, we must hold
by this principle, that our faith is founded on God. But when
we have God as our security, we ought, like persons elevated
above the heavens, boldly to tread the whole world under
our feet, or regard it with lofty disdain, rather than allow the
unbelief of any persons whatever to fill us with alarm. As to
the complaint which Christ makes, that His testimony is not
received, we learn from it that the word of God has, in all ages,
been distinguished by this peculiar feature, that they who
believed it were few; for the expression – 'you do not receive' –
belongs to the greater number, and almost to the whole body
of people. There is no reason, therefore, that we should now
be discouraged, if the number of those who believe is small.
[Commentary on John]

FEBRUARY 13

Spiritual Joy

Therefore my heart is glad, and my whole being rejoices; my flesh also dwells secure.

PSALM 16:9

In this verse the Psalmist commends the inestimable fruit of faith, of which Scripture everywhere makes mention, in that, by placing us under the protection of God, it makes us not only to live in the enjoyment of mental tranquility, but, what is more, to live joyfully and cheerfully. The principal and essential part of a happy life, as we know, is to possess tranquility of conscience and of mind. On the other hand, there is no greater unhappiness than to be tossed amidst a multiplicity of cares and fears. But ungodly people, however intoxicated they might be with the spirit of thoughtfulness or stupidity, never experience true joy or serene mental peace; rather, they feel terrible agitations which often come upon them and trouble them. ... In short, to rejoice calmly is the lot of no one other than those who have learned to place their confidence in God alone, and to commit their lives and safety to His protection. When, therefore, we are surrounded with innumerable troubles on all sides, let us be persuaded that the only remedy is to direct our eyes toward God; and if we do this, faith will not only calm our minds, but also replenish them with fullness of joy. David, however, not only affirms that he is glad inwardly; he also makes his tongue, indeed, even his flesh, to share in this joy. And not without cause, for true believers not only have this spiritual joy in the secret affections of their hearts, but also manifest it by their tongues, inasmuch as they glory in God as He who protects them and secures their salvation. [Commentary on Psalms]

FEBRUARY 14

Noah's Exemplary Faith

By faith Noah, being warned by God concerning events as yet unseen, in reverent fear constructed an ark for the saving of his household. By this he condemned the world and became an heir of the righteousness that comes by faith.

HEBREWS 11:7

[The Author shows us that Noah] feared God, having been warned of things to come that were not yet made visible; that he built an ark; that he condemned the world by building it; and that he became the heir of that righteousness that is by faith. ... [The] Apostle ever reminds us of this truth, that faith is the evidence of things not seen. And this faith's particular function is to see in God's word things which are hidden and far removed from our senses. ...

The work of building the ark was long and difficult. It might have been hindered by the scoffs of the ungodly, and thus suspended a thousand times; nor is there a doubt but that people mocked and derided the holy man on every side. That he then endured their outrageous insults with an unshaken spirit, is proof that his resolution to obey was extraordinary. But how was it that he so perseveringly obeyed God except that he had previously rested on the promise which gave him the hope of deliverance; and in this confidence he persevered even to the last. For he could not have had the courage willingly to undergo so many toils, nor could he have been able to overcome so many obstacles, nor could he have stood so firm in his purpose for so long a time, had he not beforehand possessed great confidence in God. It hence appears that faith alone is the teacher of obedience. [Commentary on Hebrews]

FEBRUARY 15

Third Petition

'Your will be done, on earth as it is in heaven.'

MATTHEW 6:10

Although the will of God, viewed in itself, is singular and simple, it is presented to us in Scripture under a twofold aspect. It is said that the will of God is done when He executes the secret counsels of His providence, however stubbornly men and women strive to oppose Him. But here we are commanded in a different sense to pray that His will may be done, namely, that all creatures may obey Him, without opposition and without reluctance. This appears more clearly from the comparison 'as it is in heaven.' For as God has the angels constantly ready to execute His commands ... so we desire that all men and women may have their will formed to such harmony with the righteousness of God, that they may freely bend in whatever direction He shall ordain. It is, no doubt, a holy desire when we bow to the will of God and acquiesce in His appointments. But this prayer implies something more. It is a prayer that God may remove all the stubbornness of men and women, which rises in unceasing rebellion against Him, and may render them gentle and submissive, that they may not wish or desire anything but what pleases Him, and meets His approval. ...

When we pray that the earth may become obedient to the will of God ... we declare that we hate and regret whatever we perceive to be contrary to the will of God, and long for its utter destruction, not only that it may be the rule of all our affections, but that we may yield ourselves without reserve to its fulfillment with all cheerfulness. [Commentary on the Harmony of the Gospels]

FEBRUARY 16

Fourth Petition

'Give us this day our daily bread ...'

MATTHEW 6:11

We are first commanded to pray that God would protect and cherish the life that He has given to us in the world, and, as we need much assistance, that He would supply us with everything that He knows we need. ... The word 'daily' is added to restrain our excessive desire, and to teach us that we depend every moment on the kindness of God, and ought to be content with that portion which He gives us. ...

Now, some of the godly are rich, who have their yearly produce stored up. Why does Christ command them to ask for what they have at home, and to ask every day for those things of which they have an abundant supply for a year? The reply is easy. These words remind us that unless God feeds us daily, the largest accumulation of all the necessities of life will be of no use to us. Though we might have an abundance of corn and wine and everything else, unless they are watered by the secret blessing of God, they will suddenly vanish, or we will be deprived of their use, or they will lose their natural power to support us, so that we shall famish in the midst of plenty. There is therefore no reason to be surprised that Christ invites the rich and poor indiscriminately to appeal to their heavenly Father for the supply of their needs. No man or woman will sincerely offer such a prayer as this unless they have learned ... to endure patiently their poverty or humble condition, and not to be intoxicated by a false confidence in their abundance (Phil. 4:12). [Commentary on the Harmony of the Gospels]

FEBRUARY 17

The Shepherd's Provision

'They shall feed along the ways; on all bare heights shall be their pasture; they shall not hunger or thirst ... for he who has pity on them will lead them, and by springs of water will guide them.'

ISAIAH 49:9-10

When God promises that pastures shall be accessible to the children of God, and shall be on the tops of the mountains, by these metaphors He declares that all who shall be under the protection of Christ shall dwell safely; for He is a careful and attentive Shepherd who supplies His flock with everything they need, so that they lack for nothing that is necessary for their greatest happiness (John 10:11). This instruction was especially necessary at the time when the Jews were about to undertake a journey through dry and barren countries, in their return to a land which lay waste and was desolate. ...

[I]t is probable that God is indirectly warning believers not to desire excessive luxury ... for we know that 'the ways' are exposed to the attacks of enemies and robbers, and that the tops of mountains are for the most part barren. The Church is governed by Christ in such a manner as not to be free from the attacks and insults of the wicked, and is led in such a manner as to frequently inhabit barren and frightening regions. But though enemies are at hand, God protects us from their violence and oppression. If we are thirsty or hungry, He is abundantly able to supply everything that is necessary for food and sustenance. And, amidst the perils and difficulties of this nature we perceive His care and concern more clearly than if we were placed beyond the reach of all danger. [Commentary on Isaiah]

FEBRUARY 18

Christ in Us

... that according to the riches of his glory he may grant you to be strengthened with power through his Holy Spirit in your inner being, so that Christ may dwell in your hearts through faith.

EPHESIANS 3:16-17

It is a mistake to imagine that the Spirit can be obtained without obtaining Christ; and it is equally foolish and absurd to dream that we can receive Christ without the Spirit. Both doctrines must be believed. ... [T]he Spirit will be found nowhere but in Christ, on whom He is said, on that account, to have rested. For He Himself says by the prophet Isaiah: 'The Spirit of the Lord is upon me' (Isa. 41:1; Luke 4:18). But neither can Christ be separated from His Spirit; for then He would be said to be dead, and to have lost all His power. For good reason, then, Paul affirms that the persons who are endowed by God with spiritual vigor are those in whom Christ dwells. He points to that part in which Christ especially dwells, 'in your hearts,' to show that it is not adequate for the knowledge of Christ to dwell on the tongue or flutter in the brain. ...

What a remarkable commendation is here bestowed on faith, that, by means of it, the Son of God becomes our own, and makes His home with us (John 14:23)! By faith we not only acknowledge that Christ suffered and rose from the dead on our account, but, accepting the offers which He makes of Himself, we possess and enjoy Him as our Savior. ... In a word, faith is not a distant view, but a warm embrace of Christ, by which He dwells in us, and we are filled with the divine Spirit. [Commentary on Ephesians]

FEBRUARY 19

The Father's Love Manifested

For God so loved the world, that he gave his only-begotten Son, that whoever believes in him should not perish but have eternal life.
JOHN 3:16

As the whole matter of our salvation must not be sought anywhere else than in Christ, so we must see why Christ came to us, and why He was offered to be our Savior. Both points are distinctly stated to us: namely, that faith in Christ brings life to all, and that Christ brought life because the heavenly Father loves the human race, and wishes that they should not perish. ... This, [John] says, is the proper look of faith, to be fixed on Christ, in whom it beholds the breast of God filled with love: this is a firm and enduring support, to rely on the death of Christ as the only pledge of that love.

The word 'only-begotten' is emphatic, to magnify the fervor of the love of God toward us. For as men and women are not easily convinced that God loves them, in order to remove all doubt, He has expressly stated that we are so very dear to God that, on our account, He did not even spare His only-begotten Son. Since, therefore, God has most abundantly testified His love toward us, whoever is not satisfied with this testimony, and still remains in doubt, offers a high insult to Christ, as if He had been an ordinary man given up at random to death. ... Christ has a right to this name [only-begotten Son] because He is by nature the only Son of God; and He communicated this honor to us by adoption, when we are engrafted into His body. [Commentary on John]

FEBRUARY 20

God's Perfect Law

The law of the LORD is perfect, reviving the soul; the testimony of the LORD is sure, making wise the simple; the precepts of the LORD are right, rejoicing the heart; the commandment of the LORD is pure, enlightening the eyes.

PSALM 19:7-8

The first commendation of the law of God is that it is 'perfect.' By this word David means that if people are duly instructed in the law of God, they lack nothing which is requisite for perfect wisdom. In the writings of heathen authors there are no doubt found true and useful sentences scattered here and there; and it is also true, that God has put into the minds of men and women some knowledge of justice and uprightness; but due to the corruption of our nature, the true light of truth is not to be found among people where revelation is not enjoyed, but only certain mutilated principles which are involved in much obscurity and doubt. David, therefore, justly claims this praise for the law of God, that it contains in it perfect and absolute wisdom. ...

David adds [further] that God's statutes rejoice the heart. This implies that there is no true and solid joy other than that which proceeds from a good conscience; and we become partakers of this joy when we are certainly persuaded that our life is pleasing and acceptable to God. No doubt, the source from which true peace of conscience proceeds is faith, which freely reconciles us to God. But to the saints who serve God with true affection of heart there also arises unspeakable joy from the knowledge that they do not labor in their service in vain, or without hope of reward, since they have God as the one who judges and approves of their life. [Commentary on Psalms]

FEBRUARY 21

Fifth Petition

'[F]orgive us our debts, as we also have forgiven our debtors.'

MATTHEW 6:12

Christ has included in two petitions all that relates to the eternal salvation of the soul and to the spiritual life: for these are the two leading points of the divine covenant, in which all our salvation consists.

He offers to us a free reconciliation by 'not counting our sins' (2 Cor. 5:19) and promises the Spirit, to engrave the righteousness of the law on our hearts. We are commanded to ask for both, and the prayer for obtaining the forgiveness of sins is placed first. In Matthew, sins are called 'debts,' because they expose us to the condemnation at the tribunal of God, and make us debtors; indeed, more, they alienate us entirely from God, so that there is no hope of obtaining peace and favor except by pardon. And so is fulfilled what Paul tells us, 'all have sinned and fallen short of the glory of God' (Rom. 3:23), 'that every mouth may be stopped, and the whole world may be held accountable to God' (Rom. 3:19). For though the righteousness of God shines (to some extent) in the saints, yet so long as they are surrounded by the flesh, they lie under the burden of sins. No one will be found so pure as not to need the mercy of God, and if we wish to partake of it, we must feel our wretchedness. ... [W]hen [Christ] commands all His disciples to come to Him daily for the forgiveness of sins, those who think that they have no need of such a remedy, are removed from the number of disciples. [Commentary on the Harmony of the Gospels]

FEBRUARY 22

Sixth Petition

'And lead us not into temptation, but deliver us from evil.'

MATTHEW 6:13

Some people have split this petition into two. This is wrong, for the nature of the subject makes it clear that it is one and the same petition. ... The meaning is, 'We are conscious of our own weakness, and desire to enjoy the protection of God, that we may remain invincible against all the assaults of Satan.' We showed from the former petition that no one can be reckoned a Christian who does not acknowledge themselves to be a sinner. And, in the same manner, we conclude from this petition that we have no strength for living a holy life, except so far as we obtain it from God. Whoever begs God to help them overcome temptations acknowledges that, unless God delivers them, they will be constantly falling. ...

The word 'temptation' is often used generally of any kind of trial. In this sense God is said to have 'tempted Abraham' (Gen. 22:1) when He tested his faith. We are tempted both by adversity and by prosperity, because each of them is an occasion for bringing to light feelings that were formerly concealed. But in this passage, [Christ] is speaking of inward temptations, which may rightly be called the scourge of the devil, as they excite our lusts. It would be foolish to ask that God would keep us free from everything that tests our faith. ... Though it is quite possible that we may feel such pricks in our minds – for, we have constant warfare with the flesh during the entire course of our lives – yet we ask that the Lord not cause us to be thrown down, or allow us to be overwhelmed, by temptations. [Commentary on the Harmony of the Gospels]

FEBRUARY 23

Heavenly Inheritance

According to his great mercy, he has caused us to be born again to a living hope …. to an inheritance that is imperishable, undefiled, and unfading, kept in heaven for you.

1 PETER 1:3-4

Every word which follows is weighty. The inheritance is said to be reserved, or preserved, that we may know that it is beyond the reach of danger. For, were it not in God's hands, it might be exposed to endless dangers. If it were in this world, how could we regard it as safe amidst so many changes? That He might free us from every fear, He testifies that our salvation is placed in safety beyond the harms which Satan can do. But as the certainty of salvation can bring us but little comfort, unless each person knows that it belongs to themselves, Peter adds the words 'for you.' For consciences will calmly rest here, that is, when the Lord cries to them from heaven, 'Behold, your salvation is in my hand and is kept for you.' But as salvation is not indiscriminately for all, He calls our attention to faith, that all who are endued with faith might be distinguished from the rest, and that they might not doubt but that they are the true and legitimate heirs of God. For as faith penetrates into heavens, so also it appropriates to us the blessings which are in heaven. [Commentary on 1 Peter]

FEBRUARY 24

Preservation of the Church

'Lift up your eyes to the heavens, and look at the earth beneath; for the heavens vanish like smoke, the earth will wear out like a garment ... but my salvation shall be forever and my righteousness will never be dismayed.'

ISAIAH 51:6

When we see so great changes in the world, we are inclined to think that the Church comes under the influence of the same violent changes; and, therefore, we need to have our minds elevated above the ordinary course of nature. Otherwise, the salvation of the Church will appear to hang on a thread, and to be blown here and there by the billows and storms. Yet we can see both in heaven and on earth how wisely God regulates all things, with what fatherly kindness He upholds and defends His workmanship and the frame of the world, and with what equity He provides for all His creatures. But in a remarkable manner He desires to watch over His Church, as He has assigned special priority to her. ...

[The prophet] urges believers to turn their eyes upwards and downwards, so as to perceive both in heaven and in earth the wonderful providence of God, by which He so beautifully preserves the order and harmony which He first established in the world. But he adds that, though heaven and earth rapidly decay, it is impossible that the Church shall fail, the stability of which is founded on God. ... [This passage] reminds us that the grace of God, which He displays in the preservation of His Church, surpasses all His other works. Everything that is contained in heaven and earth is frail and fading; but God's salvation by which He guards the Church is eternal, and therefore cannot be vulnerable to these dangers. [Commentary on Isaiah]

FEBRUARY 25

The Example of Cornelius

At Caesarea there was a man named Cornelius, a centurion of what was known as the Italian Cohort, a devout man who feared God with all his household, gave alms generously to the people, and prayed continually to God.

ACTS 10:1-2

Luke says that Cornelius was a godly man and one that feared God. Secondly, like a good householder, he was concerned to instruct his family. Next, Luke praises him for the offices of love, because he was kind toward all the people. Finally, that he prayed to God continually. In sum, Cornelius was a man of singular virtues, marked by integrity of godliness, so that his life was framed in all ways according to the rule which God prescribes for His people. ... This is very profitable to be noted, because Luke describes in the person of Cornelius how to live well. Therefore, in ordering life well, let faith and religious devotion be at the foundation, for, in their absence, all other virtues are nothing else but smoke. For good reason Luke judges the fear of God and prayer as fruits and testimonies of godliness. For religious devotion cannot be separated from the fear of God and reverence for Him, neither can any man or woman be counted as godly, save those who acknowledge God to be their Father and Lord, and who cling wholly to Him. ... Moreover, because a large part of the world corrupts and defiles the worship of God with fake trifles, Luke adds (with good reason) that Cornelius prayed continually, which signifies that he demonstrated his godliness not only with external ceremonies, but also that he worshiped God spiritually, when he exercised himself in prayer. ... Thus, let all of us exhort ourselves to persevere in prayer by the example of Cornelius. [Commentary on Acts]

FEBRUARY 26

God-Ordained Preaching

And he gave the apostles, the prophets, the evangelists, the shepherds and teachers, to equip the saints for the work of ministry, for building up the body of Christ, until we all attain to the unity of the faith and of the knowledge of the Son of God.
EPHESIANS 4:11-13

If the edification of the church proceeds from Christ alone, He surely has a right to prescribe in what manner it shall be edified. But Paul expressly states that, according to the command of Christ, no real union or perfection is attained, except by the outward preaching. We must allow ourselves to be ruled and taught by men. This is the universal rule, which extends equally to the highest and to the lowest. The Church is the common mother of all the godly, which bears, nourishes, and brings up children to God, kings and peasants alike; and this is done by the ministry. Those who neglect or despise this order choose to be wiser than Christ. Woe to the pride of such people! It is, no doubt, possible that divine influence should make us perfect without human assistance. But the present inquiry is not what the power of God can accomplish, but what is the will of God and the appointment of Christ. In employing human instruments for accomplishing their salvation, God has conferred on humanity no ordinary favor. Nor can any exercise be found better adapted to promote unity than to gather around the common doctrine – the standard of our General. 'Until we all attain.' ... [Paul] reminds his readers that the use of the ministry is not temporary, like that of a school for children, but constant, so long as we remain in the world. [Commentary on Ephesians]

FEBRUARY 27

Providence and Deliverance

For he will deliver you from the snare of the fowler and from the deadly pestilence. He will cover you with his pinions, and under his wings you will find refuge…

PSALM 91:3-4

Hence appears the immeasurable felicity of the godly mind. Innumerable are the evils that beset human life; innumerable, too, the deaths that threaten it. … Embark upon a ship, you are one step away from death. Mount a horse, if one foot slips, your life is imperiled. Go through the city streets, you are subject to as many dangers as there are tiles on the roofs. If there is a weapon in your hand or a friend's, harm awaits. All the fierce animals you see are armed for your destruction. … I pass over poisonings, ambushes, robberies, open violence, which in part besiege us at home, in part dog us abroad. Amid these tribulations must not men and women be most miserable, since, but half alive in life, they weakly draw their anxious and languid breath, as if they had a sword perpetually hanging over their neck? … Yet, when that light of divine providence has once shone upon a godly person, they are then relieved and set free not only from the extreme anxiety and fear that were pressing them before, but from every care. … Their solace, I say, is to know that their heavenly Father so holds all things in His power, so rules by His authority and will, so governs by His wisdom, that nothing can befall except He determine it. Moreover, it comforts them to know that they have been received into God's safekeeping … and that neither water, nor fire, nor iron can harm them, except in so far as it pleases God as governor to give them occasion. [Institutes (1559), I.xvii.10-11]

FEBRUARY 28

Sincere Worship

Praise the LORD! I will give thanks to the LORD with my whole heart, in the company of the upright, in the congregation.

PSALM 111:1

The best and most effective way to instill the performance of any duty is by way of example; and, accordingly, we find that the prophet, in the present instance, sets himself as an example, to lead others to engage in the celebration of God's praises. His desire to praise God consists of two parts: that he would sincerely celebrate God's praises with all his heart, and that he would do it publicly, in the assembly of the faithful. Quite appropriately, he begins with heart-praises, because it is much better to praise in secret, when no one is aware of it, than to lift up our voice and shout forth his praises with insincere lips. At the same time, the person who, in secret, pours out their heart with grateful emotions toward God, will also extol his praises publicly in swelling strains, otherwise God would be deprived of one half of the honor which is due to Him. The prophet is determined to praise God with his whole heart, that is, with an upright and honest heart; not that he hopes to come up to the full measure of his duty, but he declares that he does not want to be like the hypocrites, who [praise God] coldly and with a deceptive heart. … This is a point worth noting, lest anyone should be discouraged due to not being able to cherish such a desired hope of attaining that perfection of heart. For, however defective our praises may be, they will nevertheless be acceptable to God, provided only we strive sincerely to render unto Him this act of devotion. [Commentary on Psalms]

FEBRUARY 29

Presumptuous Sins

Keep back your servant from presumptuous sins; let them not have dominion over me!
PSALM 19:13

Now, if David, who had made so much progress in the fear of God, was not beyond the danger of sinning, how shall carnal and unrenewed people (in whom innumerable lusts exercise dominion) be able to restrain and govern themselves by their own free will? … By these words [David] expressly declares that unless God assist him, he will not only be unable to resist, but will be entirely brought under the dominion of the worst vices. This passage, therefore, teaches us not only that all humans are naturally enslaved to sin, but that the faithful themselves would also become the bond slaves of sin, if God did not unceasingly watch over them to guide them in the path of holiness, and to strengthen them for persevering in it. There is also another useful lesson to which we should pay attention, namely, that we ought never to pray for forgiveness without, at the same time, asking to be strengthened and fortified by the power of God in the future, that temptations may not gain the advantage over us. And although we may feel in our hearts the incitements of concupiscence goading and distressing us, we ought not, on that account, to become discouraged. The remedy to which we should have recourse is to pray to God to restrain us. No doubt, David could have wished to feel in his heart no stirrings of corruption; but knowing that he would never be entirely free from the remnants of sin, until at death he had put off the corrupt nature, he prays to be armed with the grace of the Holy Spirit for the combat, that iniquity might not reign victorious over him. [Commentary on Psalms]

MARCH 1

Faith and the Gospel

[Christ] bears witness to what he has seen and heard, yet no one receives his testimony. Whoever receives his testimony sets his seal to this, that God is true.
JOHN 3:32-33

Even if the whole world should refuse or withhold faith in the gospel, this ought not to prevent good men and women from giving their assent to God. They have something on which they may safely rest, when they know that to believe the gospel is nothing else than to assent to the truths which God has revealed. ...

Hence, too, we are reminded how acceptable and precious a sacrifice faith is in the sight of God. As nothing is dearer to Him than His truth, so we cannot render to Him more acceptable worship than when we acknowledge by our faith that He is true, for then we ascribe that honor which truly belongs to Him. On the other hand, we cannot offer to Him a greater insult than not to believe the gospel; for He cannot be deprived of His truth without taking away all His glory and majesty. His truth is in some sort closely linked with the gospel, and it is His will that there it should be recognized. Unbelievers, therefore, as far as lies in their power, leave to God nothing whatever; not that their wickedness overthrows the faithfulness of God, but because they do not hesitate to charge God with falsehood. ... [Faith in the gospel] ought to kindle in our minds the most ardent love of it; for how great is the honor which God confers on poor worthless people, when they, who by nature are nothing else than falsehood and vanity, are thought worthy of attesting by their signature the sacred truth of God? [Commentary on John]

MARCH 2

Faith and Works

Was not Abraham our father justified by works when he offered up his son Isaac on the altar? You see that faith was active along with his works, and faith was completed by his works...

JAMES 2:21-22

We have already said that James does not speak here of the cause of justification, or of the manner in which humans obtain righteousness, and this is plain to everyone. Rather, his object is only to show that good works are always connected with faith; and, therefore, since he declares that Abraham was 'justified by works,' he is speaking of the proof he gave of his justification.

When, therefore, the Sophists set up James against Paul, they go astray through the ambiguous meaning of a term. When Paul says that we are justified by faith, he means no other thing than that by faith we are counted righteous before God. But James has quite another thing in view, namely, to show that those who profess that they have faith must prove the reality of their faith by their works. Doubtless James did not mean to teach us here the ground on which our hope of salvation ought to rest; and it is this alone that Paul dwells upon. ...

[W]e must take notice of the twofold meaning of the word 'justified.' Paul means by it the gratuitous imputation of righteousness before the tribunal of God; and James, the manifestation of righteousness by our conduct, and that in the presence of others, as we may gather from these preceding words, 'Show me your faith' (James 2:18), etc. In this sense we fully allow that men and women are justified by works...
[Commentary on James]

MARCH 3

Sharing with the Poor

'Is not this the fast that I choose ... to share your bread with the hungry and bring the homeless poor into your house?'

ISAIAH 58:6-7

Isaiah now shows that we ought to exercise kindness toward the miserable and those who need our assistance. Uprightness and righteousness are divided into two parts: first, that we should injure nobody; and, second, that we should share our wealth and abundance with the poor and needy. And these two principles ought to be joined together; for it is not enough to abstain from acts of injustice if you refuse your assistance to the needy. Nor will it be of much good to render your aid to the needy, if at the same time you rob some of that which you share with others. You must not relieve your neighbors on goods acquired by plunder or theft; and if you have committed any act of injustice, or cruelty, or extortion, you must not – with a pretended offering – call on God to receive a share of the plunder. These two parts, therefore, must be held together, provided only that we have our love of our neighbor approved and accepted by God. By commanding them to 'share your bread with the hungry,' Isaiah intended to take away every excuse from those covetous and greedy people, who allege that they have a right to hold on to that which is their own. 'This is mine, and therefore I may keep it for myself,' they say. 'Why should I make common property of that which God has given me?' Isaiah replies: 'It is indeed yours, but on this condition, that you share it with the hungry and thirsty, not so that you eat it all by yourself.' [Commentary on Isaiah]

MARCH 4

Life-Giving Fountain

Jesus said to her, 'Everyone who drinks of this water will be thirsty again, but whoever drinks of the water that I will give him will never be thirsty again.' JOHN 4:13-14

[Jesus] distinguishes between the use of the two kinds of water; the one serves the body, and only for a time, while the power of the other gives perpetual vigor to the soul. For, as the body is liable to decay, so the aids by which it is supported must be frail and transitory. That which quickens the soul cannot but be eternal. Again, the words of Christ are not at variance with the fact that believers, to the very end of life, burn with desire for more abundant grace. For He does not say that, from the very first day, we drink so as to be fully satisfied, but only means that the Holy Spirit is a continually flowing fountain; and that, therefore, there is no danger that they who have been renewed by spiritual grace shall be dried up. And, therefore, although we thirst throughout our whole life, yet it is certain that we have not received the Holy Spirit for a single day, or for any short period, but as a perennial fountain, which will never fail us. Thus, believers thirst – keenly thirst – throughout their whole life; and yet they have abundance of life-giving water; for however small may have been the measure of grace which they have received, it gives them perpetual vigor, so that they are never entirely dry. ... The grace of Christ, therefore, does not flow to us for a short time, but overflows into a blessed immortality. [Commentary on John]

MARCH 5

Inviting Others to Christ

Jesus said to her, 'I who speak to you am [the Christ].'… So the woman left her water jar and went away into town and said to the people, 'Come, see a man who told me all that I ever did. Can this be the Christ?'
JOHN 4:26, 28-29

This circumstance is reported by John to express the ardor of the woman's zeal; for it is an indication of her haste that she leaves her pitcher, and returns to the city. And this is the nature of faith, that when we have become partakers of eternal life, we wish to bring others to share with us; nor is it possible that the knowledge of God shall lie buried and inactive in our hearts without being manifested before other people, for that saying must be true: 'I believed, even when I spoke' [Ps. 116:10]. The earnestness and promptness of the woman are so much more worthy of attention, that it was only a small spark of faith that kindled them; for scarcely had she tasted Christ when she spreads His fame throughout the whole city. In those who have already made progress in His school, sluggishness will be highly disgraceful. But [some might say that she deserves] blame on this account, that while she is still ignorant and imperfectly taught, she goes beyond the limits of her faith. I reply, she would have acted inconsiderately, if she had assumed the office of a teacher, but when she desires nothing more than to excite her fellow citizens to hear Christ speaking, we will not say that she forgot herself, or proceeded farther than she had a right to do. She merely fulfills the office of a trumpet or bell to invite others to come to Christ. [Commentary on John]

MARCH 6

Christ's Intense Suffering

I am poured out like water, and all my bones are out joint; my heart is like wax; it is melted within my breast.

PSALM 22:14

Hitherto [David] has informed us that being surrounded by wild beasts, he was not far from death. ... He now bewails, in addition to this, his inward distress; from which we learn that he was not dull or insensible to dangers. It could have been no ordinary fear which made him almost waste away, by which his bones were disjointed, and his heart poured out like water. We see, then, that David was not buffeted with the waves of affliction like a rock which cannot be moved, but was agitated within by painful troubles and temptations, which, due to the weakness of the flesh, he would never have been able to sustain had he not been aided by the power of the Spirit of God.

How these sufferings are applicable to Christ I have informed [the reader] a little before. Being a real man, He was truly subject to the infirmities of our flesh, only without the taint of sin. The perfect purity of His nature did not extinguish His human affections; it only regulated them, that they might not become sinful through excess. The greatness of His griefs, therefore, could not so weaken Him as to prevent Him, even in the midst of His most excruciating sufferings, from submitting Himself to the will of God, with a composed and peaceful mind. ... Following the example of David, we should take courage; and when, through our infirmity, we are, as it were, almost lifeless, we should direct our groaning to God, begging that He would be graciously pleased to restore us to strength and vigor. [Commentary on Psalms]

MARCH 7

Fear and Faith

God is our refuge and strength, a very present help in trouble. Therefore, we will not fear though the earth gives way, though the mountains be moved into the heart of the sea.

PSALM 46:1-2

[The Psalmist] next concludes that the faithful have no reason to be afraid, since God is always ready to deliver them, indeed, is also armed with invincible power. He shows in this that the true and proper proof of our hope consists in this, that, when things are so confused, that the heavens seem as it were to fall with great violence, the earth to remove out of its place, and the mountains to be torn up from their very foundations, we nevertheless continue to preserve and maintain calmness and tranquility of heart. It is an easy matter to give the appearance of great confidence, so long as we are not placed in imminent danger; but if, in the midst of a general crash of the whole world, our minds continue undisturbed and free of trouble, this is evident proof that we attribute to the power of God the honor which belongs to Him. When, however, the sacred poet says, 'We will not fear,' he is not to be understood as meaning that the minds of the godly are exempt from all concerns or fears, as if they were destitute of feeling, for there is a great difference between indifference and the confidence of faith. He only shows that whatever may happen they are never overwhelmed with terror, but rather gather strength and courage sufficient to allay all fear. [Commentary on Psalms]

MARCH 8

Christ's Temptations

Then Jesus was led up by the Spirit into the wilderness to be tempted by the devil.

MATTHEW 4:1

I have no doubt that God intended to exhibit in the person of His Son, as in a very bright mirror, how obstinately and perseveringly Satan opposes the salvation of men and women. ... At the same time, it ought to be observed that the Son of God voluntarily endured the temptations, which we are now considering, and fought, as it were, in single combat with the devil so that, by His victory, He might obtain a triumph for us. Whenever we are called to encounter Satan, let us remember that his attacks can be sustained and repelled in no other way than by holding out this shield: for the Son of God undoubtedly allowed Himself to be tempted so that He might be constantly set before our minds when Satan excites within us any contest of temptations. When He was leading a private life at home, we do not read that He was tempted. But when He was about to discharge the office of Redeemer, He then entered the field in the name of His whole church. But if Christ was tempted as the public representative of all believers, let us learn that the temptations that befall us are not accidental, or regulated by the will of Satan, without God's permission; but that the Spirit of God presides over our contests as an exercise of our faith. This will help us in cherishing the assured hope, that God, who is the supreme judge and disposer of combat, will not be unmindful of us, but will fortify us against those distresses that He sees that we are unable to meet. [Commentary on the Harmony of the Gospels]

MARCH 9

Anxiety and Providence

Humble yourselves, therefore, under the mighty hand of God so that at the proper time he may exalt you, casting all your anxieties on him, because he cares for you.

1 PETER 5:6-7

Peter more fully sets forth here the providence of God. For whence are these proverbial sayings, 'We shall have to howl among wolves,' and 'They are foolish who are like sheep, exposing themselves to wolves to be devoured,' except that we think that by our humility we set loose the reins to the audacity of the ungodly, so that they insult us all the more blatantly? But this fear arises from our ignorance of divine providence. Now, on the other hand, as soon as we are convinced that God cares for us, our minds are easily led to patience and humility. Lest, then, the wickedness of men and women should tempt us to become fierce of mind, the Apostle prescribes to us a remedy, just as David does in Psalm 37, so that, having cast our care on God, we may calmly rest. For all those who do not rest in the providence of God must necessarily be in constant turmoil and violently attack others. We ought the more to dwell on this thought, that God cares for us, in order, first, that we may have peace within; and, secondly, that we may be humble and meek toward others.

But we are not therefore urged to cast all our care on God, as though God wished us to have strong hearts, and to be void of all feelings; but lest fear or anxiety should drive us to impatience. [For divine providence] ... ought not to encourage the laziness of the flesh, but bring rest to faith. [Commentary on 1 Peter]

MARCH 10

The Armor of God

Put on the whole armor of God, that you may be able to stand against the schemes of the devil. For we do not wrestle against flesh and blood, but against the rulers, against the authorities, against the cosmic powers over this present darkness ...

EPHESIANS 6:11-12

God has furnished us with various defensive weapons, provided we do not lazily refuse what is offered. But almost all of us are guilty of carelessness and hesitation in using the grace offered to us; just as if a soldier, about to meet the enemy, should take off his helmet, and neglect his shield. To correct this ... laziness, Paul borrows a comparison from the military art, and bids us 'put on the whole armor of God.' ... To impress them still more deeply with their danger, Paul points out the nature of the enemy, which he illustrates by a comparative statement, 'we do not wrestle against flesh and blood.' The meaning is that our difficulties are far greater than if we had to fight with human opponents. There we resist human strength, sword is opposed to sword, man contends against man, force is met by force, and skill by skill. But here the case is very different. All amounts to this, that our enemies are such as no human power can withstand. ... Paul describes our enemy as formidable, not to overwhelm us with fear, but to stimulate our diligence and earnestness; for this is a middle course to be observed. When the enemy is neglected, they do their utmost to oppress us with sloth, and afterwards disarm us by terror; so that, even before the engagement has begun, we are vanquished. ... The devil is not an enemy who may be safely despised. [Commentary on Ephesians]

MARCH 11

God Our Shepherd

The LORD is my shepherd; I shall not want.

PSALM 23:1

Using the analogy of a shepherd, [David] commends the care which God, in His providence, had exercised toward him. His language implies that God has no less care for him than a shepherd has for the sheep committed to his charge. God, in the Scripture, frequently takes to Himself the name, and puts on the character of a shepherd, and this is no small token of His tender love toward us. As this is a lowly and homely manner of speaking ... [God] must possess an exceptionally strong affection for us. It is therefore a strange thing if, when He invites us to Himself with such gentleness and familiarity, we are not drawn or allured to Him, that we may rest in safety and peace under His guardianship. But it should be observed, that God is a shepherd only to those who, touched with a sense of their own weakness and poverty, feel their need of His protection, and who willingly abide in His sheepfold, and surrender themselves to be governed by Him. David, who excelled in both power and riches, nevertheless frankly confessed himself to be a poor sheep, that he might have God for his shepherd. ... We ought to bear in mind that our happiness consists in this, that God's hand is stretched forth to govern us, that we live under His shadow, and that His providence keeps watch and care over our welfare. Thus, even if we have an abundance of all temporal good things, let us be assured that we cannot be truly happy unless God chooses to count us among the number of His flock. [Commentary on Psalms]

MARCH 12

Sorrowful Yet Rejoicing

In this you rejoice, though now for a little while, if necessary, you have been grieved by various trials ...
1 PETER 1:6

It seems somewhat inconsistent, when Peter says that the faithful, who exulted with joy, were at the same time sorrowful, for these are contrary feelings. But the faithful know by experience how these things can exist together, much better than can be expressed in words. However, to explain the matter in a few words, we may say that the faithful are not logs of wood, nor have they so divested themselves of human feelings, but that they are affected with sorrow, fear danger, and feel poverty as an evil, and persecutions as hard and difficult to be borne. Hence they experience sorrow from evils; but it is so mitigated by faith, that they cease not at the same time to rejoice. Thus, sorrow does not prevent their joy, but on the contrary, gives place to it. Again, though joy overcomes sorrow, yet it does not put an end to it, for it does not divest us of humanity. And hence it appears what true patience is; its beginning, and, as it were, its root, is the knowledge of God's blessings, especially of that gratuitous adoption with which He has favored us; for all who raise their minds to this fact find it an easy thing calmly to bear all evils. For why is it that our minds are pressed down with grief, except that we have no participation in spiritual things? But all those who regard their troubles as necessary trials for their salvation, not only rise above them, but also turn them to an occasion of joy. [Commentary on 1 Peter]

MARCH 13

Handling Scripture Wisely

Do your best to present yourself to God as one approved, a worker who has no need to be ashamed, rightly handling the word of truth.

2 TIMOTHY 2:15

Let us therefore be 'workmen' in building the Church, and let us be employed in the work of God in such a manner that some fruit shall be seen; then we shall have no cause to be ashamed; for, although in debating we may not be equal to talkative boasters, yet it will be enough that we excel them in the desire for edification, in industry, in courage, and in the efficacy of doctrine. In short, Paul urges Timothy to labor diligently, that he may not be ashamed before God. ... 'Rightly handling the word of truth.' This is a beautiful metaphor, and one that skillfully expressed the chief goal of teaching. [Some people might say:] '[W]hat purpose is served by having sermons every day, or even the office of pastors? Has not every person an opportunity to read the Bible?' But Paul assigns teachers the duty of dividing or cutting, as if a father, in giving food to his children, were dividing the bread, by cutting it into small pieces. Paul advises Timothy to 'cut aright,' lest, when he is employed in cutting the surface – as unskillful people tend to do – he leaves the pith and marrow untouched. ... Some people mutilate the word, others tear it, others torture it, others break it in pieces; still others remain on the outside and never come to the heart of doctrine. To all these faults Paul contrasts the 'right handling,' that is, the manner of explaining that is adapted to edification; for that is the rule by which we must test all interpretations of Scripture. [Commentary on 2 Timothy]

MARCH 14

Idolatry

Those who make [idols] become like them; so do all who trust in them.

PSALM 115:8

The reason why God holds images in such great abhorrence appears very plainly from the fact that He cannot endure that the worship due to Himself alone should be taken from Him and given to them. It is an honor that belongs uniquely to God that the world should acknowledge Him to be the sole author of salvation, and should ask for and expect from Him alone all that is needed. And, therefore, as often as men and women place their confidence in any other than Himself, God is deprived of the worship that is due to Him, and His majesty is, as it were, annihilated. ... If a person carves an image of marble, wood, or brass, or if they cast one of gold or silver, this of itself would not be so detestable a thing; but when they attempt to attach God to their inventions, and to make Him, as it were, descend from heaven, then a pure fiction is substituted in God's place. It is very true that God's glory is instantly counterfeited when it is invested with a corruptible nature ... nevertheless, He is doubly injured when His truth, and grace, and power are imagined to be concentrated in idols. To make idols, and then to confide in them, are things which are almost inseparable. ... Therefore, averse to seeking God in a spiritual manner, [idolators] pull Him down from His throne and place Him under inanimate things. Thus, it happens that they address their prayers to images, because they imagine that in them God's ears, and also His eyes, and hands are near to them. [Commentary on Psalms]

MARCH 15

Heirs in Christ

It has been testified somewhere, 'What is man, that you are mindful of him, or the son of man, that you care for him? You made him for a little while lower than angels; you have crowned him with glory and honor, putting everything in subjection under his feet.'

HEBREWS 2:6-8

We found at the beginning of this epistle that Christ has been appointed by the Father as the heir of all things. Doubtless, as he ascribes the entire inheritance to one person, he excludes all others as aliens – and rightfully so, since we have all become exiles from God's kingdom. We thus have no right to take the food, then, that God has destined for His own family, unless Christ, by whom we are admitted into this family, at the same time admits us into a participation of this privilege, so that we may enjoy the whole world, together with the favor of God. Hence, Paul teaches us that Abraham was made an heir of the world by faith, that is, because he was united to the body of Christ (Rom. 4:13). If men and women, then, are precluded from all God's bounty until they receive a right to it through Christ, it follows that the dominion mentioned in the Psalm was lost to us in Adam, and that on this account it must again be restored as a gift. Now, the restoration begins with Christ as the head. …

To make the thing clearer, let us suppose two worlds – the first being the old world corrupted by Adam's sin; and the second being that world renewed later by Christ. The state of the first creation has become entirely decayed and has fallen due to human sin. Hence, this Psalm will not be fulfilled until a new restoration is accomplished by Christ. … [B]ut it will no doubt have its full accomplishment in our final redemption. [Commentary on Hebrews]

MARCH 16

True Repentance

[L]et the wicked forsake his way, and the unrighteous man his thoughts; let him return to the LORD, that he may have compassion on him, and to our God, for he will abundantly pardon.

ISAIAH 55:7

[T]he doctrine of repentance ought always to accompany the promise of salvation; for in no other way can men and women taste the goodness of God than by abhorring themselves on account of their sins, and renouncing themselves and the world. And, indeed, no one will sincerely desire to be reconciled to God and to obtain pardon of sins until they are moved by a true and earnest repentance. By three forms of expression Isaiah describes the nature of repentance: first, 'Let the wicked forsake his way'; second, 'the unrighteous man his thoughts'; third, 'let him return to the LORD.' Under the word 'way' he includes the whole course of life, and accordingly demands that they bring forth the fruits of righteousness as witnesses of their newness of life. By adding the word 'thoughts' he intimates that we must not only correct outward actions, but must begin with the heart. For even if, in the opinion of other people, we appear to change our manner of life for the better, yet we shall have made little proficiency if the heart is not also changed. Thus, repentance embraces a change of the whole person. ... We must first wash away from the mind all uncleanness, and conquer wicked inclinations, so that outward testimonies may afterwards be added. And if anyone boasts that they have been changed, and yet live in whatever way they please, it will be vain boasting. For both conversion of the heart and a change of life are required. [Commentary on Isaiah]

MARCH 17

Fighting Through Prayer

[A]nd take the helmet of salvation, and the sword of the Spirit, which is the word of God, praying at all times in the Spirit, with all prayer and supplication. To that end keep alert with all perseverance ...
EPHESIANS 6:17-18

Having instructed the Ephesians to put on their armor, Paul now enjoins them to fight by prayer. This is the true method. To call upon God is the chief exercise of faith and hope; and it is in this way that we obtain from God every blessing. ... We are exhorted to persevere in prayer. Every tendency to weariness must be counteracted by a cheerful performance of the duty. With unabated earnestness we must continue in our prayers, though we do not immediately obtain what we desire. ... There is not a moment in our lives in which our needs do not compel within us the duty of prayer. But ceaseless prayer may also be encouraged by considering, with sympathy, the needs of other believers. When is it that some members of the church are not suffering distress, and needing our assistance? If, at any time, we are colder or more indifferent about prayer than we ought to be, because we do not feel the pressure of immediate needs – let us immediately reflect on how many of our fellow believers are worn out by varied and heavy afflictions and weighed down by painful perplexity, or are reduced to terrible distress. If reflections like these do not rouse us from our lethargy, we must have hearts of stone. But should we pray for believers only? Though Paul states the claims of the godly, he does not exclude others. And yet in prayer, as in all other kinds of duties, our first concern unquestionably is due to the saints. [Commentary on Ephesians]

MARCH 18

Clean Hands, Pure Hearts

Who shall ascend the hill of the Lord? And who shall stand in his holy place? He who has clean hands and a pure heart, who does not lift up his soul to what is false and does not swear deceitfully.

PSALM 24:3-4

[David] comprehends all religion, and denotes the well-ordered life, under the purity of the hands and of the heart, and the reverence of God's name. True purity, no doubt, has its seat in the heart, but it manifests its fruits in the works of the hands. The Psalmist, therefore, very properly joins to a pure heart the purity of the whole life; for people act in a ridiculous fashion who boast of having a sound heart, if they do not show by their fruit that the root is good. On the other hand, it will not suffice to frame the hands, feet, and eyes according to the rule of righteousness, unless purity of heart precedes outward temperance. ...

A question may here be raised, why David does not say so much as one word concerning faith and calling upon God. The reason for this is easily explained. As it seldom happens that people behave themselves uprightly and innocently toward their fellow believers, unless they are so endued with the true fear of God, ... David very justly measures the piety of people toward God by the character of their conduct toward their fellow human beings. For the same reason, Christ describes 'justice, mercy, and faith' (Matt. 23:23) as the principal points of the law. [Commentary on Psalms]

MARCH 19

Peace and Protection

In peace I will both lie down and sleep; for you alone, O LORD, make me dwell in safety.

PSALM 4:8

[David] concludes by stating that, as he is protected by the power of God, he enjoys as much security and quiet as if he had been defended by all the garrisons on earth. Now, we know, that to be free from all fear, and from the torment and vexation of care, is a blessing to be desired above all other things. This verse, therefore, is a confirmation of the former sentence [in Ps. 4:7], intimating that David justly prefers the joy produced by the light of God's fatherly love before all other objects; for inward peace of mind certainly surpasses all the blessings we can imagine. Many commentators explain this passage as expressing David's hope, that his enemies will be reconciled to him, so that he may sleep with them in peace ... But in my judgment the proper meaning is this, that he will live as quietly and securely alone, as in the midst of a great army, because God defends him ... In short, David boasts that the protection of God alone was sufficient, and that under it he sleeps as securely, although destitute of all human guardianship, as if he had many to keep vigilant watch continually over him, or as if he had been defended on all sides by a great company. Let us therefore learn from his example, to yield this honor to God – to believe, that although there may appear no human help available, yet under His hand alone we are kept in peace and safety, as if we were surrounded by a great army. [Commentary on Psalms]

MARCH 20

The Gospel of Truth and Life

In him you also, when you heard the word of truth, the gospel of your salvation, and believed in him, were sealed with the promised Holy Spirit. EPHESIANS 1:13

Two phrases are here applied to the gospel: the 'word of truth,' and the 'gospel of your salvation.' Both deserve our careful attention. Nothing is more earnestly attempted by Satan than to lead us either to doubt or to despise the gospel. Paul therefore furnishes us with two shields, by which we may repel both temptations. In opposition to every doubt, let us learn to bring forward this testimony, that the gospel is not only certain truth, which cannot deceive, but it is ... the word of truth, as if, strictly speaking, there was no truth but itself. If our temptation is to despise or dislike the gospel, let us remember that its power and efficacy have been manifested in bringing us to salvation. The Apostle had formerly declared that 'it is the power of God for salvation to everyone who believes' (Rom. 1:16), but here Paul expresses more, for he reminds the Ephesians that, having been made partakers of salvation, they had learned this by their own experience. Unhappy are those people who weary themselves, as the world generally does, in wandering through many winding paths, neglecting the gospel, and pleasing themselves with wild romances – 'always learning and never able to arrive at a knowledge of the truth' (2 Tim. 3:7) or to find life! But happy are they who have embraced the gospel, and whose attachment to it is steadfast; for this, beyond all doubt, is truth and life. [Commentary on Ephesians]

MARCH 21

God Our Father

For you, O LORD, are our Father, our Redeemer from of old is your name.
ISAIAH 63:16

God permits us to reveal our hearts before Him in a familiar way. For prayer is nothing other than the opening up of our hearts before God; and it is the greatest of comforts to pour our cares, distresses, and anxieties into His lap. 'Commit your way to the Lord,' says David (Ps. 37:5). After having enumerated God's benefits, from which His goodness and power are clearly seen … Isaiah returns to this consideration, that the goodness of God is nevertheless so great as to exceed human wickedness. He calls God a 'Father' in the name of the Church; for everyone cannot address Him in this way, but it is the special privilege of the Church to address Him by a father's name. Hence it ought to be inferred that Christ, as the first-born, or rather, the only-begotten Son of God, always governed His Church; for in no other way than through Him can God be called Father. …

Redemption is here described as a testimony of that adoption; for by this proof God manifested Himself to be the Father of the people; and, therefore, believers can boldly and confidently call on God as their Father, because He gave a remarkable testimony of His fatherly kindness toward them, which encouraged them to confidence. But redemption alone would not have been enough, if a promise had not also been added; and therefore, as He once redeemed them, He promised that He would always be their Father. [Commentary on Isaiah]

MARCH 22

Saving Faith

But now the righteousness of God has been manifested apart from the law, although the Law and the Prophets bear witness to it – the righteousness of God through faith in Jesus Christ for all who believe.
ROMANS 3:21-22

As God justifies us freely by imputing the obedience of Christ to us, so we are rendered capable of this great blessing only by faith alone. ... Faith, I say, is a firm certainty of conscience, which embraces Christ as He is offered to us by the gospel. ... With regard, then, to the obtaining of righteousness before God, I say that we must necessarily hold the following five points concerning faith: First, that it is an undoubting persuasion, by which we receive the word brought by Prophets and Apostles as truth sent from God. Secondly, that what it properly looks to in the Word of God is the free promises, and especially Christ, their pledge and foundation, so that resting on the paternal favor of God, we can venture to entertain a confident hope of eternal salvation. Thirdly, that it is not a bare knowledge which flutters in the mind, but that it carries along with it a lively affection, which has its seat in the heart. Fourthly, that this faith does not spring from the shrewdness of the human mind, or the proper movement of the heart, but is the special work of the Holy Spirit, whose role it is both to enlighten the mind and impress the heart. Lastly, that this efficacy of the Spirit is not felt by all indiscriminately, but by those who are ordained to life. [On Reforming the Church, CTS, 249-50]

MARCH 23

Complete Joy

And we are writing these things so that our joy may be complete.

1 JOHN 1:4

By full joy, John expresses more clearly the complete and perfect happiness which we obtain through the gospel; at the same time, he reminds the faithful where they ought to fix all their affections. True is the saying, 'Where your treasure is, there your heart will be also' (Matt. 6:21). Whosoever, then, really perceives what fellowship with God is, will be satisfied with it alone, and will no more burn with desires for other things. 'The Lord is my portion and my cup,' says David. 'The lines have fallen from me in pleasant places' (Ps. 16:5-6). In the same manner Paul declares that all things were deemed by him as dung, in comparison with Christ alone (Phil. 3:8). John therefore has at length made a proficiency in the gospel, those persons who esteem themselves happy in having communion with God, and acquiesce in that alone; and thus they prefer it to the whole world, so that they are ready for its sake to relinquish all things. [Commentary on 1 John]

MARCH 24

Testimony to the Gospel

It is right for me to feel this way about you all, because I hold you in my heart, for you are all partakers with me of grace, both in my imprisonment and in the defense and confirmation of the gospel.

PHILIPPIANS 1:7

[I]t is no little honor that God confers on us, when we suffer persecution for the sake of His truth. For it was not in vain that it was said 'Blessed are you when others revile and persecute you and utter all kinds of evil against you falsely on my account' (Matt. 5:11). Let us therefore also remember that we must with readiness and cheerfulness embrace the fellowship of the cross of Christ as a special favor from God. In addition to bonds, Paul adds the 'defense and confirmation of the gospel,' that he may express so much the better the honorableness of the service which God has prescribed on us in placing us in opposition to His enemies, in order to bear testimony to His gospel. For it is as though He had entrusted us with the defense of His gospel. ... If only this came to the mind of everyone that is called to make a confession of their faith, that they have been chosen by Christ to be like advocates to plead His cause. For if they were sustained by this consolation they would be more courageous than to be so easily turned aside into a faithless revolt. ... [Therefore] the slaughter of so many martyrs has been accompanied at least with this advantage, that they have been like seals by which the gospel has been sealed in our hearts. Hence that saying of Tertullian, that 'the blood of the martyrs is the seed of the Church.' [Commentary on Philippians]

MARCH 25

Boldness and Humility

Peter answered him, 'Though they all fall away because of you, I will never fall away.'
MATTHEW 26:33

This passage claims our attention, so that everyone, remembering their own weakness, may earnestly seek the assistance of the Holy Spirit; and next, that no one may venture to take more upon themselves than what the Lord promises. Believers ought, indeed, to be prepared for the contest in such a manner that, having no doubt or uncertainty about the outcome and the victory, they may resist fear; for trembling and excessive anxiety are marks of distrust. But, on the other hand, they ought to guard against that stupidity that shakes off all anxiety, and fills their minds with pride, and extinguishes the desire to pray. This middle course between two faulty extremes is very beautifully expressed by Paul when he enjoins us to 'work out our own salvation with fear and trembling, for it is God who works in you, both to will and to work for His good pleasure' (Phil. 2:12-13). For, on the one hand, having humbled us, he entreats us to seek help from elsewhere; and, on the other hand, lest anxiety should induce sloth, he exhorts us to strenuous exertions. And, therefore, whenever any temptation is presented to us, let us first remember our weakness, that, being entirely thrown down, we may learn to seek elsewhere what we need; and, next, let us remember the grace which is promised, that it may free us from doubt. For those who, forgetting their weakness, and not calling on God, feel assured that they are strong, act entirely like drunken soldiers, who throw themselves rashly into the field, but, as soon as the effects of strong drink have worn off, think of nothing else than fleeing. [Commentary on the Harmony of the Gospels]

MARCH 26

Courage from God Alone

The servant girl at the door said to Peter, 'You also are not one of this man's disciples, are you?' He said, 'I am not.'

JOHN 18:17

Peter is introduced into the high priest's hall; but it cost him very dearly, for, as soon as he sets his foot within it, he is constrained to deny Christ. When he stumbles so shamefully at the first step, the foolishness of his boasting is exposed. He had boasted that he would prove to be a valiant champion, and able to meet death with firmness; and now, at the voice of a single maid ... he is confounded and throws down his arms. Such is a demonstration of the power of human beings. Certainly, all the strength that appears to be in them is smoke, which a breath immediately drives away. When we are out of the battle, we are very courageous; but experience shows that our lofty talk is foolish and groundless; and, even when Satan makes no attacks, we contrive for ourselves idle alarms which disturb us before the time. The voice of a feeble woman terrified Peter: and what is the case with us? Do we not continually tremble at the rustling of a falling leaf? A false appearance of danger, which was still distant, made Peter tremble: and are we not every day led away from Christ by childish absurdities? ... A man, filled not with fortitude but with wind, promises that he will obtain easy victory over the whole world; and yet, no sooner does he see the shadow of a thistle, than he immediately trembles. Let us therefore learn to be brave in nothing other than the Lord. [Commentary on John]

MARCH 27

Never Forsaken

My God, my God, why have you forsaken me? Why are you so far from saving me, from the words of my groaning?

PSALM 22:1

[This] verse contains two remarkable sentences which, although apparently contrary to one other, are yet always entering into the minds of the godly together. When the Psalmist speaks of being forsaken and cast off by God, it seems to be the complaint of someone in despair; for can a person have a single spark of faith remaining in them, when they believe that there is no longer any assistance available from God? And yet, in stating twice that God is his own God, and pouring forth anguished cries into his bosom, David makes a very distinct confession of his faith. Godly people will necessarily experience this inward conflict whenever God withdraws the tokens of His favor from them, so that, in whatever direction they turn their eyes, they see nothing but the darkness of night. ...

There is no one among the godly who does not daily experience this same thing. According to the judgment of the flesh, they think they are cast off and forsaken by God, while yet they apprehend by faith the grace of God, which is hidden from the eye of sense and reason; and thus, it comes to pass that contrary affections are mingled and interwoven in the prayers of the faithful. ... Between these two contrary affections the faithful are agitated and fluctuate, as Satan, on the one hand, exhibits to their view the signs of God's wrath [and] urges them on to despair ... while faith, calling them back to the promises, teaches them to wait patiently and to trust in God, until He again shows them His fatherly appearance. [Commentary on Psalms]

MARCH 28

Crucified with Christ

I have been crucified with Christ. It is no longer I who live, but Christ who lives in me. And the life I now live in the flesh I live by faith in the Son of God, who loved me and gave himself for me.

GALATIANS 2:20

'I am crucified with Christ.' This explains the manner in which we, who are dead to the law, live to God. Engrafted into the death of Christ, we derive from it a secret energy, as the twig does from the root. Again, the handwriting of the law, 'which stood against us,' Christ has nailed to the cross (Col. 2:14). Being then crucified with Him, we are freed from all the curse and guilt of the law. He who endeavors to set aside that deliverance negates the cross of Christ. But let us remember, that we are delivered from the yoke of the law, only by becoming one with Christ, as the twig draws its sap from the root, only by growing into one nature. ...

'Yet not I, but Christ who lives in me.'... He does not live by his own life, but is animated by the secret power of Christ; so that Christ may be said to live and grow in him; for as the soul enlivens the body, so Christ imparts life to His members. It is a remarkable sentiment, that believers live outside of themselves, that is, they live in Christ. This can only be accomplished by holding real and actual communication with Him. Christ lives in us in two ways. The first way consists in governing us by His Spirit and directing all our actions; the other way, in making us partakers of His righteousness, so that, while we can do nothing of ourselves, we are accepted in the sight of God. The first way relates to regeneration, the second to justification by free grace. [Commentary on Galatians]

MARCH 29

God's Presence

Lift up your heads, O gates! And be lifted up, O ancient doors, that the King of glory may come in.
PSALM 24:7

It was no ordinary token of the goodness of God that He condescended to dwell in the midst of them by a visible symbol of His presence [that is, the temple], and was willing that His heavenly dwelling place should be seen upon earth. This doctrine ought to be of use to us today; for it is an instance of the inestimable grace of God, that, as much as the weakness of our flesh will permit, we are lifted up even to God by the exercises of religion. What is the purpose of the preaching of the word, the sacraments, the holy assemblies, and the whole external government of the church, but that we may be united to God? It is thus with good reason that David extols so highly the worship of God appointed in the law, seeing that God exhibited Himself to His saints in the ark of the covenant, and thereby gave them a certain pledge of speedy assistance whenever they should call upon Him for aid. God, it is true 'dwells not in temples made with hands,' nor does He delight in outward pomp. ... But since it was God's pleasure that His ancient people ... should be lifted up to Him by earthly elements, David does not hesitate here to set forth, for the confirmation of their faith, the magnificent building of the temple, to assure them that it was not a useless theater. Rather, when they rightly worshiped God in it ... they stood as it were in His presence, and would actually experience that He was near to them. [Commentary on Psalms]

MARCH 30

Shadow of God's Wings

Be merciful to me, O God, be merciful to me, for in you my soul takes refuge; in the shadow of your wings I will take refuge, till the storms of destruction pass by.

PSALM 57:1

David had committed himself entirely to the guardianship of God, and now experienced that blessed consciousness of dwelling in a place of safety. ... The divine protection is compared to the shadow of wings, because God, as I have elsewhere observed, so as to warmly invite us to himself, is represented as stretching out his wings like a hen, or other birds, for the shelter of their young. How great our ingratitude and perversity in being so slow to accept such an endearing and gentle invitation! ... [I]t is evident, David declares, that God would prove his refuge, and the wings of God his shelter, under every tempest of affliction which blew over him. There are seasons when we are privileged to enjoy the calm sunshine of prosperity; but there is not a day of our lives in which we may not suddenly be overtaken by storms of affliction, and it is necessary that we should be persuaded that God will cover us with His wings. To hope he adds prayer. Those, indeed, who have placed their trust in God will always direct their prayers to Him; and David gives here a practical proof of his hope, by showing that he sought God in his emergencies. ... It substantially confirms and sustains our hope to recognize that God will never forsake the workmanship of His own hands – that He will perfect the salvation of His people and continue His divine guidance until He has brought them to the end of their [earthly] course. [Commentary on Psalms]

MARCH 31

Confidence in Death

For while we are still in this tent, we groan, being burdened – not that we would be unclothed, but that we would be further clothed, so that what is mortal may be swallowed up by life.

2 CORINTHIANS 5:4

The wicked also groan, because they are not content with their present situation in life. But afterward a very different disposition takes over them, that is, a clinging to life, so that they are horrified by death and do not find burdensome the long duration of their mortal life. The groaning of believers, on the other hand, arises from the fact that they know that here they are exiles from their homeland, and that they are shut up in the body as in a prison. Hence, they find burdensome this present life because in it they are not able to possess true and perfect blessedness, and because they cannot fell the bondage of sin except by death, and thus they long to be elsewhere. As, however, it is natural for all animals to desire existence, how can it be that believers are willing to cease to exist? The Apostle solves this question when he says that believers do not desire death for the sake of losing anything, but as having regard to a better life. For he admits that we have a natural aversion to leaving this life ... for no one willingly allows themselves to be stripped of their garments. Afterwards, however, he adds that the natural horror of death is overcome by confidence. For an individual will, without any reluctance, throw away a coarse, dirty, threadbare, and, in a word, tattered garment, in view of being arrayed in an elegant, handsome, new, and durable one. [Commentary on 2 Corinthians]

READINGS FOR
EASTER WEEK

SUNDAY

Christ's Kingdom Banishes Fear

And Jesus found a young donkey and sat on it, just as it is written, 'Fear not, daughter of Zion; behold, your king is coming, sitting on a donkey's colt.' JOHN 12:14-15

'Fear not.' In these words of the Prophet, as [John] the Evangelist quotes them, we ought to observe, first, that never is tranquility restored to our minds, or fear and trembling banished from them, unless we know that Christ reigns amongst us. The words of the Prophet [in Zechariah 9:9], indeed, are different; for he exhorts believers to gladness and rejoicing. But the Evangelist has here described the manner in which our hearts exult with true joy. For, we obtain that joy which springs from faith (Rom. 5:1) when the fear that torments us is removed and we are reconciled to God. This benefit, therefore, comes to us through Christ, that, freed from the tyranny of Satan, the yoke of sin being broken, guilt canceled, and death abolished, we freely boast, relying on the protection of our King, since those who are placed under His guardianship ought not to fear any danger. Not that we are free from fear, so long as we live in the world, but because confidence, founded on Christ, rises superior to all fear. Though Christ was still at a distance, yet the Prophet [Zechariah] exhorted the godly of that age to be glad and joyful because Christ was to come. 'Behold,' he said, 'your King will come; therefore, fear not.' Now that Jesus has come, in order that we may enjoy His presence, we ought more vigorously to contend with fear, that, freed from our enemies, we may peacefully and joyfully honor our King. [Commentary on John]

EASTER WEEK

MONDAY

Fellowship in Christ's Death

[T]hat I may know Christ and the power of his resurrection, and may share his sufferings, becoming like him in his death, that by any means possible I may attain the resurrection from the dead.

PHILIPPIANS 3:10-11

There is a twofold participation and fellowship in the death of Christ. One is inward – what the Scripture tends to call the 'mortification of the flesh,' or the 'crucifixion of the old man,' which Paul treats in Romans 6. The other is outward – which is termed the 'mortification of the outward man or woman.' It is the endurance of the Cross, which Paul treats in Romans 8 and here also, if I am not mistaken. For after introducing along with this the 'power of His resurrection,' Christ crucified is set before us, that we may follow Him through tribulations and distresses; and hence the resurrection of the dead is expressly made mention of, that we may know that we must die before we live. This is a continual subject of meditation for believers as long as they sojourn in this world. This, however, is a precious consolation, that in all our miseries we are partakers of Christ's Cross, if we are His members; so that through afflictions the way is opened up for us to everlasting blessedness, as we read elsewhere: 'If we have died with Him, we will also live with Him; if we suffer with Him, we will also reign with Him' (2 Tim. 2:11-12). We must all therefore be prepared for this – that our whole life shall represent nothing else than the image of death, until it produces death itself, as the life of Christ is nothing else than a prelude of death. We enjoy, however, in the meantime, this consolation – that the end is everlasting blessedness. [Commentary on Philippians]

TUESDAY

Kissing the Cross

For it was fitting that [God], for whom and by whom all things exist, in bringing many sons to glory, should make the founder of their salvation perfect through suffering. For he who sanctifies and those who are sanctified all have one source.

HEBREWS 2:10-11

The Apostle's object is to make Christ's humiliation appear glorious to the godly; for when Christ is said to have been clothed with our flesh, He seems to be classed with the common order of humanity; and the cross brought Him even lower than all men and women. We must therefore be careful that Christ not be less esteemed because He willingly humbled Himself for us. …

[This reflects] the ordinary way which God adopts in dealing with His own people; for His will is to exercise them with various trials so that they may spend their whole life under the cross. It was thus necessary that Christ, as the first-begotten, should by the cross be inaugurated into His supremacy, since that is the common lot and condition of all. … It is indeed a singular consolation, intended to mitigate the bitterness of the cross, when the faithful hear, that by sorrows and tribulations they are sanctified for glory as Christ Himself was; and hence they see a sufficient reason why they should lovingly kiss the cross rather than dread it. And when this is the case, then doubtless the reproach of the cross of Christ immediately disappears, and its glory shines forth; for who can despise what is sacred, indeed, what God sanctifies? Who can deem something disgraceful that prepares us for glory? And yet both these things are said here of the death of Christ. [Commentary on Hebrews]

WEDNESDAY

Christ's Voluntary Sacrifice

*When Jesus had finished all these sayings, he said to his disciples,
'You know that after two days the Passover is coming, and the
Son of Man will be delivered up to be crucified.'*

MATTHEW 26:1-2

[T]his last prediction of Christ's clearly shows how willingly
He offered Himself to die; and it was necessary that He should
do so, because God could not be appeased except by a sacrifice
of obedience. He intended, at the same time, to prevent the
disciples from taking offense, lest they might be altogether
discouraged by the thought that He was dragged to death of
necessity. Two purposes were thus served by this statement:
First, to testify that the Son of God willingly surrendered
Himself to die, in order to reconcile the world to the Father,
for in no other way could the guilt of sins have been expiated,
or righteousness obtained for us. Second, that He did not die
like one oppressed by violence, which He could escape; rather,
He voluntarily offered Himself to die. He therefore declares
that He is coming to Jerusalem with the express intention of
suffering death there. ... And though it was of no advantage to
the disciples to be informed, at that time, of the obedience that
He was rendering to the Father, yet afterwards this doctrine
tended in no small degree to edify their faith. Similarly, it is
of singular use to us in the present day, because we behold,
as in a bright mirror, the voluntary sacrifice, by which all
the transgressions of the world were blotted out. And, as we
contemplate the Son of God advancing with cheerfulness and
courage to death, we already behold Him victorious over death.
[Commentary on the Harmony of the Gospels]

THURSDAY

The Fearsome Voice of Christ

When Jesus said to them, 'I am he,' they drew back and fell to the ground.

JOHN 18:6

[Christ] replies mildly that He is the person whom they seek, and yet He lays them prostrate on the ground as if they had been struck down by a violent tempest, or rather by a thunderbolt. ... We may infer from this how dreadful and alarming the voice of Christ will be to the wicked, when He shall ascend His throne to judge the world. [In the Garden of Gethsemane], He stood as a lamb ready to be sacrificed; His majesty, as far as outward appearance was concerned, was utterly gone; and yet when He utters but a single word, His armed and courageous enemies fall down. And what was the word? He thunders no fearful excommunication against them, but only replied, 'I am He.' What then will be the result, when He shall come, not to be judged by a man, but to be the Judge of the living and the dead; not in that humble and despicable appearance, but shining in heavenly glory, and accompanied by His angels? He intended, at that time, to give a proof of that efficacy which the Prophet Isaiah ascribes to His voice. Among other glorious attributes of Christ, Isaiah reports that 'He shall strike the earth with the rod of His mouth, and with the breath of His lips he shall kill the wicked' (Isa. 11:4). It is true that the fulfillment of this prophecy is declared by Paul to be delayed until the end of the world (2 Thess. 2:8). Yet we daily see the wicked, with all their rage and pride, struck down by the voice of Christ ... when He speaks by His ministers. [Commentary on John]

EASTER WEEK

FRIDAY

The Wisdom of the Cross

So they took Jesus, and he went out, bearing his own cross, to the place called The Place of the Skull.... There they crucified him, and with him two others.

JOHN 19:16-18

We ought always to remember, that the wicked executioners of Christ did nothing but what had been determined by the hand and purpose of God; for God did not surrender His Son to their lawless passions, but determined that, according to His own will and good pleasure, He should be offered as a sacrifice.... [W]e ought to consider, on the one hand, the dreadful weight of His wrath against sin, and, on the other hand, His infinite goodness toward us. In no other way could our guilt be removed than by the Son of God becoming a curse for us. We see Him driven out into an accursed place, as if He had been defiled by a mass of all sorts of crimes, that there He might appear to be accursed before God and humanity. Assuredly we are prodigiously stupid if we do not plainly see in this mirror God's abhorrence toward sin; and we are harder than stones, if we do not tremble at such a judgment as this. When, on the other hand, God declares that our salvation was so dear to Him, that He did not spare His only-begotten Son, what abundant goodness and what astonishing grace do we here behold? Whoever, then, takes a right view of the causes of the death of Christ, together with the advantage which it yields to us, will not ... regard it as an offense (1 Cor. 1:23), but rather as an invaluable token and pledge of the power, and wisdom, and righteousness, and goodness of God. [Commentary on John]

SATURDAY

The Cry of Dereliction

And about the ninth hour Jesus cried out with a loud voice, saying 'Eli, Eli, lema sabachthani?' that is, 'My God, my God, why have you forsaken me?'

MATTHEW 27:46

Though in the cry which Christ uttered a power more than human was manifested, yet it was unquestionably drawn from Him by intensity of sorrow. And certainly, this was His chief conflict, and harder than all the other tortures, that in His anguish He was so far from being soothed by the assistance or favor of His Father, that He felt Himself to be in some measure estranged from Him. For not only did He offer his body as the price of our reconciliation with God, but in His soul also He endured the punishments due to us; and thus, He became, as Isaiah states, 'a man of sorrows' (Isa. 53:3). ... Now nothing is more dreadful than to feel that God, whose wrath is worse than all deaths, is the Judge. When this temptation was presented to Christ, as if, having God opposed to Him, he were already devoted to destruction, He was seized with horror, which would have been sufficient to swallow up a hundred times all the people in the world. But by the amazing power of the Spirit He achieved the victory. ... No one who considers that Christ undertook the office of Mediator on the condition of suffering our condemnation, both in His body and in His soul, will think it strange that He maintained a struggle with the sorrows of death, as if an offended God had thrown Him into the whirlpool of afflictions. [Commentary on the Harmony of the Gospels]

EASTER WEEK

SUNDAY

Christ Conquers Death

But the angel said to the women, 'Do not be afraid, for I know that you seek Jesus who was crucified. He is not here, for he has risen.'

MATTHEW 28:5-6

We now come to the closing scene of our redemption. For the lively assurance of our reconciliation with God arises from Christ having come from hell as the conqueror of death, in order to show that He had the power of a new life at His disposal. Paul states rightly, therefore, that there will be no gospel, and that the hope of salvation will be vain and fruitless, unless we believe that 'Christ is risen from the dead' (1 Cor. 15:14). For it was then that Christ obtained righteousness for us, and opened up our entrance into heaven; and, in short, then our adoption was ratified, when Christ, by rising from the dead, exerted the power of His Spirit, and proved Himself to be the Son of God. ... He went out of the grave without a witness, that the emptiness of the place might be the first witness; next, He chose to have it announced to the women by the angels that He was alive; and shortly after appearing to the women, He finally appeared to the apostles on various occasions. ... He began with the women, and not only presented Himself to be seen by them, but even gave them a commission to announce the gospel to the apostles, so as to become their instructors. ... In this manner He exhibited an example of what Paul tells us, that He chooses those things which are foolish and weak in the world to humble the loftiness of the flesh (1 Cor. 1:27-28). [Commentary on the Harmony of the Gospels]

APRIL 1

Threefold Shield

The LORD is my light and my salvation; whom shall I fear? The LORD is the stronghold of my life; of whom shall I be afraid?

PSALM 27:1

David, having been tossed with various storms, at length recovers himself and shouts triumphantly over the troubles with which he has been harassed, rejoicing that whenever God displays His mercy and favor, there is nothing to be feared. This is further intimated by the accumulation of terms that he employs, when he calls God not only 'my light,' but 'my salvation' and the 'stronghold of my life.' His object was to put a threefold shield, as it were, against his various fears, as sufficient to ward them off. ...

Let us learn, therefore, to put such a value on God's power to protect us as to put to flight all our fears. Not that the minds of the faithful can, by reason of the infirmity of the flesh, be at all times entirely devoid of fear; but immediately recovering courage, let us, from the high tower of our confidence, look down upon all our dangers with contempt. Those who have never tasted God's grace tremble because they refuse to rely on Him, and imagine that He is often angry at them, or at least far removed from them. But with the promises of God before our eyes, and the grace which they offer, our unbelief does Him grievous wrong, if we do not with unshrinking courage boldly set Him against all our enemies. When God, therefore, kindly allures us to Himself, and assures us that He will take care of our safety ... it is right that we highly extol His power, that it may ravish our hearts with admiration of Himself. [Commentary on Psalms]

APRIL 2

God's Extraordinary Love

'Listen to me, O house of Jacob, all the remnant of the house of Israel, who have been borne by me from before your birth, carried from the womb.'

ISAIAH 46:3

'Carried from the womb' is a very expressive metaphor, by which God compares Himself to a mother who carries a child in her womb. God speaks of the past time, when He began to give them testimonies of His grace. Yet the words might be taken as meaning simply that God kindly nourished the people – like an infant taken from its mother's womb – and carried it in His bosom, as the Psalmist says, 'On you was I cast from my birth, and from my mother's womb you have been my God' (Ps. 22:10). ... If one objects that God is everywhere called a 'Father' (Jer. 31:9; Mal. 1:6) and that this title is more appropriate to Him, I reply that no figures of speech can describe God's extraordinary affection toward us; for it is infinite and various; so that, if all that can be said or imagined about love were brought together into one, yet it would be surpassed by the greatness of the love of God. By no metaphor, therefore, can His incomparable goodness be described. If you understand [this passage] simply to mean that God, from the time that He bore them, gently carried and nourished them in His bosom, this will agree admirably with what we find in the Song of Moses, 'He bore them and carried them, as an eagle carries her young on her wings' (Deut. 32:11). In a word, the intention of the Prophet is to show that ... [the Jews] were not begotten in vain, and that God, who has manifested Himself to be both their Father and their Mother, will always assist them. [Commentary on Isaiah]

APRIL 3

Living and Dying in Christ

I am hard pressed between the two. My desire is to depart and be with Christ, for that is far better. But to remain in the flesh is more necessary on your account.

PHILIPPIANS 1:23-24

Paul did not desire to live with any other object in view than to promote the glory of Christ and to do good to God's people. Hence, he does not think that he derives any other advantage from living than the welfare of his brothers and sisters. But so far as concerns himself personally, it would be, he acknowledges, far better for him to die soon, because he would be with Christ. ... And assuredly this is in reality what it means to live and die to Christ, when, with indifference to ourselves, we allow ourselves to be carried and borne away wherever Christ calls us.

'My desire is to depart and be with Christ.' These two things must be read together. For death in and of itself will never be desired, because such a desire is at variance with our natural feeling, but is desired for some particular reason, or with some particular object in mind. Persons in despair have recourse to it from having a weary life; believers, on the other hand, willingly hasten forward to death because it is a deliverance from the bondage of sin, and an introduction into the kingdom of heaven. What Paul now says is this: 'I desire to die, because, by this means, I will come into immediate connection with Christ.' In the meantime, believers do not cease to regard death with horror, but when they turn their eyes to that life which follows death, they easily overcome all dread by means of that consolation. [Commentary on Philippians]

APRIL 4

Peter's Denial

And a servant girl came up to [Peter] and said, 'You also were with Jesus the Galilean.' But he denied it before them all, saying, 'I do not know what you mean.'

MATTHEW 26:69-70

Peter undoubtedly was no less courageous than any of us, and he had already given no ordinary proof of his valor, though it was exercised in a rash and improper manner; and yet, ... terrified by a woman's voice, he immediately denies his Master. Even though but recently he thought himself a valiant soldier even to death. Let us therefore remember that our strength is so far from being sufficient to resist powerful attacks, that it will give way when there is the mere shadow of a battle. But in this way God gives us the just reward of our treachery, when He disarms and strips us of all power, so that, when we have thrown off the fear of Him, we tremble for a mere nothing. For if a deep fear of God had dwelt in Peter's heart, it would have been an invincible fortress; but now, naked and defenseless, He trembles while He is still far from danger. ... In short, as a bold and open confession edifies all the children of God, and puts unbelievers to shame, so apostasy draws along with it the public ruin of faith in the Church, and the reproach of sound doctrine. The more eminent a man or woman is, therefore, they ought to be the more careful to be on their guard; for their notoriety makes it impossible for them to fall from it without doing greater harm. [Commentary on the Harmony of the Gospels]

APRIL 5

Surrounded by Death

I shall not die, but I shall live, and recount the deeds of the LORD.

PSALM 118:17

David speaks like a person emerging from the grave. The very same person who says, 'I shall not die,' acknowledges that he was rescued from death, to which he was near as one condemned to it. For a number of years his life was in imminent danger, exposed every moment to a thousand deaths, and no sooner was he delivered from one than he entered another. Thus, he declares that he would not die, because he regained life, all hope of which he had entirely abandoned. We, whose life is hidden with Christ in God, ought to meditate upon this song all our days (Col. 3:3). If we occasionally enjoy some relaxation, we are bound to join with David in saying, that we who were surrounded with death are risen to newness of life. In the meantime, we must constantly persevere through the midst of darkness; since our safety lies in hope, it is impossible that it can be very visible to us. In the second part of this verse, [David] points out the proper use of life. God does not prolong the lives of His people, that they may pamper themselves with meat and drink, sleep as much as they please, and enjoy every temporal blessing, but to magnify Him for His benefits which He is daily heaping upon them. [Commentary on Psalms]

APRIL 6

Melchizedek and Christ

For this Melchizedek, king of Salem, priest of the Most High God, met Abraham returning from the slaughter of the kings and blessed him.

HEBREWS 7:1

Let us now consider each of these particulars in which the apostle compares Christ to Melchizedek. The first likeness is in the name; for it was not without a mystery that He was called the King of Righteousness. For though this honor is ascribed to kings who rule with moderation and equity, yet this belongs really to Christ alone, who not only exercises authority justly as others do, but also communicates to us the righteousness of God, partly when He makes us to be counted righteous by a gracious reconciliation, and partly when He renews us by His Spirit, that we may lead a godly and holy life. He is then called the King of Righteousness, because of what He effects in diffusing righteousness on all His people. It thus follows that, with the exception of His kingdom, nothing but sin reigns among men and women. And therefore Zechariah, when he introduces Him (as if by a solemn decree) into the possession of His kingdom, extols Him: 'Rejoice, O daughter Zion, for behold your righteous King comes to you,' intimating that the righteousness, which is otherwise lacking in us, is brought to us by the coming of Christ.

The second likeness that the Apostle states is as to the kingdom of peace. This peace indeed is the fruit of that righteousness which he has mentioned. It thus follows that wherever Christ's kingdom extends, there peace ought to be. ... [which] is an inward peace that quiets the conscience and renders it confident before God. [Commentary on Hebrews]

APRIL 7

God's Timely Rescue

But you do see, for you note mischief and vexation, that you may take it into your hands; to you the helpless commits himself; you have been the helper of the fatherless.

PSALM 10:14

Nothing is easier than to acknowledge in general terms that God exercises care for the world and the affairs of men and women; but it is very difficult to apply this doctrine to its various uses in everyday life. And yet, all that the Scripture says concerning the power and righteousness of God will be of no use to us, and as it were, only a matter of fruitless speculation, unless everyone applies these statements to themselves, as need requires. Let us therefore learn from the example of David to reason in this way: that, since God takes notice of all the mischief and injuries that are inflicted on His good and simple people, He considers our troubles and sorrows even when He seems for a time to take no notice of them. The Psalmist adds that He does not look down from heaven ... as an idle and unconcerned spectator, but that it is His work to pass judgment upon it. ...

It is, however, our duty to wait patiently ... until God stretches forth His arm to help us. We see, therefore, the reason why it is immediately added, 'upon you the helpless commits himself.' The godly, when they are afflicted, may with confidence cast their cares into His bosom, and commit themselves to His protection. They should not, however, be in haste for the accomplishment of their wishes; but, finding relief from their burdens, they should wait until God clearly announces the proper time of interfering on their behalf has come. [Commentary on Psalms]

APRIL 8

Fountain of Grace

Blessed is the nation whose God is the LORD, the people whom he has chosen as his heritage!   PSALM 33:12

The prophet, therefore, in proclaiming that those people are blessed whom God receives into His protection, reminds us that God's counsel ... is displayed in the existence and protection of the Church, and may be seen there. Thus, we learn that it is not those who coldly speculate about the power of God, but those alone who apply it to their own present benefit, who rightly acknowledge God as the Governor of the world. Moreover, when the Psalmist places all our blessedness in this, that Yahweh is our God and a fountain of divine love toward us, He captures in a word what is necessary to be desired to make life happy. For when God condescends to provide for our salvation, to cherish us under His wings, to provide for our necessities, to aid us in all our dangers – all this flows from our adoption by Him. But lest it should be thought that men and women obtain so great a good by their own efforts and industry, David teaches us expressly that it proceeds from the fountain of God's gracious electing love, that we are accounted the people of God. It is indeed true, that, in the person of Adam, human beings were first created for the very purpose that they should be sons and daughters of God; but the estrangement that followed upon sin deprived us of that great blessing. Until God freely adopts us, we are all by nature wretched; we have no other means of attaining happiness than this, that God, of His own good pleasure, should choose us who are altogether unworthy. [Commentary on Psalms]

APRIL 9

God's Faithful Care

Into your hand I commit my spirit; you have redeemed me,
O LORD, faithful God.

PSALM 31:5

Whoever does not rely on the providence of God, so as to commit their lives to its faithful guardianship, has not yet correctly learned what it is to live. On the other hand, those who entrust the keeping of their lives to God's care, will not doubt of its safety even in the midst of death. We must therefore put our life into God's hand, not only that He may keep it safely in this world, but also that He may preserve it from destruction in death itself, as Christ's own example has taught us. As David wished to have his life prolonged amidst the dangers of death, so Christ passed out of this transitory life so that His soul might be saved in death. This is a general prayer, therefore, in which the faithful commit their lives to God, first, that He may protect them by His power, so long as they are exposed to the dangers of this world; and, secondly, that He may preserve them safe in the grave, where nothing is to be seen but destruction. We ought further to assure ourselves, that we are not forsaken by God either in life or in death; for those whom God brings safely by His power to the end of their course, He at last receives to Himself at their death. ... [I]n sum, we should not be afraid of death, which, though it destroys the body, cannot snuff out the soul. [Commentary on Psalms]

APRIL 10

Praying in Solitude

'And when you pray, you must not be like the hypocrites. For they love to stand and pray in the synagogues and at the street corners. ... But when you pray, go into your room and shut the door and pray to your Father who is in secret. And your Father who sees in secret will reward you.'

MATTHEW 6:5-6

It is a gross and shameful profanation of the name of God when hypocrites, in order to obtain glory from human beings, pray in public, or at least make a pretense of praying. But as hypocrisy is always ambitious, we should not be surprised that it is also blind. Christ, therefore, commands His disciples, if they wish to pray in the right manner, to enter into their closets. ... We must not interpret the words 'go into your closet' literally, as if Christ ordered us to avoid the presence of other people, or declared that we do not pray correctly unless there are no witnesses. Rather, He speaks comparatively, meaning that we ought to seek solitude rather than a crowd of people to watch us praying. It is certainly advantageous for believers, and gives them greater freedom to pour out their prayers and groans before God, to withdraw from the gaze of other people. Solitude is also useful for another reason, so that our minds may be more free and disengaged from all distracting thoughts. Hence, Christ Himself frequently chose the refuge of some solitary spot for the sake of prayer. ... To express it in a few words, whether people pray alone, or in the presence of others, they ought to have the same feelings, as if they were shut up in their closets, and had no other witnesses than God. [Commentary on the Harmony of the Gospels]

APRIL 11

Need for a Mediator

For there is one God, and there is one mediator between God and men, the man Christ Jesus. 1 TIMOTHY 2:5

Therefore, let us hold this as an undoubted truth which no siege engine can shake: the mind of humans has been so completely estranged from God's righteousness that it conceives, desires, and undertakes, only that which is impious, perverted, foul, impure, and infamous. The heart is so steeped in the poison of sin, that it can breathe out nothing but a loathsome stench. But if some people occasionally make a show of good, their minds nevertheless ever remain enveloped in hypocrisy and deceitful craft, and their hearts bound by inner perversity. The whole human race perished in the person of Adam. ... Therefore, since we have fallen from life into death, the whole knowledge of God the Creator that we have discussed would be useless unless faith also followed, setting forth for us God our Father in Christ. ... Therefore, although the preaching of the cross does not agree with our human inclination, we ought nevertheless to embrace it humbly if we desire to return to God our Author and Maker, from whom we have been estranged, in order that He may again begin to be our Father. Surely, after the fall of the first man no knowledge of God apart from the Mediator has had power unto salvation. For Christ not only speaks of His own age, but comprehends all ages when He says: 'This is eternal life, that they know you the only true God, and Jesus Christ whom you have sent' (John 17:3). [Institutes (1559), II.v.19-vi.1]

APRIL 12

Christian Gospel

For we did not follow cleverly devised myths when we made known to you the power and coming of our Lord Jesus Christ, but we were eyewitnesses of his majesty.

2 PETER 1:16

No doubt Peter meant in these words to include the substance of the gospel, as it certainly contains nothing except Christ, in whom are hid all the treasures of wisdom. But he distinctly mentions two things – that Christ had been manifested in the flesh, and also that power was exhibited by Him. Here, then, we have the whole gospel; for we know that He, the long-promised Redeemer, came from heaven, put on our flesh, lived in the world, died and rose again; and, in the second place, we perceive the end and fruit of all these things, that is, that He might be God with us, that He might exhibit in Himself a sure pledge of our adoption, that He might cleanse us from the defilements of the flesh by the grace of His Spirit, and consecrate us temples to God, that He might deliver us from hell, and raise us up to heaven, that He might by the sacrifice of His death make an atonement for the sins of the world, that He might reconcile us to the Father, that He might become to us the author of righteous and of life. Those who know and understand these things are fully acquainted with the gospel.

[And] let us remember that the gospel was not at the beginning made up of vague rumors, but that the apostles were the authentic preachers of what they had seen. [Commentary on 2 Peter]

APRIL 13

God's Rescue Plan

All we like sheep have gone astray; we have turned – every one – to his own way; and the LORD has laid on him the iniquity of us all.

Isaiah 53:6

If we do not perceive our wretchedness and poverty, we shall never know how desirable is that remedy which Christ has brought to us, or approach Him with due ardor of affection. As soon as we know that we are ruined, then, aware of our wretchedness, we eagerly run to avail ourselves of the remedy, which otherwise would be considered of little importance. In order, therefore, that we may appreciate Christ, let everyone consider and examine themselves so as to acknowledge that they are ruined until they are redeemed by Christ. We see here that no one is exempt, for the Prophet includes the word 'all.' The whole human race would have perished, if Christ had not brought relief. ...

By comparing them to sheep, he does not intend to downplay their guilt, as if they deserved little blame, but to state plainly that it belongs to Christ to gather from their wanderings those who resembled brute beasts. 'And the LORD has laid upon Him.' Here we have a beautiful contrast. In ourselves we are scattered; in Christ we are gathered together. By nature we go astray, and are driven headlong to destruction; in Christ we find the course by which we are conducted to the harbor of salvation. Our sins are a heavy load; but they are laid on Christ, by whom we are freed from the load. Thus, when we were ruined and estranged from God – and, indeed, were hastening to hell – Christ took upon Himself the filthiness of our iniquities, in order to rescue us from everlasting destruction. [Commentary on Isaiah]

APRIL 14

Disgrace and Glory

And they stripped him and put a scarlet robe on him, and twisting together a crown of thorns, they put it on his head and put a reed in his right hand. And kneeling before him, they mocked him, saying, 'Hail, King of the Jews!' And they spit on him and took the reed and struck him on the head.

MATTHEW 27:28-30

We are taught [in this passage] that the kingdom of Christ ought not to be judged by the sense of the flesh, but by the judgment of faith and of the Spirit. For so long as our minds grovel in the world, we look upon His kingdom not only as contemptible, but even as loaded with shame and disgrace; but as soon as our minds rise by faith to heaven, not only will the spiritual majesty of Christ be presented to us, so as to obliterate all the dishonor of the cross, but the spitting, scourging, blows, and other indignities, will lead us to the contemplation of His glory; as Paul informs us, that 'God has highly exalted him and bestowed on him the name that is above every name, so that at the name of Jesus every knee should bow' because 'He willingly emptied Himself ... even to death on a cross' (Phil. 2:8-10). If, therefore, even in the present day, the world insolently mocks at Christ, let us learn to rise above these offenses by elevated faith; and let us ... [remember] with what ornaments the Father has clothed Him, with what scepter and with what crown He has adorned Him, so as to raise Him high, not only above human beings, but even above all the angels. [Commentary on the Harmony of the Gospels]

APRIL 15

Christ in His People

'A little while, and you will see me no longer; and again a little while, and you will see me.'
JOHN 16:16

Christ had often forewarned the apostles of His departure, partly that they might bear it with greater courage, partly that they might desire more ardently the grace of the Spirit, of which they had no great desire, so long as they had Christ present with them in the body. ...

[Jesus] mitigates and soothes the disciples' sorrow for His absence by this consolation, that it will not last long; and thus, He magnifies the grace of the Spirit, by which He will be continually present with them; as if He had promised that, after a short interval, He would return, and that they would not be long deprived of His presence.

Nor ought we to think it strange when Christ says that He is 'seen,' when He dwells in the disciples by the Spirit; for, though He is not seen with the bodily eyes, yet His presence is known by the undoubted experience of faith. What we are taught by Paul is indeed true, that 'while we are at home in the body we are away from the Lord, for we walk by faith, not by sight' (2 Cor. 5:6-7). But it is equally true that believers may justly, in the meantime, glory in having Christ dwelling in them by faith, in being united to Him as members to the Head, in possessing heaven along with Him by hope. Thus, the grace of the Spirit is a mirror, in which Christ wishes to be seen by us, according to the flesh. [Commentary on John]

APRIL 16

God My Deliverer

Many are the afflictions of the righteous, but the LORD delivers him out of them all. He keeps all his bones; not one of them is broken.

PSALM 34:19-20

The Psalmist here anticipates the thought that often arises in our minds: 'How can it be that God cares about the righteous, who are continually harassed with so many calamities and trials? For what purpose does the protection of God serve, except for those who are peaceably inclined, enjoying peace and repose? And what is more unreasonable than that those who cause trouble to no one should themselves be tormented and afflicted in all sorts of ways?' So that, therefore, the temptations by which we are continually assailed may not shake our belief in God's providence, we ought to remember this lesson of instruction, that although God governs the righteous, and provides for their safety, they are yet subject and exposed to many miseries, so that, being tested by such trials, they may give evidence of their invincible constancy, and experience all the more that God is their deliverer. If they were exempted from every kind of trial, their faith would languish, they would cease to call upon God, and their piety would remain hidden and unknown. It is therefore necessary that they should endure various trials, especially for this purpose, that they may acknowledge that they have been wonderfully preserved by God amidst numberless deaths. ... David, therefore, admonishes the faithful never to lose courage, whatever evils may threaten them; since God, who can as easily deliver them a thousand times as once from death, will never disappoint their expectation. [Commentary on Psalms]

APRIL

APRIL 17

King of Righteousness

In his days may the righteous flourish, and peace abound, till the moon be no more!

PSALM 72:7

[The Psalmist] prayed that the king might be adorned with righteousness and judgment, that the just might flourish and the people prosper. This prediction receives its highest fulfillment in Christ. It was, indeed, the duty of Solomon to maintain the righteous; but it is the proper office of Christ to make men and women righteous. He not only gives to every person their own, but also reforms their hearts through the agency of His Spirit. By this means He brings righteousness back, as it were, from exile, which otherwise would be altogether banished from the world. Following the return of righteousness, one experiences God's blessing, by which He causes all His children to rejoice, enabling them to perceive that under their king, Christ, every provision is made for their enjoyment of all manner of prosperity and happiness. If anyone would rather take the word 'peace' in its proper and more restricted sense, I have no objections to it. And certainly, nothing is more desirable than peace for the consummation of a happy life, for amidst the turmoil and contentions of war, men and women derive almost no advantage from having an abundance of possessions, as they are then wasted and destroyed. Moreover, when [the Psalmist] represents the life of the king as prolonged to the end of the world, this shows more clearly that he not only meant his successors who would occupy an earthly throne, but that his mind ascends even to Christ, who, by rising from the dead, obtained for Himself celestial life and glory, that He might govern His Church forever. [Commentary on Psalms]

APRIL 18

Christ's Unshakeable Kingdom

Jesus answered, 'My kingdom is not of this world. If my kingdom were of this world, my servants would have been fighting. ... But my kingdom is not from the world.'

JOHN 18:36

This defense was made by Christ before Pilate, but the same doctrine is useful to believers to the end of the world; for if the kingdom of Christ were earthly, it would be frail and changeable, because the 'present form of this world is passing away' (1 Cor. 7:31), but now, since it is pronounced to be heavenly, this assures us of its perpetuity. Thus, even if the whole world were overturned, provided that our consciences are always directed to the kingdom of Christ, they will, nevertheless, remain firm, not only amidst shakings and convulsions, but even amidst dreadful ruin and destruction. ...

We are taught, also, the nature of this kingdom; for if it made us happy according to the flesh, and brought us riches, luxuries, and all that is desirable for the use of the present life, it would smell of the earth and of the world; but now, though our condition appears to be wretched, still our true happiness remains unimpaired. We learn from it, also, who belongs to this kingdom, namely, those who have been renewed by the Spirit of God, who contemplate the heavenly life in holiness and righteousness. Yet it deserves our attention that this passage does not say that the kingdom of Christ is not in this world; for we know that it has its seat in our hearts. ... But, strictly speaking, the kingdom of God, while it dwells in us, is a stranger to the world, because its condition is totally different. [Commentary on John]

APRIL 19

Safe in Christ

That is why [Christ] is not ashamed to call them brothers, saying 'I will tell your name to my brothers'... and again, 'I will put my trust in him.'
HEBREWS 2:11-13

Here is shown the primary cause of our obedience, namely, that God has adopted us. Christ brings none to the Father but those given Him by the Father; and this donation, we know, depends on eternal election. For those whom the Father has destined to life, He delivers to the safe-keeping of His Son, that He may defend them. This is what He says in John's Gospel: 'All that the Father gives Me will come to Me' (6:37). ... [L]et us learn to ascribe this altogether to His mercy; for otherwise we shall never be led to Him by the hand of Christ. Moreover, this doctrine supplies us with strong ground for confidence; for who can tremble under the guidance and protection of Christ? And, undoubtedly, when Christ says 'Behold, I and the children,' He really fulfills what He has elsewhere promised, that He will not allow any of those to perish whom He has received from the Father (John 1:28).

We must observe lastly that though the world rejects the gospel with mad stubbornness, yet the sheep always recognize the voice of their shepherd. Therefore, let not the impiety of almost all ranks, ages, and nations disturb us, provided Christ gathers together His own, who have been committed to His protection. ... Let us at the same time know that God's own are known to Him, and that their salvation is sealed by Him, so that not one of them shall be lost. [Commentary on Hebrews]

APRIL 20

Humility

Do nothing from selfish ambition or conceit, but in humility count others more significant than yourselves.

PHILIPPIANS 2:3

Paul gives a definition of true humility – when people esteem themselves less than others. Now, if anything in our whole life is difficult, this above everything else is so. Hence it is not surprising that humility is such a rare virtue. For as an ancient once said, 'Everyone has in himself the mind of a king, by claiming everything for himself.' See, this is pride! Afterwards from a foolish admiration of ourselves arises contempt for other Christians. And we are so far from what Paul here commands that we can hardly endure it when others are on our level, for there is no one that is not eager to be superior to others. But it might be asked, how can a person who is in fact truly distinguished above others treat them as superior when it is clear that they are far beneath them? In whatever way a person may be distinguished by illustrious gifts, they should remind themselves that such gifts have not been conferred on them so that they might be complacent and exalt themselves, or even so that they might hold themselves in high esteem. Let them, instead, strive to correct and detect their own faults, and they will have abundant opportunities for humility. On the other hand, with regard to others, let gifted persons honor whatever is excellent in them, and by means of love bury their faults. The person who observes this rule will not find it difficult to prefer others before themselves. [Commentary on Philippians]

APRIL 21

Duties of Love

But if anyone has the world's goods and sees his brother in need, yet closes his heart against him, how does God's love abide in him?

1 JOHN 3:17

[John] now speaks of the common duties of love, which flow from that chief foundation, that is, when we are prepared to serve our neighbors even to death. Here he seems to reason from the greater to the less; for those who refuse to alleviate with their possession the needs of their brothers and sisters, while their life is safe and secure, will by no means expose themselves to danger for the sake of their neighbor. Then the Apostle denies that there is love in us if we withhold help from our neighbors. ...

Let this, then, be the first proposition, that no one truly loves their brothers and sisters, unless they really show such love whenever an occasion occurs. Second, that as far as any one has the means, they are bound to assist their fellow believers, for the Lord thus supplies us with the opportunity to exercise love. Third, that the needs of every one ought to be addressed, for as any one needs food and drink or other things of which we have abundance, so they require our aid. Fourth, that no act of kindness is pleasing to God unless it is accompanied with sympathy. There are many people who seem generous, who do not feel for the miseries of their brothers and sisters. But the Apostle requires that our hearts should be stirred; which is done, when we are endued with such a feeling as to sympathize with others in their difficulties as if they were our own. [Commentary on 1 John]

APRIL 22

Food for the Soul

And a large crowd was following [Jesus], because they saw the signs that he was doing on the sick.
JOHN 6:2

Here we see, in the first place, how eager the people were to hear Christ, since all of them, forgetting themselves, took no concern about spending the night in a desert place. So much the less excusable is our indifference, or rather our sloth, when we are so far from preferring heavenly doctrine to the gnawing of hunger, that the slightest interruptions [in our meal times] immediately leads us away from meditation on the heavenly life. Very rarely does it happen that Christ finds us free and disengaged from the entanglements of the world. ... And though this disease prevails nearly throughout the whole world, yet it is certain that no one will be fit for the kingdom of God until ... they learn to desire the food of the soul so earnestly that their stomach shall not hinder them.

But as the flesh demands us to attend to its needs, we ought likewise to observe that Christ ... takes care of those who neglect themselves in order to follow him. ... We shall perhaps be told that this does not always happen, for we often see that godly people, though they have been entirely devoted to the kingdom of God, are exhausted and almost fainting with hunger. I reply, though Christ is pleased to test our faith and patience in this manner, yet from heaven He sees our needs and is careful to relieve them, as far as is necessary for our welfare; and when assistance is not immediately granted, it is done for the best reason, though that reason is concealed from us. [Commentary on John]

APRIL 23

Taming the Tongue

My heart became hot within me. As I mused, the fire burned; then I spoke with my tongue.
PSALM 39:3

[David] now illustrates the greatness of his grief by the introduction of a simile, telling us that his sorrow, being internally suppressed, became so much the more inflamed, until the turbulent passions of his soul continued to increase in strength. From this we may learn the very profitable lesson that the more strenuously people set themselves to obey God, and employ all their efforts to attain the exercise of patience, the more vigorously are they assailed by temptation: for Satan, while he is not so troublesome to people who are indifferent and careless, and seldom notices them, yet he displays all his forces in hostile array against those individuals [who seek to obey God]. If, therefore, at any time we feel turbulent emotions struggling and raising a commotion in our breasts, we should call to remembrance this conflict of David, that our courage may not fail us, or at least, that our infirmity may not drive us headlong into despair. ... Whenever, therefore, the flesh shall put forth its efforts, and shall kindle up a fire in our hearts, let us know that we are exercised with the same kind of temptation which caused so much pain and trouble to David. ... In his own person he sets before us a mirror of human weakness, that, being warned by the danger to which we are exposed, we may learn early on to seek protection under the shadow of God's wings. [Commentary on Psalms]

APRIL 24

The Happy Life

Seeing the crowds, [Jesus] went up on the mountain, and when he sat down his disciples came to him. And he opened his mouth and taught them, saying: 'Blessed are the poor in spirit, for theirs is the kingdom of heaven.'

MATTHEW 5:1-3

We know that not only the great body of people, but even the learned themselves, hold this error, thinking those people happy who are free from annoyance, attain all their wishes, and lead a joyful and easy life. Indeed, it is the general opinion that happiness should be achieved in the present state of life. Christ, therefore, in order to accustom His own people to bear the cross, exposes this mistaken opinion, that those are happy who lead an easy and prosperous life according to the flesh. For it is impossible for men and women to submit to calamities and disgrace as long as they think that patience is at odds with a happy life. The only consolation that mitigates and even sweetens the bitterness of the cross and all afflictions, is the conviction that we are happy in the midst of our miseries; for our patience is blessed by the Lord, and will soon be followed by a happy result. This teaching, I admit, is vastly different from the common opinion, but the disciples of Christ must learn the philosophy of placing their happiness beyond the world, and above the affections of the flesh. ... Let us remember, therefore, that the main purpose of this discourse is to show that those people are not unhappy who are oppressed by the reproaches of the wicked, and subject to various disasters ... because the distresses of the godly will soon be changed for the better. [Commentary on the Harmony of the Gospels]

APRIL 25

The Poor of Spirit

And he opened his mouth and taught them, saying: 'Blessed are the poor in spirit, for theirs is the kingdom of heaven.'

MATTHEW 5:2-3

Now when we have everything we want, our appetites inevitably know no limits. They are like the foaming waves of the sea; nothing can hold them back. In short, we are puffed up – like drunkards who no longer remember what temperance is. By contrast, when God allows us to be despised by other people, and when everyone has had a laugh at our expense; when we are slandered so that we are subject to hatred, envy, and spite; when false charges and accusations are brought against us; when we are poor and rejected without comfort or aid – when, in short, we have been afflicted with everything we might call adversity, then we learn the meaning of modesty, and hang our head which was previously lifted too high. Since, however, many people do not cease pandering to their pride, even when God strikes them with great blows and encourages them to humility – since, I say, there are many who are almost unteachable, that is why our Lord Jesus Christ added the words, 'in spirit' ...

Those persons are truly blessed, then, who are poor in their own estimation, that is, who willingly abase themselves and attribute nothing to themselves, who make no false claims about themselves, but allow themselves to be rejected by the world. Here we see the substance of Jesus' words, and the benefit that we may gain from them. [Sermons on the Harmony of the Gospels, CO 46:776-777]

APRIL 26

The Kingdom of Heaven

'Blessed are the poor in spirit, for theirs is the kingdom of heaven.'
MATTHEW 5:3

By this our Lord indicates that we should not amuse ourselves with what our eyes see, but that we should always focus upon the final goal. When those philosophers who valued virtue above all else wished to demonstrate that afflictions did not make a person miserable, they had to invent a person so hardened that they were like an anvil which a hammer could never dent. Ultimately this was a mere fantasy and pure stupidity on their part. ... But our Lord Jesus Christ does not lead us into speculations which have no practical effect. On the contrary, He sets us on a solid foundation, so that, as long as we rest on it, we will not be shaken. And however much the storms and winds of the world buffet us, so that it seems that heaven and earth seem to be fixed together, our happiness will always be secure, as long as we fix our gaze on the kingdom of heaven. So this is what the passage teaches: in order to taste the blessedness of which the Son of God speaks, we must learn first that this world is only a passageway; it is not our resting place, nor where we find true life. Rather, we must reach further and lift our eyes to the heavenly inheritance. Thus, all who are attached to this world, who rely on human opinion and who look to enjoy their happiness here on earth, cannot possibly grasp the importance of this teaching. Instead it will always be hateful to them. [Sermons on the Harmony of the Gospels, CO 46:779]

APRIL 27

The Kingdom of God

[Jesus] presented himself alive to them after his suffering by many proofs, appearing to them during forty days and speaking about the kingdom of God.

ACTS 1:3

We must first note that we are born and that we live as aliens and strangers from the kingdom of God, until such time as God refashions us in newness of life. Therefore, we may properly set the world, the flesh, and our sinful human nature as contrary to the kingdom of God. For the natural man or woman is entirely occupied with the things of this world, and they seek their happiness there; hence in the meantime we are as it were banished from God and He from us. But Christ, by the preaching of the gospel, lifts us up into the meditation of the life to come. ... And He reforms all our earthly affections, and, having stripped out of us the vices of our flesh, He separates us from the world. And, just as eternal death is prepared for all those who live according to the flesh, so, in a parallel fashion, God renews our inner persons that we may go forward in the spiritual life, and He draws us nearer to the perfection of the kingdom of God. ... Therefore, God reigns in and among us now, so that He may at length make us partakers of His kingdom. From this we see that Christ primarily dealt with the corruption of human beings; the tyranny of sin, whose bond-slaves we are; the curse and guilt of eternal death, to which we are all subject. He also deals with the means of our salvation, the remission of sins, the denying of the flesh, spiritual righteousness, the hope of eternal life, and other such things. [Commentary on Acts]

APRIL 28

Sharing God's Light with Others

Do all things without grumbling or disputing, that you may be blameless and innocent, children of God without blemish in the midst of a crooked and twisted generation, among whom you shine as lights in the world, holding fast to the word of life ...

PHILIPPIANS 2:14-16

The reason why [the Philippians] ought to be luminaries is that they carry the word of life, by which they are enlightened, so that they may give light also to others. Now he ... likens us to lamps; while he compares the word of God to the wick, from which the light comes. If you prefer another figure – we are candlesticks; the doctrine of the gospel is the candle, which, being placed in us, radiates light on all sides. Now Paul intimates that we do injustice to the word of God if it does not shine forth in us in purity of life. This is the significance of Christ's saying: 'Nor do people light a lamp and put it under a basket' (Matt. 5:15). We are said, however, to 'hold fast to the word of life' in such a way as to be, in the meantime, sustained by it, inasmuch as we are founded upon it. ... The sum is this: that all who are enlightened with heavenly doctrine carry about with them a light, which detects and discovers their sins, if they do not walk in holiness and chastity; but that this light has been kindled up, not merely that they themselves may be guided in the right way, but that they may also show it to others. [Commentary on Philippians]

APRIL 29

The Mourners

'Blessed are those who mourn, for they shall be comforted.'

MATTHEW 5:4

Here Jesus affirms more or less what we have already heard. For if we are poor in spirit, we cannot avoid weeping and experiencing deep anxiety. After all, we are not without feelings, as those madmen we mentioned earlier who instruct people to remain impassive – as if they were an anvil or a stone! All such things are contrary to our nature. Instead, it is inevitable that we will experience various miseries that pulverize us by cracking and breaking us so that we cannot lift our heads or breathe (in a manner of speaking), causing us to become like poor dead people. That is why our Lord Jesus Christ connects in this passage weeping and poverty of spirit. It is as if He were saying: 'When I say that nothing will take away your blessedness, however oppressed and afflicted you might be, I do not mean that you should dumbly resist regardless of your feelings, that you should be like senseless blocks of wood that are moved by nothing. No! You will weep, you will experience scarcity, disgrace, illnesses, and all other sorts of worldly troubles. You will suffer these things; they will wound you to the heart and cause you to weep. But whatever happens, this will not take away your blessedness. Why? Because this is the inevitable outcome: Wait for your consolation from on high! ...' When we remember that God has promised to comfort us, provided that we tearfully seek Him in humility and patiently obey Him, then we can be confident that all our suffering will be like salutary trials – like spurs that prick us forward to accomplish our duty. [Sermons on the Harmony of the Gospels, CO 46:781-782]

APRIL 30

God's Comfort

'Blessed are those who mourn, for they shall be comforted.'

MATTHEW 5:4

Let us weep to our God; it is to Him that our tears should be addressed. When we do this, we will experience what David said, 'Lord, you have put my tears in a bottle' (Ps. 56:8). Just as a person treasures a bottle of precious perfume or costly ointment, so David says that God collects our tears. ... When we cry before our God, we can be sure that He will not lose a single tear, but will carefully guard them all. ...

[If] we are disciples of our Lord Jesus Christ, we bear our cross and carry our gallows with us, like poor condemned criminals, mocked, insulted, slandered. Yet nothing will prevent us from always being blessed; nothing will take away our reasons for rejoicing. ... It is necessary for each person to embrace this teaching for themselves and to recognize that our Lord Jesus Christ is speaking to each one of us personally, saying 'To be poor, you must be poor in spirit, truly humbled; you must become as nothing in your heart. When you do this, know that even though the world judges you as miserable – and your natural instincts may say as much – nevertheless, you can respond to me with a bold 'Amen' and accept the blessedness that I extend to you. In the end you will learn that you have not been deceived, but have received your inheritance. Then you will recognize that God rejoices over His children after He has allowed them to experience sadness in the world and that God fills His children to the full after He has allowed them to experience poverty.' [Sermons on the Harmony of the Gospels, CO 46:783-784]

MAY 1

Power and Fatherly Love

The nations rage, the kingdoms totter; he utters his voice, the earth melts. The LORD of hosts is with us, the God of Jacob is our fortress.

PSALM 46:6-7

[The Psalmist's] confident boasting arises from this, that God has chosen us for His peculiar people, to show forth His power in preserving and defending us. On this account, the Prophet, after having celebrated the power of God by calling Him the 'LORD of hosts,' immediately adds another epithet, 'the God of Jacob,' by which He confirms the covenant made of old with Abraham, that his posterity, to whom the inheritance of the promised grace belongs, should not doubt that God was also favorable to them. That our faith may rest truly and firmly in God, we must take into consideration at the same time these two parts of His character – His immeasurable power, by which He is able to subdue the whole world under Him; and His fatherly love which He has manifested in His word. When these two things are joined together, there is nothing which can hinder our faith from defying all the enemies which may rise up against us, nor must we doubt that God will support us, since He has promised to do it; and as to power, He is sufficiently able also to fulfill His promise, for He is the God of armies. From this we learn that those persons err egregiously in the interpretation of Scripture, who ... do not rest assured that He will be a Father to them, inasmuch as they are of His flock, and partakers of His adoption. [Commentary on Psalms]

MAY 2

Words of Christ

When [the disciples] had rowed about three or four miles, they saw Jesus walking on the sea ... and they were frightened. But he said to them, 'It is I; do not be afraid.'

JOHN 6:19-20

John here holds out to us, as in a mirror, what kind of knowledge of Christ we may obtain without the word, and what advantage may be reaped from that knowledge. For if Jesus presents a simple demonstration of His divinity, we immediately fall into our imaginations, and every person forms an idol for himself instead of Christ, ... [and this] is immediately followed by trembling and a confused terror of heart. But when Christ begins to speak, we then obtain from His voice clear and solid knowledge, and then also joy and delightful peace dawns upon our minds. For there is great weight in these words: 'It is I; do not be afraid.' We learn from them that it is in Christ's presence alone that we have abundant grounds of confidence, so as to be calm and at ease. But this belongs exclusively to the disciples of Christ; for we shall afterwards see in John 18:6 that wicked men and women were struck down by the same words, 'It is I.' The reason for the distinction is that He is sent as a Judge to the reprobate and unbelievers for their destruction; and, therefore, they cannot bear His presence without being immediately overwhelmed. But believers, who know that He is given to them to make propitiation, as soon as they hear His name, which is a sure pledge to them both of the love of God and of their salvation, take courage as if they had been raised from death to life. [Commentary on John]

MAY

MAY 3

Children of the Church

The princes of the peoples gather as the people of the God of Abraham. For the shields of the earth belong to God; he is highly exalted!

PSALM 47:9

This passage contains two very important and instructive truths. In the first place, we learn from it that all who would be considered among the children of God ought to seek to have a place in the Church, and to join themselves to it, that they may maintain fraternal unity with all the godly. Secondly, that when the unity of the Church is spoken of, it is to be considered as consisting in nothing else but a genuine agreement to yield obedience to the word of God, that there may be one sheepfold and one Shepherd. Moreover, those who are exalted in the world in respect of honors and riches, are here admonished to divest themselves of all pride, and willingly and submissively to bear the yoke in common with others, that they may show themselves the obedient children of the Church. [Commentary on Psalms]

MAY 4

The Call to Harmony

So if there is any encouragement in Christ... complete my joy by being of the same mind, having the same love, being in full accord and of one mind.   PHILIPPIANS 2:1-2

There is an extraordinary tenderness in this exhortation, in which Paul entreats by all means the Philippians to cherish harmony among themselves lest, in the event of their being torn apart by mutual contentions, they should expose themselves to the deceptions of the false apostles. For when there are disagreements, there is invariably a door opened for Satan to spread ungodly doctrines, while agreement is the best bulwark for repelling them. ... 'Complete my joy.' Here again we see how little anxiety Paul had for himself, provided only that it went well with the Church of Christ. He was kept shut up in a prison and bound with chains. He was considered worthy of capital punishment. He was subject to tortures even as the executioner was near at hand. Yet all these things did not prevent him from experiencing unmingled joy, as long as he saw that the churches were in a good condition. Now what he considers to be the chief indication of a prosperous condition of the Church is when mutual agreement prevails in it, along with the harmony of Christian brothers and sisters. Thus Psalm 137:6 teaches us in a similar manner that our crowning joy is the remembrance of Jerusalem. ... The sum is this – that the [Philippians] should be joined together in their views and inclinations. For he makes mention of agreement in doctrine and mutual love. [Commentary on Philippians]

MAY 5

Soldiers of the Gospel

I have thought it necessary to send to you Epaphroditus my brother and fellow worker and fellow soldier, and your messenger and minister to my need, for he has been longing for you ...

PHILIPPIANS 2:25-26

After having encouraged the Philippians by the promise of his own coming, along with Timothy, Paul fortifies them also for the present, by sending Epaphroditus to them, so that they would not be without a pastor while Paul waited the completion of his own affairs. ... Now Paul recommends Epaphroditus with many distinctions – that he is his brother, and helper in the affairs of the gospel, that he is his fellow soldier – and with these terms he intimates the nature of ministers of the gospel. For they are engaged in continuous warfare, for Satan will not allow them to promote the gospel without enduring conflict. Let those, then, who would seek to edify the Church know that war is promised and prepared for them. This is indeed common to all Christians – to be soldiers in the camp of Christ, for Satan is the enemy of all. But it is more particularly applicable to the ministers of the word, who go before the army and bear the battle standard. Paul could especially boast of his military service, in that he endured the strain of every kind of contest as by a miracle. He accordingly commends Epaphroditus, because he had been a companion to him in his conflicts. ... 'He has been longing for you.' It is a sign of a true pastor that, even when at a great distance and involved in a godly endeavor, he was nevertheless affected with concern for his flock, and longed for them. And, upon learning that his sheep were distressed on his account, he was concerned for their grief. [Commentary on Philippians]

MAY 6

The Meek

'Blessed are the meek, for they shall inherit the earth.'

MATTHEW 5:5

Experience shows us that people who are powerful and successful are those who are the boldest and most audacious, while ordinary people keep their mouths shut and dare not to complain, even though others may rob them and fleece them. Thus, common sense tells us that persons who are meek will be exposed to all sorts of insults and abuse, unable to find even some small corner to breath; and that they will be pursued as if they were a lamb amidst a great pack of wolves. But even so our Lord Jesus Christ is not deceiving us when He makes this promise, saying that 'the meek will inherit the earth.'

Indeed, this teaching might make no sense to the profane and worldly; but believers have tasted enough of it to know that these teachings have not been made in vain. ... For we know that God has given us the Lord Jesus Christ as our Shepherd. Now, truly, His most important work is to preserve our souls until we attain the eternal salvation which He has purchased for us. Nevertheless, even in this transitory life He wishes to be the guardian of our bodies. Let us therefore be His sheep, because He is not a shepherd of wolves. We cannot look to Jesus Christ as our Shepherd if we choose to live like wild beasts, throwing off restraint, ... taking up arms to avenge ourselves and trying to create as many problems as possible. What He wants is for us to hear His voice, just like sheep and lambs – let them be our example! [Sermons on the Harmony of the Gospels, CO 46:785, 787]

MAY 7

Heirs and Pilgrims

'Blessed are the meek, for they shall inherit the earth.'

MATTHEW 5:5

Let us recognize, therefore, that if we exercise self-control and are patient ... we will inherit the whole earth, and that, with thanksgiving, God will give to us the grace to enjoy His blessings here on earth with free and open hearts. So too, we will always enjoy peace, whatever troubles we may encounter.

Nevertheless, we should note that this promise today is not totally accomplished in every situation – it is enough that we experience it in part. It is for good reason that Scripture states that the last day is truly the day of our redemption, when God's children will be revived and restored. Thus, let us patiently wait to possess this promised inheritance at the appearing of our Lord Jesus Christ, confident that the earth has been given to us. And let us be content to run the race set before us and finish our earthly pilgrimage. Regardless of where we may be; regardless of the oppression we experience and the losses we endure, let us be content to trust God's promise (along with the testimony of our conscience) that we will possess all things as His children and heirs. Furthermore, let us not envy those who boast that they have reached the summit, when, like brute beasts, they devour everything by their pride, violence, and tyrannies. ... Let us place our Lord's protection above every impulse to retaliate or defend ourselves. For certainly, God's power to protect and sustain us is infinite, and He will demonstrate that He is stronger than all things. [Sermons on the Harmony of the Gospels, CO 46:788-789]

MAY 8

Hungry, Yet Satisfied

'Blessed are those who hunger and thirst for righteousness,
for they shall be satisfied.'

MATTHEW 5:6

When Scripture says 'Blessed are those who hunger' it means the same thing as we saw previously, namely, that those are blessed who mourn and are poor of spirit, who find their refuge and relief in God. Why then does Saint Matthew add the word 'righteousness'? The sense is altogether appropriate, for Matthew wishes to make it clear that children of God will not only experience hunger and thirst – that is, they will not only be deprived of help and comfort, victims of oppression – but they will be in the right, since they will have done nothing to deserve such poor treatment. It's not that they demand special privilege or be granted special favors for having injured no one. They do not try to plead their case by illicit means. All they request is that they be treated fairly and not tormented without cause. ... How wretched they would appear to be, were it not for that promise which is given here, that 'they shall be satisfied.'...

Let us learn, therefore, to rest in this hope, that in the end we will be filled and that God will supply everything we lack. If today we are like those on death's precipice, with no inner strength, no outside help, and in the most desperate condition, let this firm hope sustain us, as we look to God who is eager to satisfy those who are hungry. ...

And although God allows us to suffer affliction, even when we are in the right, nevertheless, let us not be overwhelmed with sadness and despair, but let us hold firm to the expectation that, in the end, God will provide for all our needs. [Sermons on the Harmony of the Gospels, CO 46, 789-791]

MAY 9

Faith and Works

Jesus answered them: 'This is the work of God, that you believe in him whom he has sent.' JOHN 6:29

Christ reminds them of one work, that is, faith, by which He means that all that is undertaken without faith is vain and useless.... We may think it strange that God approves of nothing but faith alone; for the love of our neighbor ought not to be despised, and the other exercises of religion do not lose their place of honor. So then, though faith may hold the highest rank, still other works are not superfluous. The reply is easy, for faith does not exclude either the love of our neighbor or any other good work, because it contains them all within itself. Faith is called the only work of God, because by means of it we possess Christ, and thus become the children of God, so that He governs us by His Spirit. So then, because Christ does not separate faith from its fruits, we need not be surprised if He makes it to be the first and the last.... It ought always to be remembered that, in order to have a full perception of the power of faith, we must understand who Christ is, in whom we believe, and why He was given to us by the Father....

Now faith brings nothing to God; rather, it places men and women before God as empty and poor, that they may be filled with Christ and His grace. [Faith] is therefore – if we may be allowed the expression – a passive work, to which no reward can be paid, and it bestows on men and women no other righteousness than that which they receive from Christ. [Commentary on John]

MAY 10

Comfort in Affliction

Hear this, all peoples! Give ear, all inhabitants of the world, both low and high, rich and poor together! My mouth shall speak wisdom; the meditation of my heart shall be understanding.
PSALM 49:1-3

[A]s God's providence of the world is not presently apparent to us, we must exercise patience … as we anticipate a favorable outcome. That it is our duty to maintain a resolute struggle with our afflictions, however severe these may be, and that it would be foolish to find our happiness in the enjoyment of such fleeting possessions as the riches, honors, or pleasures of this world – these are precepts which even the pagan philosophers have affirmed, yet they have uniformly failed to set before us the true source of consolation. However admirably they discourse about a happy life, they confine themselves entirely to commending virtue, and do not call our attention to the fact that it is God who governs the world, and to whom alone we can turn with confidence in the most desperate of circumstances. Slender comfort, then, can be derived upon this subject from the teaching of philosophy. If, therefore, the Holy Spirit in this psalm calls our attention to truths that are sufficiently familiar to experience, it is so that He may raise our minds from them to the higher truths of the divine government of the world, assuring us of the fact that God sits supreme, even when the wicked are triumphing most in their success … and that a day is coming when God will dash the cup of pleasure out of the hands of His enemies, and give joy to the hearts of His friends, by delivering them out of their severest distresses. This alone is the consideration that can impart solid comfort to us under our afflictions. [Commentary on Psalms]

MAY 11

Word and Spirit

*Then [Christ] opened their minds to understand the
Scriptures.*
LUKE 24:45

As the Lord had formerly discharged the office of Teacher, with
little or no improvement on the part of the disciples, He now
begins to teach them inwardly by His Spirit; for words are idly
wasted on the air, until the minds are enlightened by the gift of
understanding. It is truth, indeed, that the word of God is like
a lamp (Ps. 119:105) but it shines in darkness and amidst the
blind, until the inward light is given by the Lord, to whom it
uniquely belongs to enlighten the blind (Ps. 146:8). And hence
it is evident how great is the corruption of our nature, since the
light of life exhibited to us in the heavenly oracles is of no avail
to us. Now if we do not perceive by the understanding what is
right, how would our will be sufficient for yielding obedience?
We ought, therefore, to acknowledge that we come short in
every respect, so that the heavenly doctrine proves to be useful
and efficacious to us, in so far as the Spirit both forms our
minds to understand it, and our hearts to submit to its yoke;
and, therefore, that in order for us to be properly qualified to
become His disciples, we must lay aside all confidence in our
own abilities, and seek light from heaven … and give ourselves
up to be governed by God. Nor is it without reason that Paul
bids men and women to become fools, that they may be wise
to God (1 Cor. 3:18); for no darkness is more dangerous for
quenching the light of the Spirit than reliance on our own
wisdom. [Commentary on the Harmony of the Gospels]

MAY 12

Renouncing All Things

Indeed, I count everything as loss because of the surpassing worth of knowing Christ Jesus my Lord. For his sake I have suffered the loss of all things and count them as rubbish, in order that I may gain Christ.

PHILIPPIANS 3:8

But it is asked whether it is necessary for us to renounce riches, and honors, and nobility of descent, and even external righteousness, that we may become 'partakers of Christ' (Heb. 3:14). For are not all these things gifts of God, which in themselves, are not to be despised? I answer that the Apostle does not speak here so much of the things themselves, as of the quality of them. It is indeed true that the kingdom of heaven is like a precious pearl, which no one should hesitate to sell everything they own so as to purchase it (Matt. 13:46). There is, however, a difference between the substance of things and the quality. Paul did not think it necessary to disown his ethnic background, his tribe and connection to Abraham ... that he might become a Christian, but rather to renounce dependence upon his descent. ... Paul, therefore, divested himself – not of works, but of that mistaken confidence in works, with which he had been puffed up. As to riches and honors, when we have divested ourselves of attachment to them, we will be prepared also to renounce the things themselves, whenever the Lord will require this from us, and so it ought to be. It is not expressly necessary that you be a poor man or woman, in order that you may be a Christian; but if it pleases the Lord and it should be so, you ought to be prepared to endure poverty. In sum, it is not lawful for Christians to have anything apart from Christ. [Commentary on Philippians]

MAY 13

Resurrection and Ascension

If then you have been raised with Christ, seek the things that are above, where Christ is seated at the right hand of God. Set your minds on things that are above, not on things that are on the earth. For you have died, and your life is hidden with Christ in God.

COLOSSIANS 3:1-3

Ascension follows resurrection: hence, if we are the members of Christ, we must ascend into heaven, because He, on being raised from the dead, was 'received up into heaven' (Mark 16:19) so that He might draw us up with Him. Now, we seek those things which are above when in our minds we are truly sojourners in this world, and are not bound to it. ... No one can rise again with Christ, if they have not first died with Him. ... Why has Paul taught that we must seek those things that are above? It is because the life of the pious man or woman is above. Why does he now teach that the things which are on earth are to be left behind? Because they are dead to the world. ...

It is worthy of observation that our life is said to be hid, so that we may not murmur or complain if our life, being buried under the shame of the cross, and under various distresses, differs nothing from death, but may patiently wait for the day of revelation. And so that our waiting may not be painful, let us observe those expressions, 'in God,' and 'with Christ,' which intimate that our life is out of danger, although that may not appear to be the case. For ... God is faithful, and therefore will not deny what has been committed to Him (2 Tim. 1:12). [Commentary on Colossians]

MAY 14

Mercy and Pity

'Blessed are the merciful, for they shall receive mercy.'

MATTHEW 5:7

Everything that we've said to this point shows that if we experience a lot of miseries, annoyances, oppressions and injuries, we can still be happy because God blesses all our afflictions when we look to Him. In this verse, our Lord Jesus Christ takes believers one step further, teaching us that we should not only be meek and patient when afflicted and tormented, but we must extend sympathy toward others in their suffering and be so touched with compassion for the difficulties and troubles that they are enduring that we look for ways to help them, as if their pain was ours. We should recognize that even as God has brought us together and wishes that we be one body ... so each individual should take their share of the suffering so as to lighten the burden of those who can bear no more. ...

Now to summarize, mercy is nothing other than the pain that we feel at someone else's sorrow. A person may be healthy and content, with plenty to drink and eat, and with no danger threatening them. Nevertheless, when they see their neighbor suffering, they must feel for them, share their sorrow and shoulder a part of the burden to lighten their load. That is what mercy is. ... So, when we see those who are sick, poor, and destitute, and others who are troubled and distressed (whether of body or mind), we should think, 'Alas, this person and I are of the same body.' And then we should demonstrate by our deeds that we are merciful. We can insist a thousand times that we feel pity for those who are suffering, but all our claims amount to nothing unless we actually help them. [Sermons on the Harmony of the Gospels, CO 46:792-793]

MAY 15

Mercy to the Merciful

'Blessed are the merciful, for they shall receive mercy.'

MATTHEW 5:7

This verse has a promise added to it because we are so very slow to extend pity to others. So too, what God's Son says here is completely contrary to our natural inclination and very difficult for us to believe. The promise thus gives us an entry-point. For if the passage only said 'Blessed are the merciful,' we would all reject it out of hand. But when our Lord Jesus Christ reminds us that we also have need of mercy, both from our heavenly Father and from other people, and that we can only obtain mercy if we are merciful – this should cause us to think about ourselves more carefully. ... Take for example those who have everything they could desire in this world – they will still experience a lot of crosses in life. Even princes, kings, and mighty lords are not immune from terrible ordeals, suffering sometimes in body, sometimes in mind. And even if they might wish to build for themselves a nest above the clouds so as to escape all trouble, nevertheless, God keeps them in their place and shows that they are mere mortals and frail creatures. If those who seem already to have attained a kind of paradise for themselves need mercy, what should be said for the rest of us?

Thus, were we to think carefully about these matters, we would most certainly extend mercy to our needy neighbors whenever we see their miseries and afflictions. ... Although the world has contempt for all this, nevertheless God will overrule so that when we are in need, He will not deny us our reward – we will receive mercy when we have given it. [Sermons on the Harmony of the Gospels, CO 46:793-794]

MAY 16

Beginning of Repentance

Now when they heard this they were cut to the heart, and said to Peter and the rest of the apostles, 'Brothers, what shall we do?'

ACTS 2:37

Luke now declares the fruit of Peter's sermon, so that we may know that the power of the Holy Spirit was manifested not only in the diversity of tongues, but also in the hearts of those who heard. And he notes a double-fruit: first, that they were touched with the feeling of sorrow; and, secondly, that they were obedient to Peter's counsel. This is the beginning of repentance and the entrance into godliness, to be sorry for our sins and to be wounded with the feeling of our misery. For as long as men and women are careless, they cannot receive teaching as they should. And for this reason, the word of God is compared to a sword (Heb. 4:12), because it mortifies our flesh, that we may be offered to God for a sacrifice. But to this pricking of the heart, there must also be a readiness to obey. Cain and Judas were both pricked of the heart, but despair kept them from submitting themselves to God (Gen. 4:13; Matt. 27:3). For when the mind is oppressed with horror, it can do nothing but flee from God. And surely, when David affirms that a contrite spirit and a humble heart is a sacrifice acceptable to God, he speaks of voluntary pricking; for, in the case of the wicked, the pricking is mixed with fretting and fuming. Therefore, we must be of good heart and lift up our mind with this hope of salvation, so that we may be ready to give ourselves entirely over to God, and to follow whatsoever He commands. [Commentary on Acts]

MAY 17

Pure in Heart

'Blessed are the pure in heart, for they shall see God.'

MATTHEW 5:8

Everyone readily agrees that the main virtue which we should possess is purity of heart and sincerity. For, without these qualities, every other virtue – however highly regarded – is only smoke and rubbish before God. Everyone praises integrity, but the sad truth is that no one wants to follow its precepts. For we recognize that without trickery and maliciousness it is impossible to live among men and women, especially since the wicked always have their nets ready to trap us. Thus, we think it necessary to follow their example. However, after we have affirmed the importance of living sincerely and without pretense, and having a pure and clean heart, we invariably resort to tricks and deception to accomplish our goals. So, when our Lord Jesus Christ says 'Blessed are those who have a clean and pure heart,' on the face of it He is repeating a common maxim. But if we consider how people usually live, how they indulge in their cunning and in bent and crooked ways, we can see that it was with good reason that our Lord Jesus Christ reminded His disciples of the importance of sincerity and integrity. [Sermons on the Harmony of the Gospels, CO 46:797-798]

MAY 18

Enjoying God

'Blessed are the pure in heart, for they shall see God.'

MATTHEW 5:8

Our Lord Jesus Christ says that if the world mocks our innocence, and if our innocence seems to subject us to greater harm, then we should all the more rejoice in our reward – that we shall see God. Our eyes may not be keen enough to perceive how to acquire worldly profits, comfort, convenience, pleasure and prestige. But when we gaze on other things instead, we will have a better view of what is promised to us here: we will rejoice in God's presence, the source of our blessedness, joy, and glory. ... Now, it is true that we cannot presently see God, for to see Him we would have to be like Him, as St. John claims in his epistle (1 John 3:2). And we are very far from that! The joy of seeing God, which is mentioned here, cannot be ours before the last day, when we will be conformed to the glory of God. ...

In the meantime, it is adequate for us to know that our Lord Jesus Christ declares here that, as His disciples, we should (first of all) not practice cunning, nor boast that we perceive more light than is permitted us, nor give false pretentions so as to deceive and cheat others. People may not think we're successful in this world, since we act with integrity. We will allow many opportunities for gain to pass us by, and accept loss if our actions might offend God. ... We know, however that even if the world condemns us, we have a reward that fully satisfies and comforts us: we will have God to enjoy. For the word 'see' in Scripture means 'enjoy.' [Sermons on the Harmony of the Gospels, CO 46:799-800]

MAY 19

Sacrifice of Prayer

The one who offers thanksgiving as his sacrifice glorifies me; to one who orders his way rightly I will show the salvation of God.

PSALM 50:23

[T]here is nothing for which we are more frequently guilty than forgetfulness of the benefits of the Lord. Scarcely one out of a thousand blessings attracts our notice; and if it does, it is only slightly so, as if it were in passing. [Moreover,] we do not assign that importance to the duty of praise which it deserves. We are apt to neglect it as something trivial, and altogether commonplace; whereas, in fact, it constitutes the chief exercise of godliness, in which God would have us to be engaged during the whole of our lives. In the words [of this passage], the sacrifice of praise is asserted to form the true and proper worship of God. The phrase 'glorifies me' implies that God is truly and properly worshiped, and the glory which He requires yielded to Him, when His goodness is celebrated with a sincere and grateful heart; but that all the other sacrifices to which hypocrites attach such importance are worthless in His estimation, and no part whatsoever of His worship. Under the phrase 'offers thanksgiving,' however, is comprehended, as I have already noted, both faith and prayer. There must be an experience of the goodness of the Lord before our mouths can be opened to praise Him for it, and this goodness can only be experienced by faith. Hence, it follows that the whole of spiritual worship is comprehended under what is either presupposed in the exercise of praise, or what flows from it. [Commentary on Psalms]

MAY 20

Peacemakers

'Blessed are the peacemakers, for they shall be called sons of God.'
MATTHEW 5:9

Our Lord next adds, 'Blessed are the peacemakers.' This word has been commonly misunderstood. For we take it to mean 'peaceful,' when it has a far richer meaning. For a person might be 'peaceful' without being a 'peacemaker' – that is, without pursuing peace with others. ... Now, to avoid ambiguity, we need to preserve the natural sense of this passage, namely, that we must endeavor to cultivate peace everywhere. But we must remember to begin with ourselves. ... Imagine a person who is quarrelsome, who is impatient and reckless in all their actions. Yet if that person hears some commotion, they go and appease the situation, saying, 'Enough, let's have peace!' ... What authority would such a person have if, one moment, they lose their temper and bluster and storm, and the next moment they try to promote peace all around them? Let us learn, therefore, that to make peace, we must first be peaceable. ...

Be assured, then, that we are banished from the school of our Lord Jesus Christ and His Church, when we stir up quarrels and hostility among other people. By contrast, in order to be His disciples, we must not only be peaceable ourselves, but make every effort to overcome all hostility, to put out the fire once it is kindled and to avoid all kinds of disputes. And when we see someone giving themselves over to hatred, we should intervene as early as possible. We should not wait for Satan to claim victory, but should intervene first. That, in short, is what we must remember. [Sermons on the Harmony of the Gospels, CO 46:801, 803]

MAY 21

Children of God

'Blessed are the peacemakers, for they shall be called sons of God.'

MATTHEW 5:9

Now, in order to impress this teaching upon us, our Lord Jesus Christ says that those who pursue peace 'shall be called children of God.' Could there be anything more desirable than to be recognized and acknowledged as a child of God, and to call upon Him as our Father? Imagine our situation if that were not the case. If God were to reject us, what would remain for us? Even if we had all that the world could offer, would not everything be cursed and turned to confusion if God were against us? For we can have no true confidence of prosperity and goodness unless we experience God's favor and fatherly love toward us. This, then, is what we should strive for – knowing God as our father and having the privilege of calling ourselves His children. Moreover, as Jesus states here, we cannot attain this blessing unless we are peacemakers. For with good reason, God is called the God of peace. We must be like Him in this respect, or we do not belong to Him, whatever we profess with our lips. This, then, is a proof that God is our Father and that we want to live in obedience to Him – namely, that we dismantle all dissension, as much as lies in our power. [Sermons on the Harmony of the Gospels, CO 46:803]

MAY 22

Persecuted for Righteousness' Sake

'Blessed are those who are persecuted for righteousness' sake, for theirs is the kingdom of heaven.'
MATTHEW 5:10

Now to suffer persecution for righteousness' sake is a singular comfort. For it ought to occur to us how much honor God bestows upon us in thus furnishing us with the special badge of His soldiery. I say this not only of those who labor for the defense of the gospel but also those who in any way maintain the cause of righteousness by suffering persecution for righteousness. Therefore, whether in declaring God's truth against Satan's falsehoods or in taking up the protection of the good and the innocent against the wrongs of the wicked, we must undergo the offenses and hatred of the world, which may imperil either our life, our fortunes, or our honor. Let us not grieve or be troubled in thus far devoting our efforts to God, or count ourselves miserable in those matters in which He has with His own lips declared us blessed. Even poverty, if it is judged in itself, is misery; likewise, exile, contempt, prison, disgrace; finally, death itself is the ultimate of all calamities. But when the favor of our God breathes upon us, every one of these things turns into happiness for us. … What then? … If we are cast out of our own house, then we will be the more intimately received into God's family. If we are vexed and despised, we but take all the firmer root in Christ. If we are branded with disgrace and ignominy, we but have a fuller place in the Kingdom of God. If we are slain, entrance into the blessed life will thus be open to us. [Institutes (1559), III.viii.7]

MAY 23

The World's Opposition

'Blessed are you when others revile you and persecute you and utter all kinds of evil against you falsely on my account. Rejoice and be glad, for your reward is great in heaven, for so they persecuted the prophets who were before you.'

MATTHEW 5:11-12

When we are unjustly afflicted, provided we have a clean conscience before God, we must not lose courage, thinking our situation is worse than that of unbelievers. Why? Because we are seeking our happiness on high. In the meantime, we must prepare for battle. And when someone assures us of the rest that awaits us, of our victory and the glory which accompanies it, let us lift our eyes and minds to the realm above.

Moreover, we are encouraged not only to endure patiently the injuries and harsh treatment, but also the reproaches, slander, and false accusations directed against us. This is still harder, since a brave person will endure beatings, and even death itself, more easily than suffer humiliation and disgrace. ... Thus, we must arm ourselves with more than human resolve if we are to endure calmly all the insults, reproaches, and blame which the wicked unfairly impose upon us. Now, as Paul states, this is what awaits us: Since our hope is in the living God, he writes, we are bound to suffer distress and shame; we will be subject to suspicion; people will spit in our face. In this way God is testing us. We must be prepared to face these things and to take up our Lord Jesus Christ's teaching as our shield for the battle. [Sermons on the Harmony of the Gospels, CO 46:811-812]

MAY 24

Blessed Holy Spirit

On the last day of the feast, the great day, Jesus stood up and cried out, 'If anyone thirsts, let him come to me and drink. Whoever believes in me as the Scripture has said, "Out of his heart will flow rivers of living water".' Now this he said about the Spirit.

JOHN 7:37-39

By his secret watering the Spirit makes us fruitful to bring forth the buds of righteousness. Accordingly, He is frequently called 'water' as in Isaiah: 'Come, everyone who thirsts, come to the waters' (Isa. 55:1). Also, 'I shall pour out my Spirit upon those who thirst, and rivers upon the dry land' (Isa. 44:3). To these verses Christ's statement corresponds: 'If anyone thirsts, let them come to me and drink' (John 7:37). Although sometimes He is so called because of His power to cleanse and purify, as in Ezekiel, where the Lord promises 'clean water' in which He will 'wash away the filth' of His people (Ezek. 36:25). From the fact that the Spirit restores and nourishes unto vigor of life those on whom He has poured the stream of His grace, He gets the names 'oil' and 'anointing' (1 John 2:20, 27). On the other hand, persistently and boiling away and burning up our vicious and inordinate desires, He enflames our hearts with the love of God and with zealous devotion. From this effect upon us He is also justly called 'fire' (Luke 3:16). ... [B]y the inspiration of His power the Spirit so breathes divine life into us that we are no longer actuated by ourselves, but are ruled by His action and prompting. Accordingly, whatever good things are in us are the fruits of His grace; and without Him our gifts are darkness of mind and perversity of heart. [Institutes (1559), III.i.3]

MAY 25

Pardon for Sin

Purge me with hyssop, and I shall be clean; wash me, and I shall be whiter than snow.

PSALM 51:7

The truth is that we cannot properly pray for the pardon of sin until we have come to a persuasion that God will be reconciled to us. Who can venture to open their mouth in God's presence unless they are assured of His fatherly favor? And since pardon is the first thing we should pray for, it is plain that there is no inconsistency in having a persuasion of the grace of God, and yet proceed to beg for His forgiveness. As proof for this, I might refer to the Lord's Prayer in which we are taught to begin by addressing God as our Father, and then afterwards to pray for the remission of sins. God's pardon is full and complete; but our faith cannot take in His overflowing goodness. Thus, it is necessary that it should distil to us drop by drop. ... The mention made here to purging with hyssop and of washing or sprinkling, teaches us, in all our prayers for the pardon of sin, to have our thoughts directed to the great sacrifice by which Christ has reconciled us to God. ... If sinners would find mercy, they must look to the sacrifice of Christ, which expiated the sins of the world, glancing, at the same time for the confirmation of their faith, to baptism and the Lord's Supper; for it would be vain to imagine that God, the Judge of the world, would receive us again into His favor in any other way than through a satisfaction made to His justice. [Commentary on Psalms]

MAY 26

Going to the World

And [the disciples] went out and preached everywhere, while the Lord worked with them and confirmed the message by accompanying signs.

MARK 16:20

Mark here notices briefly those events of which Luke continues the history in his [book of Acts], that the voice of a small and dispersed body of men resounded even to the farthest ends of the world. For exactly in proportion as the fact was less credible, so much more clearly was there displayed in it a miracle of heavenly power. Every person would have thought that, by the death of the cross, Christ would either be altogether extinguished, or so completely overwhelmed, that He would never be again mentioned except with shame and loathing. The apostles, whom He had chosen to be His witnesses, had wickedly deserted Him, and had subsequently concealed themselves in darkness. Such was their ignorance and lack of education, and such was the contempt in which they were held, that they hardly ventured to utter a word in public. Was it to be expected that men who were unlearned, and were held in no esteem, and had even deserted their Master, should, by the sound of their voice, reduce so many scattered nations into subjection to Him who had been crucified? There is great emphasis, therefore, in the words, 'they went out and preached everywhere' – men who had recently shut themselves up, trembling and silent, in their prison. For it was impossible that so sudden a change should be accomplished in a moment by human power; and therefore, Mark adds, 'The Lord worked with them,' by which he means that this was truly a divine work. [Commentary on the Harmony of the Gospels]

MAY 27

Guardian of Our Salvation

'And this is the will of him who sent me, that I should lose nothing of all that he has given me, but raise it up on the last day.'

JOHN 6:39

[Jesus] now testifies that this is the design of the Father, that believers may find salvation secured in Christ. ... By this He means that He is not the guardian of our salvation for a single day, or for a few days, but that He will take care of it to the end, so that He will conduct us, as it were, from the beginning to the end of our course; and, therefore, He mentions that final resurrection. This promise is highly necessary for us, who miserably groan under so great weakness of the flesh. ... Indeed, at every moment the salvation of the whole world might be ruined, were it not that believers, supported by the hand of Christ, advance boldly to the day of resurrection. Let this, therefore, be fixed in our minds, that Christ has stretched out His hand to us, that He may not desert us in the midst of the course, but that, relying on His goodness, we may boldly raise our eyes to the last day.

There is also another reason why He mentions the resurrection. It is because, so long as our 'life is hidden' (Col. 3:3) we are like dead people ... [with] one foot in the grave. ... Thus, there remains no other support of our faith and patience but this, that we disregard the condition of the present life, and apply our minds and our senses to the last day, and pass through the obstructions of the world, until the fruit of our faith at last appear. [Commentary on John]

MAY 28

Pursuit of Happiness

'For where your treasure is, there your heart will be also.'

MATTHEW 6:21

By this statement, Christ proves that those people are unhappy who have their treasure laid up on earth, because their happiness is uncertain and of short duration. Men and women who are covetous cannot be prevented from breathing in their hearts a wish for heaven; but Christ lays down an opposite principle, that people are surrounded and confined wherever they imagine the greatest happiness to be. Hence, it follows that those who desire to be happy in the world renounce heaven. We know how carefully the philosophers conducted their inquiries respecting the supreme good. It was the chief point on which they concentrated their efforts, and rightly so, for it is the principle on which the regulation of our lives entirely depends, and the object to which all our senses are directed. If honor is considered the supreme good, the minds of men and women must be entirely occupied with ambition; if money, covetousness will immediately predominate; if pleasure, it will be impossible to prevent people from sinking into gross indulgence. We all have a natural desire to pursue happiness; and, as a consequence, our false imaginations carry us away in every direction. But, if we were honestly and firmly convinced that our happiness is in heaven, it would be easy for us to trample upon the world, to despise earthly blessings ... and to rise toward heaven. For this reason, Paul, with the intention of exciting believers to look upwards, and to exhort them to meditate on the heavenly life, presents to them Christ, in whom alone they ought to seek perfect happiness (Col. 3:1). [Commentary on the Harmony of the Gospels]

MAY 29

Fountain that Satisfies

On the last day of the feast, the great day, Jesus stood up and cried out, 'If anyone thirsts, let him come to me and drink.'

JOHN 7:37

It is highly useful to us that the Evangelist introduces Christ exclaiming aloud, 'If anyone thirsts, let him come to Me.' For we infer from it that the invitation was not addressed to one or two persons only, or in a low and gentle whisper, but that this doctrine is proclaimed to all, in such a manner that none may be ignorant of it, but those who ... will not receive this loud and distinct cry. ...

By this clause [Christ] exhorts all to partake of His blessings, provided that, out of a conviction of their own poverty, they desire to obtain assistance. For it is true that we are all poor and destitute of every blessing, but it is far from being true that all are roused by a conviction of their poverty to seek relief. Hence, it happens that many persons are not affected by a perception of their emptiness, until the Spirit of God, by His own fire, kindles hunger and thirst in their hearts. It belongs to the Spirit, therefore, to cause us to desire His grace. ...

To the exhortation a promise is added: for though the word 'let him come' conveys an exhortation, still it contains within itself a promise; because Christ testifies that He is not a dry and worn-out cistern, but an inexhaustible fountain, which abundantly satisfies all who will come to drink. Hence it follows that, if we ask from Him what we want, our desire will not be disappointed. [Commentary on John]

MAY 30

Power and Goodness

Once God has spoken; twice have I heard this: that power belongs to God, and that to you, O Lord, belongs steadfast love.

PSALM 62:11-12

God is strong to put a restraint upon the wicked, and crush their proud and nefarious plans and ... [at the same time,] He is ever mindful of His goodness in protecting and defending His own children. Men and women who discipline themselves to contemplate these two attributes, which ought never to be dissociated in our minds from the idea of God, are certain to stand tall and immoveable under the fiercest assaults and temptations. ... The world's opinion of God is that He sits in heaven as an idle and unconcerned spectator of events that are happening. Should we then be surprised that men and women tremble under every difficulty, when they thus believe themselves to be the sport of blind chance? ...

There is an obvious reason, then, for the Psalmist to couple together ... His power and His clemency. They are the two wings with which we fly upwards to heaven; the two pillars on which we rest and may defy the surges of temptation. Does danger, in brief, spring up from any quarter? Then, let us call to memory that divine power which can banish all harms, and as this sentiment prevails in our minds, our troubles cannot fail to fall prostrate before it. Why should we fear – how can we be afraid when the God who covers us with the shadow of His wings, is the same who rules the universe with His nod, holds in secret chains the devil and all the wicked, and effectually overrules their designs and intrigues? [Commentary on Psalms]

MAY 31

Powerful Word

For the word of God is living and active, sharper than any two-edged sword, piercing to the division of soul and of spirit, of joints and of marrow, and discerning the thoughts and intentions of the heart.

HEBREWS 4:12

It appears evident that the word of God is not equally efficacious in everyone. Among elect persons it exerts its own power when, humbled by a true knowledge of themselves, they flee to the grace of Christ; and this can never happen, except when it penetrates into their innermost heart. For hypocrisy – which occupies an incredible and labyrinthine space in the human heart – must be sifted. So too, it is necessary that we be not slightly pricked or torn, but thoroughly wounded, so that, being laid low under a sense of eternal death, we may be taught to die to ourselves. In short, we will never be renewed in our whole mind until our old self is slain by the edge of the spiritual sword. ... [The faithful] cannot otherwise be brought to obey God than by having, as it were, their own will slain; nor can they receive the light of God's wisdom, unless they have the wisdom of their flesh destroyed. ...

The sum of the whole then is this – that as soon as God opens His sacred mouth, all our faculties ought to be open to receive His word; for He would not have His word scattered in vain, so as to disappear or fall neglected on the ground. ... [H]e has put power in His word for this purpose, that it may scrutinize all the parts of the soul, search the thoughts, discern the affections, and, in a word, show itself to be the judge. [Commentary on Hebrews]

JUNE 1

Spiritual Worship

Offer to God a sacrifice of thanksgiving, and perform your vows to the Most High, and call upon me in the day of trouble; I will deliver you, and you shall glorify me.

PSALM 50:14-15

There is in all human beings by nature a strong and ineffaceable conviction that they ought to worship God. Incapable of worshiping Him in a pure and spiritual manner, it becomes necessary that they should invent some contrived appearance as a substitute ... [and] they persist in it to the very end. Men and women have always, as a result, been found addicted to ceremonies until they have been brought to the knowledge of that which constitutes true and acceptable religion. Praise and prayer are here considered to represent the whole of the worship of God. ...

The Psalmist specifies only one part of divine worship, when he enjoins us to acknowledge God as the author of all our mercies, and to ascribe to Him the praise which is justly due to His name: and adds, that we should have recourse to His goodness, cast all our cares into His breast, and seek by prayer that deliverance which He alone can give, and thanks for which one must afterwards render to Him. Faith, self-denial, a holy life, and patient endurance of the cross, are all sacrifices which please God. But since prayer is the offspring of faith ... and since genuine praise indicates holiness of heart, we need not be surprised that these two points of worship should here be employed to represent the whole. Praise and prayer are set in opposition to ceremonies and mere external religious observance in order to teach us that the worship of God is spiritual. [Commentary on Psalms]

JUNE 2

Fruitless Ministry

And he said, 'Go, and say to this people: "Keep on hearing, but do not understand; keep on seeing, but do not perceive." Make the heart of this people dull, and their ears heavy and blind their eyes; lest they ... turn and be healed.'

ISAIAH 6:9-10

The Lord therefore forewarns Isaiah that he will have to deal with obstinate people, on whom he will produce little effect. ... This [passage] contains a most useful doctrine, which will be of perpetual use in the church of God; for all who shall labor faithfully in the ministry of the word will be laid under the necessity of meeting with the same results. We, too, have experienced it more than we could have wished; but it has been shared by all the servants of Christ, and therefore we ought to endure it with greater patience, though it is a very grievous stumbling block to those who serve God with a pure conscience. ... Satan powerfully excites his followers to raise a dislike of instruction on the pretense of it being not merely useless but even injurious, that it renders people more obstinate and leads to their destruction. At the present day, those who have no other reproach to bring against the doctrine of the gospel maintain that the only effect produced by the preaching of it has been that the world has become worse. But whatever may be the result, still God assures us that our services are acceptable to Him, because we obey His command; and although our labor appears to be fruitless, and people rush forward to their destruction and become more rebellious, we must continue; for we do nothing at our own suggestion and ought to be satisfied with the approval of God. [Commentary on Isaiah]

JUNE 3

Light of the Gospel

Again, Jesus spoke to them saying, 'I am the light of the world. Whoever follows me will not walk in darkness, but will have the light of life.'

JOHN 8:12

It is a beautiful commendation of Christ, when He is called 'the light of the world'; for, since we are all blind by nature, a remedy is offered, by which we may be freed and rescued from darkness and made partakers of the true light. Nor is it only to one person or to another that this benefit is offered, for Christ declares that He is the 'light of the whole world'; for by this universal statement He intended to remove the distinction, not only between Jews and Gentiles, but between the learned and ignorant, between persons of distinction and the common people. ...

[M]en and women will never present themselves to Christ to be illuminated, until they have known both that this world is darkness, and that they themselves are altogether blind. Let us therefore know that, when the manner of obtaining this light is pointed out to us in Christ, we are all condemned for blindness, and everything else which we consider to be light is compared to darkness, and to a very dark night. ... Hence it follows, that apart from Christ there is not even a spark of true light. There may be some appearance of brightness, but it resembles lightning, which only dazzles the eyes. It must also be observed, that the power and office of illuminating is not confined to the personal presence of Christ; for though He is far removed from us with respect to His body, yet He daily sheds His light upon us, by the doctrine of the gospel, and by the secret power of His Spirit. [Commentary on John]

JUNE 4

Contemplating God

O God, you are my God; earnestly I seek you; my soul thirsts for you; my flesh faints for you, as in a dry and weary land where there is no water. So I have looked upon you in the sanctuary, beholding your power and glory.

PSALM 63:1-2

It is apparent that God was ever in [David's] thoughts, though he was wandering in the wilderness under such circumstances of destitution. Even when so situated, in a wild and dangerous solitude, where the very horrors of the place were enough to have distracted his holy meditations, he trained himself to meditate on the power and glory of God, just as if he had been in the sanctuary. ... It is noticeable of ignorant and superstitious persons that they seem full of zeal and fervor as long as they come in contact with the ceremonies of religion, while their devotion evaporates immediately when these things are withdrawn from them. David, on the contrary, when these things were removed, continued to hold them in his memory and rise, through their assistance, to fervent longings after God. We may learn from this that, when deprived at any time of the outward means of grace, we should direct the eye of our faith to God in the worst of circumstances, and not forget Him whenever the symbols of holy things are removed from our sight. The great truth, for example, of our spiritual regeneration, though but once represented to us in baptism, should remain fixed in our minds through our whole life. The mystical union that exists between Christ and His members should be a matter of our reflection, not only when we sit at the Lord's table, but at all other times. [Commentary on Psalms]

JUNE 5

Messianic Banquet

'I tell you I will not drink again of this fruit of the vine until that day when I drink it new with you in my Father's kingdom.'

MATTHEW 26:29

[T]he disciples were warned both of their Master's approaching death, and of the new and heavenly life: for the more nearly the hour of Christ's death approached, there was the greater necessity for them to be confirmed, that they might not altogether fall away. Again, as He intended to place His death before their eyes in the Holy Supper, as in a mirror, it was not without reason that He again declared that He was now leaving the world. But as this information was full of sadness, a consolation is immediately added, that they have no occasion for shrinking from the thought of His death, which will be followed by a better life. It is as if He had said: 'It is true, indeed, that I am now hastening to my death, but it is in order that I may pass from it to a blessed immortality, not to live alone without you in the kingdom of God, but to have you associated with me in the same life.' Thus, we see how Christ leads His disciples by the hand to the cross, and thence raises them to the hope of the resurrection. And as it was necessary that they should be directed to the cross of Christ, that by that ladder they might ascend to heaven; so now, since Christ has died and been received into heaven, we ought to be led from the contemplation of the cross to heaven, that death and the restoration of life may be found to agree. [Commentary on the Harmony of the Gospels]

JUNE 6

Revering God's Word

'You shall not take the name of the LORD your God in vain.'

DEUTERONOMY 5:11

Today, do not men and women audaciously speak of the name of God as they please? And when they argue about holy Scripture over a pot of wine at the tavern, do they even think to humble themselves before it, recognizing their sinfulness and weakness, asking God for His Holy Spirit to treat these divine mysteries as they deserve? Not at all! Instead, these arguments are nothing but a mockery – sure proof that there is very little religion in the world today. We see how some make a game of Holy Scripture, drawing it into jesting proverbs.... Others discourse in flights of fancy, 'Why is this? And why is that?' And then when one comes to the high mysteries of God, if they annoy us, we would like all that abolished. ... So then let us understand that God recommends to us the honor and authority of His Word – that we must receive with all humility everything contained in Holy Scripture, making ourselves teachable to what is contained in it. ... We must always do Him this honor of taking all our senses captive and saying, 'Lord, we are your disciples; we receive peaceably what it has pleased you to teach us, knowing that it is for our profit and salvation.' Without exception, then, let everything contained in Holy Scripture be received with reverence; and when it is a question of the holy mysteries of God, let us not judge them according to our understanding; and if things do not seem to us to be good and proper, let us keep a tight rein on ourselves, and let God always have His way and His word complete freedom. [Sermons on Deuteronomy, CO 26:281-282]

JUNE 7

Learning Wisdom

I have more understanding than all my teachers, for your testimonies are my meditation.
PSALM 119:99

When [the Psalm writer] claims the credit of being superior in knowledge to his instructors, he does not mean to deny that they also had learned from the word of God. ... But he gives God thanks for enabling him to surpass, in proficiency, those from whom he had learned the first elements of knowledge. ... The faithful, it is true, are instructed by the pains and labors of their teachers, but it is in such a way that God must still be regarded as enlightening them. And this is the reason that the student surpasses the master; for God means to show, as it were, with the finger, that He uses the service of human teachers in such a way that He Himself remains the chief teacher. ... In short, [the Psalmist] affirms that whoever yields themselves with humility before God, and keeps their thoughts in subjection to His word and endeavors diligently to meditate upon the Law – those persons will thereby derive sufficient wisdom to enable them ... to match with the most pre-eminent teachers through the whole course of life. ...

[N]othing is better for us than to learn at God's mouth, since those people only are perfectly wise who are taught in His school. At the same time, the faithful are here commanded to remain sober, that they may not look for wisdom anywhere else than in God's word, and that ambition or curiosity may not incite them to vain boasting. In short, all here are encouraged, ... however intelligent they may be, to yield themselves willingly to the lessons of heavenly wisdom revealed in the divine word. [Commentary on Psalms]

JUNE 8

Kingdom of Christ

He will swallow up death forever; and the Lord God will wipe away tears from all faces and the reproach of his people he will take away from all the earth, for the LORD has spoken.

ISAIAH 25:8

The Prophet promises that there will be perfect happiness under the reign of Christ, and in order to express this the more fully, he employs various metaphors admirably adapted to the subject. That happiness is real, and not temporary or fading, which not even death can take away; for amidst the highest prosperity, our joy is not a little diminished by the consideration that it will not always last. He therefore connects two things, which render happiness full and complete. The first is that the life is perpetual; for to those who in other respects are happy for a time, it is a wretched thing to die. The second is that this life is accompanied by joy; for otherwise it may be thought that death would be preferable to a sorrowful and afflicted life. ...

But it is asked, to what period must we refer these promises? For, in this world, we must contend with various afflictions, and must fight continually; and not only are we 'appointed to death' (Ps. 44:22), but we 'die daily' (1 Cor. 15:31). ... Where or when, therefore, are these things fulfilled? They must undoubtedly be referred to the universal kingdom of Christ. ... [and] extended even to the second coming of Christ, which on that account is called the 'day of redemption' and the 'day of restoration.' ... Let us therefore direct all our hope and expectation to this point, and let us not doubt that the Lord will fulfill all these things in us when we have finished our [earthly] course. [Commentary on Isaiah]

JUNE 9

The Christian Race

But one thing I do; forgetting what lies behind and straining forward to what lies ahead, I press on toward the goal for the prize of the upward call of God in Christ Jesus.

PHILIPPIANS 3:13-14

Paul compares our life to a race course, the boundaries of which God has marked out for us as we run. For as it would profit runners nothing to have left the starting line unless they went forward toward the goal, so we must also pursue the course of our calling until death, and must not cease until we have obtained what we seek. Furthermore, as the way is marked out for the runners, that they may not exhaust themselves for no reason by wandering in this direction and that, so there is also a goal set before us, toward which we ought to direct our race single-mindedly. God does not permit us to wander about for no reason. Third, as runners need to be free from entanglements, and not stop their race on account of any impediments, but must continue to run, surmounting every obstacle, so we need to be careful not to apply our mind or heart to anything that may divert our attention. On the contrary, we must make it our goal that, free from every distraction, we may apply our entire mind's focus exclusively on God's calling. ... When he says that he does this 'one thing,' and forgets all things that are behind, he indicates his concentration, and excludes everything that might distract him. ... Thus, Paul teaches us that he does not think of what he has been or done, but he simply presses forward toward the appointed goal, and that, too, with such energy, he runs as it were with outstretched arms. [Commentary on Philippians]

JUNE 10

Freedom from Sin

'If you abide in my word, you are truly my disciples, and you will know the truth, and the truth will set you free.'

JOHN 8:31-32

[Jesus] commends the knowledge of the gospel from the fruit which we derive from it, or – which is the same thing – from its effect, namely, that it restores us to freedom. This is an invaluable blessing. Hence it follows that nothing is more excellent or desirable than the knowledge of the gospel. All men and women feel and acknowledge that slavery is a very wretched state; and since the gospel delivers us from it, it follows that we derive from the gospel the treasure of a blessed life.

We must now ascertain what kind of liberty is here described by Christ, namely, that it sets us free from the tyranny of Satan, sin, and death. And if we obtain it by means of the gospel, it is evident from this that we are by nature the slaves of sin. Next, we must ascertain what is the method of our deliverance. For as long as we are governed by our sense and by our natural disposition, we are in bondage to sin; but when the Lord regenerates us by His Spirit, He likewise makes us free, so that, loosed from the snares of Satan, we willingly obey righteousness. But regeneration proceeds from faith, and hence it is evident that freedom proceeds from the gospel. ... [T]he reason why the gospel ought to be considered as having achieved our deliverance is that it offers and gives us to Christ to be freed from the yoke of sin. [Commentary on John]

JUNE 11

Praise and Perseverance

I will come into your house with burnt offerings; I will perform my vows to you, that which my lips uttered and my mouth promised when I was in trouble.

PSALM 66:13-14

We are taught [in this passage] that when God at any time helps us in our adversity, we do an injustice to His name if we forget to celebrate our deliverances with solemn acknowledgments. More is spoken about in this passage than thanksgiving. [The Psalmist] speaks of vows that he made during the time of his affliction, and these demonstrated the constancy of his faith. The exhortation of the Apostle James is worthy of special notice: 'Is any among you suffering? Let him pray. Is anyone cheerful? Let him sing praise' (James 5:13). How many there are who lavish their hypocritical praises upon God during times of good fortune, but who, as soon as they are reduced to difficulties, become despondent in the fervor of their love and become violent, fretful, and impatient. The best evidence of true piety is when we sigh to God under the pressure of our afflictions, yet show by our prayers a holy perseverance in faith and patience – and then, afterwards, come forward with expressions of our gratitude.

The phrase 'which my lips uttered' is not a meaningless addition, but implies that [the Psalmist] had never allowed himself to be so overwhelmed with grief as not to throw his desires into the express form of a pledge, promising that he would cast himself for safety into the hands of God. [Commentary on Psalms]

JUNE 12

The Preached Word

For the word of God is living and active, sharper than any two-edged sword, piercing to the division of soul and of spirit, of joints and of arrow, and discerning the thoughts and intentions of the heart.

HEBREWS 4:12

It must be further noticed here that the apostle speaks of God's word, which is brought to us by the ministry of men. For crazy and even dangerous are those notions that, though the internal word is efficacious, yet that which proceeds from the mouth of a man is lifeless and destitute of all power. Indeed, I admit that the power does not proceed from the tongue of a man, nor exists in mere sound, but that the whole power is to be ascribed altogether to the Holy Spirit; there is, however, nothing in this to hinder the Spirit from putting forth His power in the word preached. For God, as He speaks not by Himself, but by men, dwells carefully on this point, so that His truth may not be objected to in contempt, because men are its ministers. So Paul, by saying that the gospel is the power of God (Rom. 1:16), intentionally adorned with this distinction his own preaching, though he saw that it was slandered by some and despised by others. And when in another place (Rom. 10:8) he teaches us that salvation is conferred by the doctrine of faith, he expressly states that it was the doctrine which was preached. We indeed find that God constantly commends the truth administered to us by men, in order to induce us to receive it with reverence. [Commentary on Hebrews]

JUNE 13

Christ Guards the Christian's Soul

And as they were stoning Stephen, he called out, 'Lord Jesus, receive my spirit.'

ACTS 7:59

[T]his prayer was a witness to Stephen's confidence; and surely his courage and forgiving spirit were so great that as he saw the stones flying about his ears (which would ultimately crush him) and as he heard curses and abuse hurled against his head, he yet depended meekly upon the grace of Christ. In a similar fashion, the Lord will sometimes have His servants brought to the end of their lives, for the purpose that their salvation may appear all the more wonderful. ... We see how Stephen leaned not on the judgment of the flesh; rather, assuring himself that even in destruction he would be saved, he suffered death with a quiet mind. For, undoubtedly, he was assured of this, that our life is hid with Christ in God (Col. 3:3). Therefore, casting off all care of the body, he was content to commit his soul into the hands of Christ. ...

It is hence fitting that, with David, we daily commit our souls into the hands of God (Ps. 31:6) ... so that God may deliver our life from all dangers. But when we must die, indeed, and we are called to heaven, we must fly to [Stephen's] prayer, that Christ will receive our spirit. ... This is an inestimable comfort, to know that our souls do not wander up and down when they flit out of our bodies but that Christ receives them and will faithfully keep them, if we commend them into His hands. This hope ought to encourage us to suffer death patiently. Indeed, those who commend their souls to Christ with an earnest affection of faith, will resign themselves entirely to His pleasure and will. [Commentary on Acts]

JUNE 14

Fearing God

'And do not fear those who kill the body but cannot kill the soul. Rather fear him who can destroy both soul and body in hell.'

MATTHEW 10:28

To stimulate His disciples to despise death, Christ employs the very powerful argument that men and women, who have been created for heavenly immortality, should have little regard for this frail and perishing life. The statement amounts to this, that if believers consider the purpose for which they were born, and what their condition is, they will have no reason to be so frantic in desiring an earthly life. But the words have still a richer and fuller meaning: for Christ teaches us here that the fear of God is dead in those men and women who, through dread of tyrants, depart from a confession of their faith. ... We must pay attention to the distinction between two opposite kinds of fear. If the fear of God is extinguished by the dread of men, is it not evident that we pay greater deference to them than to God Himself? Hence it follows that when we have abandoned the heavenly and eternal life, we reserve nothing more for ourselves than to be like the beasts that perish (Ps. 49:12). God alone has the power of bestowing eternal life, or of inflicting eternal death. ... Christ's words [in this verse] ought therefore to be explained as follows: 'Acknowledge that you have received immortal souls, which are subject to God's provision alone, and are not affected by the power of human beings. The consequence will be, that no terrors or alarms which people may employ will shake your faith.' [Commentary on the Harmony of the Gospels]

JUNE 15

God of Invention

For he is rightly instructed; his God teaches him.

ISAIAH 28:26

Having pointed out the wisdom of God, even in the smallest matters, Isaiah bids us in a similar way to raise our eyes to higher subjects, that we may learn to behold with greater reverence His wonderful and hidden judgments. A passing observation on the twenty-sixth verse may be made, and indeed ought to be made, that not only agriculture, but likewise all the arts which contribute to human advantage are the gifts of God, and that all that belongs to skillful invention has been imparted by Him to the human mind. Men and women have no right to be proud on this account, or to arrogate to themselves the praise of invention, as we see that the ancients did, who, out of their ingratitude to God, ranked in the number of the gods those whom they considered to be the authors of any ingenious contrivance. Hence arose deification and that pantheon of gods which the pagans created in their own fancy ... [and] the innumerable other gods, celebrated by human tongues and by human writings. The prophet shows that such arts ought to be ascribed to God alone, from whom they have been received, who alone is the inventor and teacher of them. If we ought to form such an opinion about agriculture and mechanical arts, what shall we think of the learned and exalted sciences, such as medicine, jurisprudence, astronomy, geometry, logic, and other such sciences? Shall we not much more consider them to have proceeded from God? Shall we not in them also behold and acknowledge His goodness, that His praise and glory may be celebrated both in the smallest and in the greatest affairs? [Commentary on Isaiah]

JUNE 16

Christ's Kingdom Invincible

*[T]hey lifted their voices together to God and said,
'Sovereign Lord, who made the heaven and the earth and
the sea and everything in them, who through the mouth of
our father David ... said by the Holy Spirit, "Why did the
Gentiles rage, and the peoples plot in vain?"'*

ACTS 4:24-25

This is a singular comfort, in that we hear that God is on our
side, so long as we go to war under the kingdom of Christ. Here
we may persuade ourselves, that however many opponents
(whether high or low) wickedly conspire together against this
kingdom, yet they shall not prevail, for what is the whole
world compared to God? But we must first of all know and
assure ourselves of this, that God will continually maintain the
kingdom of His Son, of which He Himself is the author, so that
we may establish His decree (which cannot be broken) against
the rashness of men and women. And, trusting in the Lord's
help, let us not hesitate to despise all human plots and schemes,
though they are terrible. ... Furthermore, when the Psalmist
teaches [in 2:1-2] that the kingdom of Christ shall endure, in
spite of the strength of the adversaries, he also shows that there
shall be many adversaries, which shall attempt to overthrow
the same. On one side, the Psalmist describes the kings
raging, and on the other, the people in an uproar – whereby
he signifies that all human estates shall be hostile to [Christ's
kingdom]. ... Therefore, we must know this for certain, that
the kingdom of Christ shall never be quiet in the world; hence,
when we are called on to fight, we should not be afraid as if it
were a strange thing. [Commentary on Acts]

JUNE 17

Grace and Perseverance

Summon your power, O God, the power, O God, by which you have worked for us.
                                                            PSALM 68:28

Men and women are always inclined to arrogate to themselves the glory of their achievements instead of tracing their successes to God, and David here reminds the people once more that they had not triumphed by their own strength, but by the power given to them from above. If they had performed with vigor on the field of battle, he would have them remember that it was God who inspired them with this valor, and would guard them against the pride which ignores and disparages the divine goodness. As a consideration that might serve to promote further humility in their minds, he reminds them of their continued dependence on God's favor and protection into the future. For, it is a great source of presumptuous confidence that we do not feel our own helplessness, and do not allow such helplessness to engender humility toward God for the supply of our needs.

Another lesson which the passage teaches us is that we need more than that God should visit us at first with His initial grace; for, we stand constantly in need of His assistance throughout our entire lives. If this is true in literal warfare, where our conflict is with flesh and blood, how much more is it true in matters of the soul? It is impossible that we could stand one moment in the context with such enemies as Satan, sin, and the world, if we did not receive from God the grace which secures our perseverance. [Commentary on Psalms]

JUNE 18

Christ Our King

Jesus answered: 'My kingdom is not of this world.'

JOHN 18:36

The happiness promised us in Christ does not consist in outward advantages – such as leading a joyous and peaceful life having rich possessions, being safe from all harm, and abounding with delights such as the flesh commonly longs after. No, our happiness belongs to the heavenly life! In the world the prosperity and well-being of a people depend partly on an abundance of all good things and domestic peace, partly on strong defenses that protect them from outside attacks. In like manner, Christ enriches His people with all things necessary for the eternal salvation of souls and fortifies them with courage to stand unconquerable against all the assaults of spiritual enemies. ... Thus, it is that we may patiently pass through this life with its misery, hunger, cold, contempt, reproaches, and other troubles – content with this one thing: that our King will never leave us destitute, but will provide for our needs until, our warfare ended, we are called to triumph. Such is the nature of His rule, that He shares with us all that He has received from the Father. Now He arms and equips us with His power, adorns us with His beauty and magnificence, enriches us with His wealth. These benefits then give us the most fruitful occasion to glory, and also provide us with confidence to struggle fearlessly against the devil, sin, and death. Finally, clothed with His righteousness, we can valiantly rise above all the world's reproaches; and just as He Himself freely lavishes His gifts upon us, so may we, in return, bring forth fruit to His glory. [Institutes (1559), II.xv.4]

JUNE 19

God's Many Blessings

Yes, the LORD will give what is good, and our land will yield its increase.
PSALM 85:12

If it is objected that these two subjects – the spiritual kingdom of Christ, and the fruitfulness of the earth – are improperly intermingled, it may be easily observed in reply that there is nothing at all incongruous in this, when we consider that God, while He bestows upon His people spiritual blessings, gives them, in addition to these, some taste of His fatherly love in the outward benefits which relate to the life of the body. This is evident from the testimony of Paul, who states 'godliness is of value in every way, as it holds promise for the present life and also for the life to come' (1 Tim. 4:8). But let it be noted that the faithful are generally only granted a limited portion of the comforts of this transitory life, that they may not be lulled to sleep by the allurements of the earth. I have therefore said that, while on earth, they only taste of God's fatherly love, and are not filled with an overflowing abundance of the good things of this world. Moreover, we are taught from this verse that the power and capacity of the earth to produce fruit for the sustenance of our bodies was not given to it all at once – as the heathen imagine God at the first creation to have adapted each element to its proper office, while He now sits in heaven in a state of laziness and repose – but that the earth is from year to year rendered fruitful by the secret influence of God, who intends thereby to give us a demonstration of His goodness. [Commentary on Psalms]

JUNE 20

Fear and Anguish

And taking with him Peter and the two sons of Zebedee, he began to be sorrowful and troubled. Then he said to them, 'My soul is very sorrowful, even to death; remain here, and watch with me.'

MATTHEW 26:37-38

The weakness which Christ took upon Himself must be distinguished from ours, for there is a great difference. In us there is no affection unaccompanied by sin, because they all exceed due bounds and proper restraint; but when Christ was distressed by grief and fear, He did not rise against God, but continued to be regulated by the true rule of moderation. We need not be surprised that, since He was innocent, and pure from every stain, the affections which flowed from Him were pure and stainless. …

The kinds of feelings by which Christ was tempted is also worthy of notice. Matthew says that He was affected by grief and anxiety; Luke says that He was seized with anguish; and Mark adds that He trembled. And from where did this sorrow, anguish, and fear come, but because He felt that death had something in it more sad and dreadful than the separation of the soul and body? And, certainly, He underwent death, not merely that He might depart from earth to heaven, but rather that, by taking upon Himself the curse to which we were liable, He might deliver us from it. He had no horror of death, therefore, simply as a passage out of the world, but because he had before His eyes the dreadful tribunal of God, and the Judge Himself armed with inconceivable vengeance; and because our sins, the load of which was laid upon Him, pressed Him down with their enormous weight. [Commentary on the Harmony of the Gospels]

JUNE 21

Quietness and Salvation

This is what the Sovereign LORD, the Holy One of Israel says: 'In repentance and rest you shall be saved; in quietness and trust shall be your strength.'

ISAIAH 30:15

This verse consists of two clauses, a command and a promise. He enjoins the people to be of a quiet disposition, and next promises that their salvation will be certain. The people do not believe this promise, and consequently they do not obey the command; for how would they render obedience to God, in whom they do not believe, and on whose promises they do not rely? We need not wonder, therefore, that they do not enjoy peace and repose; for these cannot exist without the promises, and as soon as the promises have been embraced, souls that were restless and uneasy are made calm. Thus, unbelief alone produces that anxiety; and therefore, the prophet justly reproves it, and shows that it is the source of the whole evil. Though our condition is not entirely the same as that of the Jews, yet God commands us to wait for His assistance with quiet dispositions, not to murmur, or be troubled or perplexed, or to distrust His promises. This doctrine must belong equally to all believers; for the whole purpose of Satan's plots is to distress them, and cast them down from their condition. In a similar manner Moses long before addressed them, 'The LORD will fight for you, and you have only to be silent' (Exod. 14:14). Not that He wished them to sleep or be idle, but He commanded them to have this peace in their hearts. If we have it, we shall feel that it yields us sufficient protection; and if not, we shall be punished for our levity and rashness. [Commentary on Isaiah]

JUNE 22

The Believer's Combat

'You are of your father the devil and your will is to do your father's desires. He was a murderer from the beginning, and does not stand in the truth, because there is no truth in him.'

JOHN 8:44

The fact that Satan is a liar arises not from his nature having been always contrary to the truth, but because he fell from it by a voluntary fall. This description of Satan is highly useful to us, that every person for themselves may endeavor to beware of his snares, and, at the same time, to repel his violence and fury; for 'he prowls around like a roaring lion, seeking someone to devour' (1 Pet. 5:8) and has a thousand stratagems at his command for deceiving. So much the more ought believers to be supplied with spiritual arms for fighting, and so much the more earnestly ought they to keep watch with vigilance and sobriety. Now, if Satan cannot lay aside this disposition, we ought not to be alarmed at it, as if it were a new and uncommon occurrence, when many and various errors spring up; for Satan stirs up his followers like bellows, to trick the world by their deceptions. And we should not be surprised that Satan puts forth such strenuous efforts to extinguish the light of the truth; for it is the only life of the soul. So, then, the most important and most deadly wound for killing the soul is falsehood. ...

[Thus, Christians should] first consider with what enemy they carry on war, and, next, to take upon themselves the protection of Christ their Captain, under whose banner they fight. [Commentary on John]

JUNE 23

Our Heavenly Citizenship

But our citizenship is in heaven, and from it we await a Savior, the Lord Jesus Christ.

PHILIPPIANS 3:20

Paul teaches here that nothing is to be considered of any value except God's spiritual kingdom, because believers ought to lead a heavenly life in this world. ... We are, it is true, intermingled here on earth with unbelievers and hypocrites; indeed, there appears to be more chaff in the granary of the Lord than wheat. Furthermore, we are exposed to the common inconveniences of earthly life. We also require food and drink and other necessities. But, nevertheless, we must be conversant with heaven in our minds and affections. For, on the one hand, we must pass quietly through this life and, on the other hand, we must be dead to the world that Christ may live in us, and that we, in our turn, may live to Him. ... From the connection that we have with Christ, He proves that our citizenship is in heaven, for it is not proper that the members should be separate from their Head. Accordingly, as Christ is in heaven, in order that we may be united with Him, it is necessary that we should in spirit dwell apart from this world. Besides, 'where your treasure is, there your heart will be also' (Matt. 6:21). Christ, who is our blessedness and glory, is in heaven; let our souls, therefore, dwell with Him on high. On this account Paul expressly calls Him 'Savior.' How does salvation come to us? Christ will come to us from heaven as a Savior. Hence it would be unbefitting that we should be consumed with the things of this earth. [Commentary on Philippians]

JUNE 24

God Protects His Church

For they conspire with one accord; against you they make a covenant – the tents of Edom and the Ishmaelites, Moab and the Hagrites, Gebal and Ammon and Amalek, Philistia with the inhabitants of Tyre.

PSALM 83:5-7

The same Spirit who inspired that pious king [David] with such invincible strength dictated this psalm for the benefit of the whole Church, to encourage her with unhesitating confidence to look to God for aid. And in our own day He sets before us these words, in order that no danger or difficulty may prevent us from calling upon God. When the whole world conspires together against us, we have as it were a wall of brass for the defense of Christ's kingdom in these words, 'Why do the kings of the earth rage?', etc. (Ps. 2:1). It will be in no small degree profitable for us to contemplate this as an example [of] … what has been the lot of the Church of God from the beginning. … [T]he condition of the Church in old times will strengthen us to continue to exercise patience until God suddenly displays His power, which, He is perfectly able to do … to frustrate all the attempts of the world. To remove from the minds of the godly all misgivings as to whether help will be imparted to them from heaven, the prophet clearly affirms that those who abuse the Church are guilty of making war against God, who has taken her under His protection. The principle upon which God declares that He will be our helper is contained in these words, 'He who touches you, touches the apple of His eye' (Zech. 2:8). [Commentary on Psalms]

JUNE 25

Joy of Providence

The righteous see [God's deliverance] and are glad, and all wickedness shuts its mouth. Whoever is wise, let him attend to these things; let them consider the steadfast love of the LORD.

PSALM 107:42-43

The joy mentioned here arises from this, that there is nothing more calculated to increase our faith than the knowledge of the providence of God; because without it, we would be harassed with doubts and fears, being uncertain whether or not the world was governed by chance. For this reason, it follows that those who aim at the subversion of this doctrine, by depriving God's children of true comfort and vexing their minds by unsettling their faith, forge for themselves a hell on earth. For what can be more awful and tormenting than to be constantly racked with doubt and anxiety? ...

[The Psalmist] indirectly warns of that false persuasion which prevails in the world whereby the most daring heaven-despisers esteem themselves to be the wisest of people. ... [S]ome of the greatest of philosophers were so mischievous as to devote their talents to obscure matters and conceal the providence of God and, entirely overlooking His agency, ascribed everything to secondary causes. Chief among these was Aristotle, a man of genius and learning; but being a pagan whose heart was perverse and depraved, it was His constant aim to entangle and perplex God's overruling providence by a variety of wild speculations; so much so, that it may with too much truth be said that He employed His naturally acute mental powers to extinguish all light. ... And, therefore, so that it may be inscribed on our hearts we must make God's works the theme of our attentive and constant meditation. [Commentary on Psalms]

JUNE 26

Love One Another

And let us consider how to stir up one another to love and good works, not neglecting to meet together, as is the habit of some, but encouraging one another, and all the more as you see the Day drawing near.
HEBREWS 10:24-25

There is an evil that prevails everywhere among human beings whereby every one sets themselves above others – this is especially manifested when people, who seem to excel in some matter, refuse to allow their inferiors to be on an equal footing with themselves. And then, there is so much contempt in almost everyone that people would gladly make churches for themselves if they could; for they find it so difficult to accommodate themselves to the ways and habits of other people. The rich enjoy one another; and hardly one rich person in a hundred can be found who grants to the poor the name and rank of a 'brother.' Unless we share similar habits, or some enticements or advantages draw us together, it is very difficult to maintain sustained harmony among ourselves. It is extremely important, therefore, for all of us to heed this admonition to be stimulated to love and not to envy, and not to separate from people whom God has joined to us, but to embrace with brotherly kindness all those who are united to us in faith. ... A most happy outcome would result if everyone of us were to pursue this one goal, to provoke each one to love one another and to allow no mutual emulation except for doing good works. For undoubtedly, contempt for one another, bitterness, envy, an inflated view of ourselves, and other sinful impulses, clearly show that our love is either very cold, or that it does not exist at all. [Commentary on Hebrews]

JUNE 27

In Christ's Family

While [Jesus] was still speaking to the people, behold, his mother and his brothers stood outside, asking to speak to him. But he replied to the man who told him, 'Who is my mother, and who are my brothers?' And stretching out his hand toward his disciples, he said, 'Here are my mother and my brothers!'

MATTHEW 12:46-49

These words were unquestionably intended to reprove Mary's eagerness, and she certainly acted improperly in attempting to interrupt the progress of Jesus' discourse. At the same time, by disparaging the relationship of flesh and blood, our Lord teaches a very useful doctrine; for He admits all His disciples and believers to the same honorable rank, as if they were His nearest relatives, or rather He places them in the place of His mother and brothers. ... He tells us also that there is no tie of relationship more sacred than spiritual relationship, because we ought not to think of Him according to the flesh, but according to the power of His Spirit which He has received from the Father to renew men and women, so that those who are by nature the polluted and accursed seed of Abraham begin to be by grace the holy and heavenly children of God. ... To sum up the whole, this passage first teaches us to behold Christ with the eyes of faith; and, secondly, it informs us that everyone who is regenerated by the Spirit, and gives Himself up entirely to God for true justification, is thus admitted to the closest union with Christ, and becomes one with Him. [Commentary on the Harmony of the Gospels]

JUNE 28

Days Determined by God

So they were seeking to arrest [Jesus], but no one laid a hand on him, because his hour had not yet come. JOHN 7:30

[The chief priests and the Pharisees] did not lack the will to do Christ mischief; they even made the attempt, and they had strength to do it. Why, then, amidst such strong desire are they rendered impotent, as if they had their hands and feet bound? The Evangelist replies, 'because His hour had not yet come,' by which he means that, against all their violence and furious attacks, Christ was guarded by the protection of God. And, at the same time He meets the offense of the cross; for we have no reason to be alarmed when we learn that Christ was dragged to death, not through the caprice of human beings, but because He was destined for such a sacrifice by the decree of the Father. And hence we ought to infer a general doctrine; for though we live from day to day, still the time of everyone's death has been fixed by God. It is difficult to believe that, while we are subject to so many accidents, exposed to so many open and concealed attacks both from people and beasts, and liable to so many diseases, we are safe from all risk until God is pleased to call us away. ... Hence, each of us, casting all our cares on God, should follow our own calling, and not be led away from the performance of our duties by any fears. Yet let no one go beyond their own bounds; for confidence in the providence of God must not go farther than God Himself commands. [Commentary on John]

JUNE 29

Highway of the Lord

And a highway shall be there, and it shall be called the Way of Holiness ... And the ransomed of the Lord shall return and come to Zion with singing ...
ISAIAH 35:8, 10

The Prophet therefore extols this inestimable kindness, when he represents God as journeying along with His people; for if He does not point out the road, our feet will always lead us astray, for we are altogether inclined to vanity. Besides, though the road is before us, and though it is plainly before our eyes, yet we shall not be able to distinguish it from the wrong road. ... But the Prophet shows that we shall be in no danger of going astray, when we follow God as the leader of the way. ... We may draw from this a profitable doctrine, namely that God not only begins, but conducts to the end, the work of our salvation, that His grace in us may not be useless and unprofitable. As He opens up the way, so He paves it, and removes obstacles of every description, and is Himself the leader during the whole journey. In short, He continues His grace toward us in such a manner that He at length brings it to perfection. And this ought to be applied to the whole course of our lives. Here we walk as on a road, moving forward to that blessed inheritance. Satan presents numerous obstructions, and dangers surround us on every side; but the Lord, who goes before and leads us by the hand will not leave us in the midst of the journey, but at length will perfectly finish what He has begun in us by His Spirit (Phil. 1:6). [Commentary on Isaiah]

JUNE 30

Teaching and Praying

'Therefore, brothers, pick out from among you seven men of good repute, full of the Spirit and of wisdom, whom we will appoint to this duty. But we will devote ourselves to prayer and to the ministry of the word.'

ACTS 6:3-4

Pastors must not think that they have accomplished their duty and need do no more when they have daily spent some time in teaching. There is another manner of study, another manner of zeal, another manner of hard work required, to which they should indeed boast to be entirely devoted. The apostles add [to their duties] praying, not because they alone should pray (for this is a common exercise of all godly persons), but because they have particular reasons to pray above all others. There is no man or woman who ought not to be concerned for the common salvation of the Church. How much more, then, should the pastor labor energetically in this regard, who has been explicitly enjoined to carefully carry out this duty? Moses certainly exhorted other people to pray, but he went before them as a kind of standard-bearer (Exod. 17:11). And it is not without reason that Paul often makes mention of his prayers (Rom. 1:10). Again, we must always remember that we shall waste all our efforts in plowing, sowing, and watering, unless the increase come from heaven (1 Cor. 3:7). Therefore, it is not enough to take great pains in teaching, unless we request blessings from the hands of the Lord, that our labor not be in vain and unfruitful. Hence, it appears for good reasons that the exercise of prayer is commended to ministers of the word. [Commentary on Acts]

JULY 1

Christ in All the Creed

And there is salvation in no one else, for there is no other name under heaven given among men by which we must be saved.

ACTS 4:12

We see that our whole salvation and all its parts are comprehended in Christ. We should therefore take care not to derive the least portion of it from anywhere else. If we seek salvation, we are taught by the very name of Jesus that it is of Him (1 Cor. 1:30). If we seek any other gifts of the Spirit, they will be found in His anointing. If we seek strength, it lies in His dominion; if purity, in His conception; if gentleness, it appears in His birth. For by His birth He was made like us in all respects that He might learn to feel our pain (Heb. 2:17; 5:2). If we seek redemption, it lies in His passion; if acquittal, in His condemnation; if remission of the curse, in His cross (Gal. 3:13); if satisfaction, in His sacrifice; if purification, in His blood; if reconciliation, in His descent into hell; if mortification of the flesh, in His tomb; if newness of life, in His resurrection; if immortality, in the same; if inheritance of the heavenly Kingdom, in His entrance into heaven; if protection, if security, if abundant supply of all blessings, in His Kingdom; if untroubled expectation of judgment, in the power given to Him to judge. In short, since rich store of every kind of good abounds in Him, let us drink our fill from this fountain, and from no other. [Institutes (1559), II.xvi.19]

JULY

JULY 2

God the Father

I believe in God the Father Almighty, Creator of heaven and earth.

APOSTLES' CREED

By this we confess that we have all our trust fixed in God the Father, whom we acknowledge to be Creator of ourselves and of absolutely all things that have been created, which have been established by the word, His eternal Wisdom (who is the Son) and by His power (who is His Holy Spirit). And, as He once established, so now He sustains, nourishes, activates, preserves, by His goodness and power, apart from which all things would immediately collapse and fall into nothingness.

But when we call Him almighty and creator of all things, we must ponder such omnipotence of His whereby He works all things in all, and such providence whereby He regulates all things. ... By faith we are persuaded that whatever happens to us, happy or sad, prosperous or adverse, whether it pertains to the body or to the soul, comes to us from Him (sin only excepted, which is to be imputed to our own wickedness); also, by His protection we are kept safe, defended, and preserved from any unfriendly force causing us harm. In short, nothing comes forth from Him to us ... which is not conducive to our welfare, howsoever things may commonly seem at one time prosperous, at another adverse. ...

For this reason, we must take care to give thanks for this very great goodness of His, to ponder it with our hearts, proclaim it with our tongue, and to render such praises as we are able. We should so reverence such a Father with grateful piety and burning love, as to devote ourselves wholly to His service and honor Him in all things. [Institutes (1536), 49]

JULY 3

Jesus, God's Son

And I believe in Jesus Christ, his only Son, our Lord.

APOSTLES' CREED

By this we confess that we believe in Jesus Christ who we are convinced is the only Son of God the Father. He is the Son, not as believers are – by adoption and grace only – but by nature, begotten of the Father from eternity. ... [M]oreover we believe that Christ, sent by the Father out of divine kindness and mercy, descended to us for our sake to release us from the devil's tyranny, to which we had been bound; from the bonds of sin, by which we were held tied; from the bondage of death, both of body and of soul, into which we had been thrust; from eternal punishment, to which we had been given over (since we did not have the ability to release and extricate ourselves from it). We confess that He, sent by the Father out of divine kindness and mercy, descended to us to take on our flesh, which He joined to His divinity. Thus, it was for our benefit that He who was to become our Mediator was true God and man. For since ... our sin interposed a cloud between us and our God, who could reach Him? Human beings? And yet all men and women together with their parent Adam bristled with dread at the Lord's sight. An angel? And yet even the angels had need of a Head, in whom they might cleave to their God. What then? The matter was hopeless if the very majesty of God would not descend to us, since it was not in us to ascend to Him. And so, God's Son became for us Immanuel, that is, God with us (Isa. 7:14). [Institutes (1536), 50-51]

JULY 4

Jesus' Life and Death

He was conceived of the Holy Spirit, born of the Virgin Mary, suffered under Pontius Pilate, was crucified, dead and buried.
APOSTLES' CREED

We believe Him to have been conceived a man for us by the wonderful and unspeakable power of the Holy Spirit, in the womb of the sacred virgin. Born a mortal man from her, in order to accomplish our salvation (for whose sake he had come), he delivered up His body to a most miserable death, and poured out His blood as the price of redemption.

He suffered, moreover, under Pontius Pilate, condemned indeed by the judge's sentence, as a criminal and wrongdoer, in order that we might, by His condemnation, be absolved before the judgment seat of the highest Judge. He was crucified upon a cross, which had been cursed by God's law, that He might bear our curse which our sins deserved (Gal. 3:10). He died, that by His death He might conquer death which was threatening us, and might swallow it which was to have swallowed us. He was buried, that through His grace we might be buried to sin, freed from the sway of the devil and of death. [Institutes (1536), 54-55]

JULY 5

Heeding Christ's Voice

*So, Jesus again said to them, 'Truly, truly, I say to you, I am
the door of the sheep. All who came before me are thieves
and robbers, but the sheep did not listen to them.'*

JOHN 10:7-8

What Christ means is simply this, that all the elect of God,
though they were tempted to go astray in innumerable ways,
were kept in obedience to the pure faith, so that they were not
exposed as a prey to Satan, or to his ministers. ...

This passage ought to strike us with the deepest shame;
first, because we are so ill-accustomed to the voice of our
Shepherd, that there are hardly any who do not listen to it
with indifference; and next, because we are so slow and lazy
to follow Him. ... [T]he greater part of those who boast that
they are Christ's disciples kick fiercely against Him. Lastly, as
soon as the voice of any stranger has sounded in our ears, we
hurry about to and fro; and this lightness and unsteadiness
sufficiently shows how little progress we have hitherto made
in the faith. But if the number of believers is smaller than
might be desired, and if out of this small number a large
proportion is continually dropping away, faithful teachers
have this consolation to support them, that the elect of God,
who are Christ's sheep, listen to them. It is our duty, indeed,
to labor diligently, and to strive by every possible method, that
the whole world may be brought, if possible, into the unity of
the faith; but let us, in the meantime, be well satisfied with
belonging to the number. [Commentary on John]

JULY 6

Aroma of Holiness

[B]ut as he who called you is holy, you also be holy in all your conduct, since it is written, 'You shall be holy, for I am holy.'

1 PETER 1:15-16

Peter reasons from the end for which we are called. God sets us apart as a peculiar people for Himself; then we ought to be free from all pollutions. And he quotes a sentence which had been often repeated by Moses. For as the people of Israel were on every side surrounded by pagans, from whom they might have easily adopted the worst examples and innumerable corruptions, the Lord frequently recalled them to Himself as though He had said, 'You have to do with me, you are mine; then abstain from the pollutions of the Gentiles.' We are too ready to look to other people, so as to follow their common way of living. Thus it happens, that some lead others in crowds to all kinds of evil, until the Lord by His calling separates them.

In bidding us to be holy like Himself, the proportion is not that of equals; but we ought to advance in this direction as far as our condition will bear. And as even the most perfect are always very far from coming up to the mark, we ought daily to strive more and more. And we ought to remember that we are not only told what our duty is, but that God also adds, 'I am He who sanctifies you.'

It is added, 'In all manner of conversation,' or 'in your whole conduct.' There is then no part of our life which is not to be redolent with this good odor of holiness. [Commentary on 1 Peter]

JULY 7

Love, Grace, Peace

To all those in Rome who are loved by God and called to be saints: Grace to you and peace from God our Father and the Lord Jesus Christ.

ROMANS 1:7

Paul in no way ascribes the praise of our salvation to ourselves, but derives it altogether from the fountain of God's free and paternal love toward us; for He makes this the first thing – God loves us. And, what is the cause of His love, except His goodness alone? On this depends our calling, by which in His own time He seals His adoption to those whom He had before freely chosen. ...

Nothing is more desirable than to have God propitious to us, and this is signified by the word 'grace'; and then to have prosperity and success in all things flowing from Him, and this is intimated by the word 'peace.' For however much life seems to smile on us, if God is angry with us, then even blessing itself is turned into a curse. Hence, the very foundation of our happiness is the favor of God, by which we enjoy true and solid prosperity, and by which also our salvation is promoted even when we face adversity. And then as Paul prays to God for peace, we must understand that whatever good comes to us, it is the fruit of divine kindness. Nor should we ignore the fact that he prays at the same time to the Lord Jesus Christ for these blessings. Worthily indeed is this honor rendered to Him, who is not only the administrator and dispenser of His Father's bounty to us, but also who works all things in connection with Him. [Commentary on Romans]

JULY 8

Descent into Hell

He descended into Hell.

APOSTLES' CREED

But we must seek a surer explanation, apart from the Creed, of Christ's descent into hell. The explanation given to us in God's word is not only holy and pious, but also full of wonderful consolation. If Christ had died only a bodily death, it would have been ineffectual. No – it was expedient at the same time for him to undergo the severity of God's vengeance, to appease His wrath and satisfy His just judgment. For this reason, He must also grapple hand to hand with the armies of hell and the dread of everlasting death. A little while ago we referred to the prophet's statement that 'the chastisement of our peace was laid upon Him,' 'He was wounded for our transgressions' by the Father, 'He was bruised for our infirmities' (Isa. 53:5). By these words he means that Christ was put in place of evildoers as surety and pledge – submitting Himself even as the accursed – to bear and assume all the punishments that they ought to have sustained. All – with this one exception: 'He could not be held by the pangs of death' (Acts 2:24). No wonder, then, if He is said to have descended into hell, for He suffered the death that God in His wrath had inflicted upon the wicked. [Institutes (1559), II.xvi.10]

JULY 9

Christ's Resurrection and Return

On the third day he rose again from the dead; he ascended into heaven, and sits at the right hand of the Father; thence he shall come to judge the living and the dead.

APOSTLES' CREED

We believe that 'He ascended into heaven.' By this ascent the entrance to the Kingdom of Heaven, which had been closed to all in Adam, He opened to us. Indeed, He entered in our flesh, as if in our name, that already in Him we may possess heaven through hope, and thereafter may sit, so to speak, among the heavenly ones.

We believe likewise that just as He was manifested in the flesh 'He sits there at the Father's right hand.' By this is meant that He has been appointed and declared King, Judge, and Lord over all. All creation, without exception, has been subjected to His lordship, in order that, by His power, He may lavish spirituals gifts upon us. Therefore, He sanctifies us, cleanses the filth of our sins, governs and leads us, until we reach to Himself, through death, which will bring an end indeed to our imperfection, but a beginning to our blessedness. ...

Finally, we believe that 'He will descend' in the same visible form from heaven, as He was seen to ascend, namely on the last day, when He will appear at once to all, with the ineffable majesty of His reign to judge the living and the dead. ...

Since therefore we see the whole sum of our salvation and also all its parts comprehended in Christ, we must take care not to think that the least particle of our salvation is lodged elsewhere. For in Him alone have all the heavenly treasures been hid. [Institutes (1536), 56-57]

JULY 10

Death and Resurrection

'For this reason the Father loves me, because I lay down my life that I may take it up again.'
JOHN 10:17

There is indeed another and higher reason why the Father loves the Son, for it was not in vain that a voice was heard from heaven [saying] 'This is my beloved Son, with whom I am well pleased' (Matt. 3:17). But as He was made man on our account, and as the Father delighted in Him, in order that He might reconcile us to Himself, we need not wonder … that our salvation is dearer to Himself than His own life. This is a wonderful commendation of the goodness of God to us, and ought rightly to arouse our whole souls into rapturous wonder, that not only does God extend to us the love that is due to the only-begotten Son, but He refers it to us as God's highest cause. …

'That I may take it up again.' As the disciples might be deeply grieved on account of what they had heard about the death of Christ, and as their faith might even be greatly shaken, He comforts them by the hope of His resurrection, which would speedily take place; as if He said, that He would not die on the condition of being swallowed up by death, but in order that He might soon rise again as conqueror. And even in the present day, we ought to contemplate the death of Christ, so as to remember, at the same time, the glory of His resurrection. Thus, we know that He is life, because, in His contest with death, He obtained a splendid victory, and achieved a noble triumph. [Commentary on John]

JULY 11

The Holy Spirit

I believe in the Holy Spirit.

APOSTLES' CREED

Here we confess that we believe in the Holy Spirit, but that He is with the Father and the Son, the third person of the most holy Trinity, consubstantial and co-eternal with the Father and the Son, almighty, and Creator of all things. For these are three distinct persons, but one essence, as has been said. As these are deep and hidden mysteries, they ought rather to be adored than investigated. ...

We are persuaded that there is for us no other guide and leader to the Father than the Holy Spirit, just as there is no other way than Christ; and that there is no grace from God, save through the Holy Spirit. Grace is itself the power and action of the Spirit: through grace God the Father, in the Son, accomplishes whatever good there is; through grace He justifies, sanctifies, and cleanses us, calls and draws us to Himself, that we may attain salvation.

Therefore, the Holy Spirit, while dwelling in us in this manner, illumines us with His light, in order that we may learn and plainly recognize what an enormous wealth of divine goodness we possess in Christ. He kindles our hearts with the fire of love, both toward God and toward neighbor, and day by day He boils away and burns up the vices of our inordinate desire, so that if there are in us any good works they are the fruits and powers of His grace. But our gifts, apart from Him, are darkness of mind and perversity of heart. And all these gifts depend not upon any duties or merits of ours, but are given freely to us from the divine bounty, and gratuitously. [Institutes (1536), 57-58]

JULY 12

Faith as Spiritual Resurrection

Jesus said to her, 'I am the resurrection and the life. Whoever believes in me, though he die, yet shall he live, and everyone who lives and believes in me shall never die.'

JOHN 11:25-26

Why then is Christ the resurrection? Because by His Spirit He regenerates the children of Adam, who had been alienated from God by sin, so that they begin to live a new life. ... Away now with those who idly say that men and women are prepared for receiving the grace of God by the movement of nature. For the fact that human beings live and breathe, and are endued with sense, understanding and will – all this tends to their destruction, because there is no party or faculty of the soul that is not corrupted and turned aside from what is right. Thus, death everywhere holds dominion, for the death of the soul is nothing else than its being estranged and turned aside from God. Accordingly, those who believe in Christ, though they were formerly dead, begin to live, because faith is a spiritual resurrection of the soul, and – so to speak – animates the soul itself that it may live to God; according to that passage, 'the dead will hear the voice of the Son of God, and those who hear will live' (John 5:25). This is truly a remarkable commendation of faith, that it conveys to us the life of Christ, and thus frees us from death. ... What is still more, [physical] death itself is a sort of emancipation from the bondage of death. [Commentary on John]

JULY 13

Marvelous Redemption

Oh sing to the LORD a new song; sing to the LORD, all the earth! Sing to the LORD, bless his name; tell of his salvation from day to day.
PSALM 96:1-2

[T]he Psalmist is exhorting the whole world, and not merely the Israelites, to the exercise of devotion. Nor could this be done, unless the gospel were universally spread about as the means of conveying the knowledge of God. The saying of Paul must necessarily hold true, 'How then will they call on him in whom they have not believed?' (Rom. 10:14) The same Apostle proves the calling of the Gentiles by making testimony of it, 'Praise the Lord, all you Gentiles, and let all the people extol him' (Rom. 15:11). Besides, the Psalmist requires a 'new song,' not one which was common and had formerly been raised. He must therefore refer to some unusual and extraordinary display of the divine goodness. Thus, when Isaiah speaks of the restoration of the Church, which was wonderful and incredible, he says 'Sing unto the Lord a new song' (Isa. 42:10). The Psalmist intimates, therefore, that the time would come when God would erect His kingdom in the world in a manner altogether unanticipated. ... Additional terms are used to commend the salvation here described. It is called His 'glory' and His 'marvelous works'; which is equivalent to saying that it was glorious and admirable. ... [W]hen God appeared as Redeemer of the whole world, He displayed a kind of mercy and favor which He had never before bestowed. ... [W]e can never be said to have rightly apprehended the redemption achieved by Christ, unless our minds have been raised to the discovery of something incomparably wonderful. [Commentary on Psalms]

JULY 14

Anxiety and Cares

'Therefore, I tell you, do not be anxious about your life, what you will eat, or what you will drink, nor about your body, what you will put on. Is not life more than food and the body more than clothing?'

MATTHEW 6:25

When Christ forbids them to be anxious, this is not to be taken literally, as if He intended to take away all cares from His people. We know that men and women are born in a condition where they have some cares; and, indeed, this is not the least part of the miseries that the Lord has laid upon us as a punishment, in order to humble us. ... We ought to remember this promise: though unbelievers 'rise up early and go late to rest, eating the bread of anxious toil,' yet believers will obtain rest and sleep through the kindness of God (Ps. 127:2). Though the children of God are not free from toil and anxiety, yet, properly speaking, we do not say that they are anxious about life, because, through their reliance on the providence of God, they enjoy calm repose. Hence, it is easy to learn how far we ought to be anxious about food. Each of us ought to labor, as far as our calling requires and the Lord commands. And, each of us ought to be motivated by our own needs to call upon God. This kind of anxiety holds an intermediate place between lazy carelessness and the unnecessary torments by which unbelievers kill themselves. But if we give proper attention to the words of Christ, we shall find that He does not forbid every kind of care, but only what arises from distrust. [Commentary on the Harmony of the Gospels]

JULY 15

Natural Knowledge of God

For although they knew God, they did not honor him as God or give thanks to him, but they became futile in their thinking, and their foolish hearts were darkened.

ROMANS 1:21

No idea of God can be formed without including His eternity, power, wisdom, goodness, truth, justice, and mercy. His eternity appears evident, because He is the maker of all things – His power because He holds all things in His hand and continues their existence – His wisdom, because He has arranged things in such an exquisite order – His goodness, for there is no other cause than Himself, why He created all things, and no other reason, why He should be induced to preserve them – His justice, because in His government He punishes the guilty and defends the innocent – His mercy, because He bears with so much forbearance the perversity of men and women; and His truth, because He is unchangeable. The person then who has a right notion of God ought to give Him the praise due to His eternity, wisdom, goodness, and justice. Since men and women have not recognized these attributes of God, but have dreamed of Him as though He were an empty phantom, they are rightly said to have wickedly robbed Him of His own glory. Nor is it without reason that Paul adds, 'that they were not thankful,' for there is no one who is not indebted to God for numberless benefits. ... And thus, their foolish mind, being involved in darkness, could understand nothing aright, but was carried away headlong, in various ways, into errors and delusions. Their unrighteousness was this – they quickly choked by their own depravity the seed of right knowledge, before it grew up to ripeness. [Commentary on Romans]

JULY 16

God's Universal Church

I believe in the holy catholic church.

APOSTLES' CREED

First, we believe in the holy catholic church, that is the whole number of the elect, whether angels or human beings. Among humans, both those dead and still living. Among the living, in whatever lands they live, or to wherever nation they have been scattered – to be one church and society, and one people of God. Christ our Lord, is Leader and Ruler of it; He is the Head of the one body, inasmuch as (through divine goodness) they have been chosen in Him before the foundation of the world, in order that all might be gathered into God's Kingdom.

Now this society is catholic, that is, universal, because there could not be two or three churches. But all God's elect are so united and conjoined in Christ that, as they are dependent on one Head, they also grow together into one body, being joined and knit together as are the limbs of one body. These are made truly one, who live together in one faith, hope, and love, and in the same Spirit of God, called to the inheritance of eternal life.

It is also holy, because as many as have been chosen by God's eternal providence to be adopted as members of the church – all these are made holy by the Lord. ...

Moreover, since the church is the people of God's elect, it cannot happen that those who are truly its members will ultimately perish, or come to a bad end. For their salvation rests on such a sure and solid foundation, that, even if the whole fabric of the world were to fall, it itself could not tumble and fall. [Institutes (1536), 58-59]

JULY 17

Community of Believers

I believe in the communion of saints.

APOSTLES' CREED

In the catholic church all the elect (who with true faith worship God together) have reciprocal communication and participation in all goods. By this one does not deny that individuals have various gifts – as Paul teaches that the gifts of the Spirit have been divided and variously distributed (1 Cor. 12:4-11), but not without each person occupying their unique place in the civil order. ... [T]he community of believers looks to the end that they may share among themselves, with kindness and due charity, all such goods both of the spirit and of the body insofar as is fair and according as use demands. And obviously whatever gift of God is reserved of each person, all are truly made sharers of it, even though by God's dispensation it has been especially given to one, not to others. Just as the members of one body share among themselves by some sort of community, each nonetheless has his particular gift and distinct ministry; for ... they are gathered and fastened together into one body. This is the catholic church, the mystical body of Christ. [Institutes (1536), 63]

JULY 18

Hinge of Salvation

I believe in the forgiveness of sins.

APOSTLES' CREED

Now the church itself stands and consists in this forgiveness of sins, and is supported by this as by a foundation. Since forgiveness of sins is the way that leads to God, and the means by which He is reconciled to us, for this reason forgiveness of sins alone opens for us the entrance into the church – which is the city of God; and the tabernacle which the Most High has sanctified as His dwelling place – and keeps and protects us therein. Believers receive this forgiveness, when oppressed, afflicted, and confounded by the awareness of their own sins, they are stricken by the sense of divine judgment, become displeased with themselves, and as it were groan and toil under a heavy burden. And by this hatred of sin and by their own confusion, they mortify their flesh and whatever derives from it. ...

It seemed good to the Lord, to show Himself in this order to men and women that after they have divested themselves of all arrogance through recognition of their own poverty, have wholly cast themselves down, and have plainly become worthless to themselves, then at long last they may begin to taste the sweetness of the mercy which the Lord holds out to them in Christ. ... On the other hand, those who do not strive by these steps to God will never attain this forgiveness of sins, which is the hinge of salvation. [Institutes (1536), 63-64]

JULY 19

Death Conquered

I believe in the resurrection of the body and the life everlasting.
APOSTLES' CREED

We believe in the resurrection of the flesh. That is, it will come to pass that all human bodies will at one and the same time be raised from corruption into incorruption, from mortality into immortality. And even those who previously died will receive their flesh – whether they had been eaten by worms, or decayed in the earth, or had been reduced to ashes, or scattered in some other way. But those who still survive at that time, will also put off the corruption of their flesh. All will, by a sudden change, cross over into an immortal nature: the godly indeed into glory of life, the reprobate into condemnation of death.

Lastly, we believe in eternal life. That is, it will come to pass that at that time the Lord will receive His own people, glorified in body and soul, into blessedness, a blessedness which will endlessly endure, beyond all chance of change or corruption. This will be a true and complete perfecting into life, light, righteousness, when we shall cleave inseparably to the Lord, who like an inexhaustible fountain, contains the fullness of these in Himself. That blessedness will be the Kingdom of God, crammed with all brightness, joy, power, happiness – things far removed now from human sense, and which (as Paul says) neither ear has heard, nor eye seen, nor the human mind perceived (1 Cor. 2:9). On the other hand, the ungodly and the reprobate, who have not sought and reverenced God with pure faith, inasmuch as they will have no part in God and His Kingdom, will be cast with the devils into eternal death. [Institutes (1536), 64]

JULY 20

Genuine Repentance

But they flattered [God] with their mouths; they lied to him with their tongues. Their heart was not steadfast toward him; they were not faithful to his covenant.

PSALM 78:36-37

Here the Israelites are charged with deceitfulness, because they neither confessed their guilt with sincerity of heart, nor truly ascribed to God the glory of their deliverance. We should not suppose that they make no acknowledgment [of their sin] at all; but it is intimated that the confession of their mouth, since it did not proceed from the heart, was forced and not voluntary. This is certainly worthy of being noticed; for from it we learn not only our duty to guard against that gross hypocrisy which consists in uttering one thing with the tongue before people, while we think a different thing in our hearts, but also that we ought to beware of a kind of hypocrisy which is more hidden, and which consists in this, that the sinner, being constrained by fear, flatters God in a slavish manner, while yet, if he could, he would shun the judgment of God. The greater part of men and women are mortally infected with this disease; for although the divine majesty elicits from them some kind of awe, yet they would prefer that the light of divine truth be completely extinguished. It is, therefore, not enough to give our assent to the divine word, unless that assent is accompanied with true and pure affection, so that our hearts may not be double or divided. The Psalmist points out that the cause and source of this dissimulation resides in the fact that they were not steadfast and faithful. [Commentary on Psalms]

JULY 21

Christ the Good Shepherd

'I am the good shepherd. The good shepherd lays down his life for the sheep.'
JOHN 10:11

[Christ] now assumes the character of a shepherd, and indeed affirms that He is the only shepherd. Indeed, there is no other to whom this honor and title strictly belongs; for, as to all the faithful shepherds of the Church, it is He who raises them up, endows them with the necessary qualifications, governs them by His Spirit, and works by them; and therefore, they do not prevent Him from being the only governor of His Church. ...

From the extraordinary affection which He bears toward the sheep, He shows how truly He acts toward them as a shepherd; for He is so anxious about their salvation, that He does not even spare His own life. Hence it follows, that those who reject the guardianship of so kind and amiable a shepherd are exceedingly ungrateful, and deserve a hundred deaths, and are exposed to every kind of harm. The remark of Augustine is exceedingly correct, that this passage informs us what we ought to desire, what we ought to avoid, and what we ought to endure, in the government of the Church. Nothing is more desirable than that the Church should be governed by good and diligent shepherds. Christ declares that He is 'the good shepherd' who keeps His Church safe and sound, first, by Himself, and next, by His agents. Whenever there is good order, and fit men hold the government, then Christ shows that He is actually the shepherd. But there are many wolves and thieves who, wearing the garb of shepherds, wickedly scatter the Church. [Commentary on John]

JULY 22

Rain, Lightning, Wind

He it is who makes the clouds rise at the end of the earth, who makes lightnings for the rain and brings forth the wind from his storehouses.

PSALM 135:7

The Psalmist gives several particulars to illustrate that nothing takes place of itself, but by the hand and counsel of God. Our understanding cannot comprehend a one-thousandth part of God's works, and He brings forth only a few examples to prove the doctrine of divine providence which He had just announced. He speaks of the clouds rising from the ends of the earth; for the vapors which rise out of the earth form clouds, when they accumulate more densely together. Now who would think that the vapors which we see ascending upwards would shortly darken the sky and gather ominously above our heads? ... The Psalmist mentions another circumstance that calls for our wonder, namely that lightning is mixed with rain, two things that are quite opposite in their nature from one another. If custom did not make us familiar with this spectacle, we would conclude this mixture of fire and water to be a phenomenon altogether unbelievable. The same may be said of the phenomena of the winds. ... All people readily acknowledge that God is the author of rain, thunder, and wind, in so far as He originally established this order of things in nature; but the Psalmist goes further than this, stating that when it rains, this is not effected by a blind instinct of nature, but as a consequence of the decree of God, who is pleased at one time to darken the sky with clouds, and at another time, to brighten it again with sunshine. [Commentary on Psalms]

JULY 23

Firm Assurance

'I give them eternal life, and they will never perish, and no one will snatch them out of my hand. My Father, who has given them to me, is greater than all, and no one is able to snatch them out of the Father's hand.' JOHN 10:28-29

It is an inestimable fruit of faith, that Christ bids us to be convinced of our security when we are brought by faith into His sheepfold. But we must also observe on what foundation this certainty rests. It is because He will be a faithful guardian of our salvation, for He testifies that our salvation is 'in His hand.' And if this were not enough, He says that they will be safely guarded by the power of His Father. This is a remarkable passage, by which we are taught that the salvation of all the elect is not less certain than the power of God is invincible. Besides, Christ did not intend to throw this word foolishly into the air, but to give a promise which should remain deeply fixed in their minds; and, therefore, we infer that the statement of Christ is intended to show that the elect are absolutely certain of their salvation. We are surrounded, indeed, by powerful adversaries, and so great is our weakness, that we are every moment in imminent danger of death; but as He who guards what we have entrusted to Him (2 Tim. 1:12) is greater or more powerful than all, we have no reason to tremble as if our life were in danger. ... In short, our salvation is certain, because it is in the hand of God. [Commentary on John]

JULY 24

Jesus at Prayer

And after he had dismissed the crowds, he went up on the mountain by himself to pray.
MATTHEW 14:23

[I]n discharging all the parts of His office as Mediator, [Jesus] showed Himself to be God and man, and exhibited proofs of both natures, as opportunity permitted. Though He had all things at His disposal, He showed Himself to be a human being by praying; and this He did not do hypocritically, but manifested sincere and human affections toward us. ... In going up on the mountain, [Jesus] sought to benefit from more leisure for praying, with all distractions removed. We know how easily the slightest interruptions destroy the fervor of prayer, or at least make it languish and cool. Though Christ was in no danger of this fault, yet He intended to warn us by His example that we ought to be exceedingly careful to avail ourselves of every means of assistance to set our minds free from all the snares of the world, so that we may look directly toward heaven. Now in this respect solitude has a powerful influence, by disposing those who engage in prayer, when God is their only witness, to be more on their guard, to pour their heart into His bosom, to be more diligent in self-examination; and, in a word – remembering that they have to deal with God – to rise above themselves. At the same time, it must be observed, that He did not lay down a fixed rule, as if we were never permitted to pray except in isolation; for Paul commands us to 'pray in every place, lifting holy hands' (1 Tim. 2:8) and Christ Himself sometimes prayed in the presence of others...
[Commentary on the Harmony of the Gospels]

JULY 25

God's Angels

The angel of the LORD encamps around those who fear him, and delivers them.

PSALM 34:7

David here discourses in general on God's fatherly favor toward all the godly; and as the life of men and women is exposed to innumerable dangers, he at the same time teaches us that God is able to deliver them. The faithful especially, who are as sheep in the midst of wolves, beset as it were with death in every form, are constantly harassed with the dread of some approaching danger. David therefore affirms, that the servants of God are protected and defended by angels. The purpose of the Psalmist is to show, that although the faithful are exposed to many dangers, yet they may rest assured that God will be the faithful guardian of their life. But in order to confirm them all the more in this hope, he adds that ... He defends them by the power and ministration of angels. The power of God alone would indeed be sufficient in itself to perform this; but in mercy to our infirmity, [God] bestows angels as His ministers. ... [Angels] are distinguished by the general term 'ministering spirits sent out to serve for the sake of those who are to inherit salvation' (Heb. 1:4), and the Scriptures in other places teach us that whenever it pleases God, and whenever He knows it to be for their benefit, many angels are appointed to take care of each of His people. ... [Thus], however great the number of our enemies and the dangers which surround us, yet the angels of God, armed with invincible power, constantly watch over us, and array themselves on every side to aid and deliver us from all evil. [Commentary on Psalms]

JULY 26

Awaiting Christ's Return

And let us consider how to stir up one another to love and good works, not neglecting to meet together, as is the habit of some, but encouraging one another, and all the more as you see the Day drawing near.
HEBREWS 10:24-25

Were someone to ask how the Apostle could say that those who were still far removed from the appearance of Christ could see the day near at hand, I would answer thusly: from the beginning of the kingdom of Christ, the Church was established in such a way that the faithful were taught that the Judge was coming soon. Nor, indeed, were they deceived by a false notion, when they were prepared to welcome Christ almost every moment; for such was the condition of the Church from the time the gospel was promulgated, that the entirety of the period might properly be called 'the last days.' Hence, those people who have been dead for many centuries lived in the last days no less than we. The worldly-wise and scoffers – who think it ridiculous what we believe regarding the resurrection of the flesh and the last judgment – laugh at our simplicity in this respect. But so that our faith might not fail through their mockery, the Holy Spirit reminds us that a thousand years are to God as one day (2 Pet. 3:8), so that whenever we think of the eternity of the heavenly kingdom no time period should appear long to us. And further, since Christ, after having completed all things necessary for our salvation, has ascended into heaven, it is only reasonable that we who are continually looking for His second coming should regard every day as though it were the last. [Commentary on Hebrews]

JULY 27

Standing on God's Grace

Therefore, since we have been justified by faith, we have peace with God through our Lord Jesus Christ. Through him we have also obtained access by faith into this grace in which we stand...

ROMANS 5:1-2

Our reconciliation with God depends only on Christ; for He only is the beloved Son, and we are all by nature the children of wrath. But this favor is communicated to us by the gospel; for the gospel is the ministry of reconciliation, by the means of which we are in a manner brought into the kingdom of God. Hence, Paul rightly sets before our eyes in Christ a sure pledge of God's favor, that he might more easily draw us away from every confidence in works. And as he teaches us by the word 'access,' that salvation begins with Christ, he excludes those [works of] preparation by which the foolish imagine that they can anticipate God's mercy. It's as if he said, 'Christ does not come to you, nor does He help you, on account of your merits.' He afterwards immediately adds, that it is through the continuation of the same favor that our salvation becomes certain and sure; by which he intimates that perseverance is not established on our power and diligence, but on Christ. At the same time, by saying that we 'stand,' he indicates that the gospel ought to strike deep roots into the hearts of the godly, so that being strengthened by its truth, they may stand firm against all the devices of Satan and of the flesh. And by the word 'stand' he means that faith is not a persuasion that changes from day to day; but that it is unchanging, and that it sinks deep into the heart, so that it endures through life. [Commentary on Romans]

JULY 28

Steadfastness of Faith

Therefore, as you received Christ Jesus the Lord, so walk in him, rooted and built up in him and established in the faith ...

COLOSSIANS 2:6-7

Paul intimates by three metaphors what steadfastness of faith he requires from them. The first is in the word 'walk.' For he compares the pure doctrine of the gospel, as they had learned it, to a path that is sure, so that if anyone remains on it they will be kept from all danger of mistake. He exhorts them, accordingly, if they would not go astray, not to turn aside from the path they have entered upon. The second metaphor is taken from trees. For as a tree that has sunk its roots deep has sufficient support to withstand all the assaults of winds and storms, so if anyone is deeply and thoroughly planted in Christ, as in a firm root, it will not be possible for Satan to topple them from their position by his machinations. On the other hand, those who have not fixed their roots in Christ will be 'carried about by every wind of doctrine' (Eph. 4:14), just as a tree that is not supported by any root. The third metaphor is that of a foundation, for a house that is not supported by a foundation quickly falls to ruins. The case is the same with those who lean on any foundation other than Christ, or at least are not securely founded on Him. ... These two things should be observed in the Apostle's words. First, that the stability of those who rely upon Christ is immoveable, and their path is not at all wavering, or liable to error. And second, that we must indeed make progress in Christ until we have taken deep root in Him. [Commentary on Colossians]

JULY 29

Prayers Deferred

Now Jesus loved Martha and her sister and Lazarus. So, when he heard that Lazarus was ill, he stayed two days longer in the place where he was. JOHN 11:5-6

[John] the Evangelist passes on to another narrative, which contains a miracle eminently worthy of being recorded. For not only did Christ give a remarkable proof of His divine power in raising Lazarus [from the dead], but He likewise placed before our eyes a lively image of our future resurrection. …

[But] these two things appear to be inconsistent with each other, that Christ remains two days beyond the Jordan, as if He did not care about the life of Lazarus, and yet the Evangelist says that Christ loved him and his sisters; for, since love produces anxiety, He should have hastened to them immediately. As Christ is the only mirror of the grace of God, we are taught by this delay on His part, that we ought not to judge the love of God from the condition which we see before our eyes. When we have prayed to Him, He often delays His assistance, either that He may increase still more our ardor in prayer, or that He may exercise our patience, and, at the same time, accustom us to obedience. Let believers then implore the assistance of God, but let them also learn to suspend their desires, if He does not stretch out His hand to give assistance as soon as they may think that necessity requires; for, whatever may be His delay, He never sleeps, and never forgets His people. Yet let us also be fully assured that He wishes all whom He loves to be saved. [Commentary on John]

JULY 30

Nature of Our Redemption

And you, who once were alienated and hostile in mind, doing evil deeds, he has now reconciled in his body of flesh by his death, in order to present you holy and blameless and above reproach before him.

COLOSSIANS 1:21-22

[I]t was necessary that the Son of God should become man, and be a partaker of our flesh, that He might be our brother; it was necessary that He should by dying become a sacrifice, that He might make His Father propitious to us.

'That He might present us holy.' Here we have the second and principal part of our salvation – newness of life. For the entire blessing of redemption consists mainly in these two things, remission of sins and spiritual regeneration (Jer. 31:33). What he has already spoken of was a great matter, that righteousness has been procured for us through the death of Christ, so that, our sins being remitted, we are acceptable to God. Now, however, he teaches us that there is in addition to this another benefit equally distinguished – the gift of the Holy Spirit, by which we are renewed in the image of God. This, also, is a passage worthy of observation, as showing that a gratuitous righteousness is not conferred upon us in Christ, without our being at the same time regenerated by the Spirit to the obedience of righteousness. ... The former we obtained by gratuitous acceptance; and the latter by the gift of the Holy Spirit, when we are made new creatures. There is however an inseparable connection between these two blessings of grace. Let us, however, take notice that this ... will not be perfected until Christ shall appear for the restoration of all things. [Commentary on Colossians]

JULY 31

Pride Before a Fall

On an appointed day Herod put on his royal robes, took his seat upon the throne, and delivered an oration to them. And the people were shouting, 'The voice of a god, and not of a man!' Immediately an angel of the Lord struck him down...

ACTS 12:21-23

This valuable history not only shows (as if in a magnifying glass) what end is prepared for the enemies of the Church, but also how much God hates pride. The Scripture states that 'God opposes the proud' (1 Pet. 5:5). God Himself provided a vivid picture of this in the person of Herod. Assuredly, men and women cannot extol themselves higher than is their rightful position without making war with God. ... [W]e must observe the narrative of Herod's history, for all things went well with him after he had miserably persecuted the Church; he imposed his will on the surrounding nations by taming them with hunger, so that they came crawling back to him, as if God had rewarded him well for his wicked fury. This was no small trial for the godly, who might have thought to themselves that God did not care for them and who feared that Herod's power would only increase his tyranny and cruelty. But the Lord had another purpose, for He set the oppressor of the Church on high, so that he might have the greater fall. ... In a similar way, when in our own day we see bloody enemies of the Church lifted high upon the wings of fortune into heaven, there is no reason why we should be discouraged. But let us rather call to mind that saying of Solomon, 'Pride goes before destruction, and a haughty spirit before a fall' (Prov. 16:18). [Commentary on Acts]

AUGUST 1

Held Safe by God

Nevertheless, I am continually with you; you hold my right hand.
PSALM 73:23

God is always near His chosen ones, for although they sometimes turn their backs upon Him, He nevertheless has His fatherly eye always turned toward them. When the Psalmist speaks of God 'holding him by the right hand,' he means that he was, by the wonderful power of God, drawn back from that deep gulf into which the reprobate cast themselves. He then ascribes it wholly to the grace of God that he was enabled to restrain himself from breaking forth into open blasphemies, and from hardening himself in error, and that he was also brought to condemn himself of foolishness – this he ascribes entirely to the grace of God, who stretched out His hand to hold him up, and prevent him from a fall which would have caused his destruction. From this we see how precious our salvation is in the sight of God. For, when we wander far from Him, He yet continues to look upon us with a watchful eye, and to stretch forth His hand to bring us to Himself. We must indeed beware of perverting this doctrine by making it a pretext for idleness; but experience nevertheless teaches us that when we have sunk into drowsiness and insensibility, God exercises His care for us, and that even when we are fugitives and wanderers from Him, He is still near us. ... The reason then why we do not succumb, even in the severest conflicts, is nothing else than because we receive the aid of the Holy Spirit ... [who] upholds us when we stumble, and even lifts us up when we have fallen. [Commentary on Psalms]

AUGUST 2

Faithful Endurance

But recall the former days when, after you were enlightened, you endured a hard struggle with sufferings, sometimes being publicly exposed to reproach and affliction, and sometimes being partners with those so treated.

HEBREWS 10:32-33

In order to stimulate them, and rouse their eagerness to go forward, the author reminds them of the evidences of piety which they had previously demonstrated. For it is a shameful thing to begin well and to faint in the middle of the course – and still more shameful to go backwards after having made great progress. The memory of past warfare, then, if it had been conducted faithfully and diligently under the banner of Christ, is useful to us in the long run, not as a pretext for laziness ... but to render us more active in finishing the final leg of our course. For Christ has not enlisted us with the understanding that, after a few years, we would ask for a discharge like soldiers who have served their time, but that we should pursue our warfare even to the end.

He further strengthens his exhortation by saying that they had already performed great exploits at a time when they were still new recruits. Hence, it would be all the more shameful if they now fainted after having been tested a long time. ... It is as if he had said: 'As soon as you were initiated into the faith of Christ, you underwent hard and difficult contests; now, this training should have made you stronger, so as to become more courageous.' ... Whenever those things which we have done or suffered for Christ come to our mind, therefore, let them be for us like goads to stir us on to higher accomplishments. [Commentary on Hebrews]

AUGUST 3

Faith Triumphs

Immediately the father of the child cried out and said, 'I believe; help my unbelief!'

MARK 9:24

The godly heart feels in itself a division because it is partly imbued with sweetness from its recognition of the divine goodness, partly grieves in bitterness from an awareness of its calamity; partly rests upon the promise of the gospel, partly trembles at the evidence of its own iniquity; partly rejoices at the expectation of life; partly shudders at death. This variation arises from imperfection of faith, since in the course of the present life it never goes so well with us that we are wholly cured of the disease of unbelief and entirely filled and possessed by faith. Hence arise those conflicts; when unbelief, which reposes in the remains of the flesh, rises up to attack the faith that has been inwardly conceived. ... To bear these attacks faith arms and fortifies itself with the word of the Lord. And when any sort of temptation assails us – suggesting that God is our enemy because He is unfavorable toward us – faith, on the other hand, replies that while He afflicts us He is also merciful because His chastisement arises out of love rather than wrath. While one is stricken by the thought that God is avenger of iniquities, faith sets over against this the fact that His pardon is ready for all iniquities whenever the sinner betakes himself to the Lord's mercy. Thus, the godly mind, however strange the ways in which it is vexed and troubled, finally surmounts all difficulties, and never allows itself to be deprived of assurance of divine mercy. Rather, all the contentions that try and weary it result in the certainty of this assurance. [Institutes (1559), III.ii.18, 21]

AUGUST 4

Faith in Christ

He was foreknown before the foundation of the world but was made manifest in the last times for the sake of you who through him are believers in God ...   1 PETER 1:20-21

The phrase 'through Him are believers in God' expresses what faith is. For since God is incomprehensible, faith could never reach to Him, unless it had an immediate regard to Christ. Indeed, there are two reasons why we could not believe in God, unless Christ intervened as a Mediator. First, the greatness of the divine glory must be taken into account, and at the same time the littleness of our capacity. Our acuteness is no doubt very far from being capable of ascending so high as to comprehend God. Hence all knowledge of God without Christ is a vast abyss which immediately swallows up all our thoughts. ... Let us therefore remember that Christ is not in vain called the image of the invisible God (Col. 1:15); but this name is given to Him for this reason, because God cannot be known except in Him.

The second reason is that, as faith unites us to God, we shun and dread every access to Him, unless a Mediator comes who can deliver us from fear. For sin, which reigns in us, renders us hateful to God and Him to us. ... It is thus evident that we cannot believe in God except through Christ, in whom God in a manner makes Himself small, that He might accommodate Himself to our comprehension; and it is Christ alone who can tranquilize consciences, so that we may dare to come in confidence to God. [Commentary on 1 Peter]

AUGUST 5

Loving Life – Hating Life

'Truly, truly I say to you, unless a grain of wheat falls into the earth and dies, it remains alone; but if it dies, it bears much fruit. Whoever loves his life loses it, and whoever hates his life in this world will keep it for eternal life.'

JOHN 12:24-25

[I]f we must die in order that we may bring forth fruit, we ought patiently to permit God to mortify us. But as [Jesus] draws a contrast between the love of life and the hatred of it, we ought to understand what it is to 'love' and 'hate life.' He who, under the influence of immoderate desire of the present life, cannot leave the world but by constraint, is said to 'love life'; but he who, despising life, advances courageously to death, is said to 'hate life.' Not that we ought absolutely to hate life, which is justly reckoned to be one of the greatest of God's blessings; but because believers ought cheerfully to lay it down, when it prevents them from approaching Christ. ... In short, to love this life is not in itself wrong, provided that we only pass through it as pilgrims, keeping our eyes always fixed on our object. For the true limit of 'loving life' is, when we continue in it as long as it pleases God, and when we are prepared to leave it as soon as he shall order us, or – to express it in a single word – when we carry it, as it were, in our hands, and offer it to God as a sacrifice. Whoever carries his attachment to the present life beyond this limit, 'destroys his life'; that is, he consigns it to everlasting ruin. [Commentary on John]

AUGUST 6

Troubles and Blessings

'I will be with him in trouble; I will rescue him and honor him. With long life I will satisfy him and show to him my salvation.'

PSALM 91:15-16

We are taught here the additional lesson, that believers will never be exempt from troubles and embarrassments. God does not promise them a life of ease and luxury, but deliverance from their troubles. Mention is made of 'honoring Him,' suggesting that the deliverance which God extends, and which is spoken of in this psalm, is not of a mere temporary nature, but will result at last in their being advanced to perfect happiness. …

It may seem strange that 'long life' should be mentioned in the last verse as promised to believers, since many of the Lord's people are soon taken out of the world. But let me repeat an observation that has been made elsewhere, that those divine blessings which are promised in relation to the present perishing world, are not to be considered as good in a universal and absolute sense, or fulfilled in all persons in a set and predictable fashion. Wealth and other worldly comforts must be looked upon as affording some experience of the divine favor or goodness, but it does not follow that the poor are objects of divine displeasure; soundness of body and good health are blessings from God, but we must not imagine on this account that He regards with disapproval the weak and the infirm. Long life should be classified among benefits of this kind, and would be bestowed by God on all His children, were it not for the advantage they gain from being taken out of the world early. [Commentary on Psalms]

AUGUST 7

God's Intimate Care

'Are not two sparrows sold for a penny? And not one of them will fall to the ground apart from your Father. But even the hairs of your head are all numbered.'

MATTHEW 10:29-30

Since God is the guardian of our life, we may safely rely on His providence; indeed, we do Him injustice if we do not entrust to Him our life, which He is pleased to take under His charge. ... There are two things to be observed. First, Christ gives a very different account of God's providence from what is given by many who talk like philosophers, and tell us that God governs the world, but yet imagine providence to be a confused sort of arrangement, as if God did not keep His eye on each of His creatures. Now, Christ declares that each of the creatures in particular is under His hand and protection, so that nothing is left to chance. Unquestionably, the will of God is contrasted with contingency or uncertainty. And yet we must not be understood to uphold the fate of the Stoics. For it is one thing to imagine a necessity which is involved in a complicated chain of causes, and quite another thing to believe that the world, and every part of it, is directed by the will of God. ...

The second thing to be observed is that we ought to contemplate providence ... as a ground of confidence and excitement to prayer. When [Christ] informs us that 'the hairs of your head are all numbered,' it is not to encourage trivial speculations, but to instruct us to depend on the fatherly care of God which is exercised over these frail bodies. [Commentary on the Harmony of the Gospels]

AUGUST 8

God Waters the Earth

You make springs gush forth in the valleys; they flow between the hills; they give drink to every beast of the field. ... Besides them the birds of the heavens dwell; they sing among the branches.

PSALM 104:10-12

The Psalmist here describes another example of both the power and goodness of God, namely, that He makes fountains to gush out in the mountains, and to run down through the midst of the valleys. Although it is necessary for the earth to be dry, to render it a fit habitation for us, yet unless we had water to drink and unless the earth opened her veins, all kinds of living creatures would perish. ... Rivers run even through some great and desolate wildernesses, where the wild beasts enjoy some blessing of God; and no country is so barren as not to have trees growing here and there, on which birds fill the air with the melody of their singing. Since even those regions where all lies waste and uncultivated, furnish manifest tokens of the divine goodness and power, with what admiration ought we to regard that most abundant supply of all good things, which is to be seen in cultivated and favorable regions? Surely in countries where not only one river flows, or where not only grass grows for the feeding of wild beasts, or where the singing of birds is heard not only from a few trees, but where a manifold and varied abundance of good things everywhere presents itself to our view, our stupidity is more than brutish, if our minds, by such manifestations of the goodness of God, are not fixed in devout meditation on His glory. [Commentary on Psalms]

AUGUST 9

The Christian's Journey

But one thing I do: forgetting what lies behind and straining forward to what lies ahead, I press on toward the goal for the prize of the upward call of God in Christ Jesus.

PHILIPPIANS 3:13-14

[The gospel of Christ] is a doctrine not of the tongue but of life. It is not apprehended by the understanding and memory alone, as other disciplines are, but it is received only when it possesses the whole soul, and finds a seat and resting place in the inmost affection of the heart. Accordingly, either let them stop boasting of what they are not, in contempt of God, or let them show themselves disciples worthy of Christ their teacher. ... Let each one of us, then, proceed according to the measure of our puny capacity and set out upon the journey we have begun. No one shall set out so inauspiciously as not daily to make some headway, though it be slight. Therefore, let us not cease to act that we may make some unceasing progress in the way of the Lord. And let us not despair at the slightness of our success; for even though attainment may not correspond to desire, when today outstrips yesterday the effort is not lost. Only let us look toward our mark with sincere simplicity and aspire to our goal; not fondly flattering ourselves, nor excusing our own evil deeds, but with continuous effort striving toward this end: that we may surpass ourselves in goodness until we attain to goodness itself. It is this, indeed, which through the whole course of life we seek and follow. But we shall attain it only when we have cast off the weakness of the body, and are received into full fellowship with Him. [Institutes (1559), III.vi.4-5]

AUGUST 10

Rejoicing in Suffering

Not only that, but we rejoice in our sufferings, knowing that suffering produces endurance, and endurance produces character, and character produces hope ...

ROMANS 5:3-4

When he states that the saints rejoice in tribulations, Paul should not be understood as saying that the saints had no fears, or avoided adversities, or were not distressed by those tribulations when they occurred. ... But rather, in the midst of their grief and sorrow the saints experience great consolation, because they recognize that whatever they endure is given to them for good by the hand of a most generous Father – that is why they are rightly said to rejoice. For whenever salvation is promoted, there is good reason for rejoicing.

We are then taught here what is the purpose of our tribulations, if indeed we would prove ourselves to be children of God. These trials ought to habituate us to patience; and if they do not achieve this, then the work of the Lord is rendered void and to no effect due to our corruption. ... Those then who do not learn patience [in trials], do not, it is certain, make good progress. Nor can anyone object that there are passages recorded in Scripture where the saints have made complaints filled with despondency; for the Lord sometimes depresses and afflicts His people for a time to such an extent that they can hardly breathe, and can hardly remember any source of consolation. But in a moment God brings to life those whom He had nearly sunk into the darkness of death. So that what Paul says is always accomplished in them – 'We are afflicted in every way, but not crushed; perplexed, but not driven to despair; persecuted, but not forsaken; struck down, but not destroyed' (2 Cor. 4:8-9). [Commentary on Romans]

AUGUST 11

Sheepfolds and Philosophy

See to it that no one takes you captive by philosophy and empty deceit...

COLOSSIANS 2:8

Paul makes use of a very appropriate term, for he alludes to plunderers, who, when they cannot carry off the flock by violence, drive away some of the animals through fraud. Thus, he compares Christ's Church to a sheep-fold, and the pure doctrine of the gospel to the enclosures of the fold. He intimates, accordingly, that we who are the sheep of Christ rest in safety when we hold the unity of faith, while, on the other hand, he likens the false apostles to plunderers that carry us away from the fold. Would you then be considered as belonging to Christ's flock? Would you remain in his sheep-fold? Then do not deviate a nails-breadth from purity of doctrine. For unquestionably Christ will play the part of the good Shepherd by protecting us if we but listen to His voice, and reject those who are strangers. In short, John 10 is the exposition of this passage before us.

'By Philosophy.' Since many people have mistakenly imagined that philosophy is here condemned by Paul, we must point out what he means by this term. In my opinion, he means everything that people contrive of themselves when wishing to be wise by means of their own understanding, adding a fake pretext of reason to give it a false appearance. ... [I]n one word, this sort of 'philosophy' is nothing else than a persuasive speech, which insinuates itself into the minds of men and women by elegant and plausible arguments. ... Of such a nature will the subtleties of the philosophers be, if they are inclined to add anything of their own to the pure word of God. [Commentary on Colossians]

AUGUST 12

Jesus Experienced Human Feelings

'Now is my soul troubled. And what shall I say? "Father, save me from this hour"? But for this purpose I have come to this hour. Father, glorify your name.'

JOHN 12:27-28

[I]t was highly useful, and even necessary for our salvation, that the Son of God should have experienced such feelings. In His death we ought chiefly to consider His atonement, by which He appeased the wrath and curse of God, which He could not have done without taking upon Himself our guilt. The death which He underwent must therefore have been full of horror, because He could not render satisfaction for us, without feeling, in His own experience, the dreadful judgment of God; and hence we come to know more fully the enormity of sin for which the heavenly Father exacted so dreadful a punishment from His only-begotten Son. Let us therefore know, that death was not a sport and amusement to Christ, but that He endured the severest torments on our account.

Nor was it unsuitable that the Son of God should be troubled in this manner; for the divine nature, being concealed, and not exerting its force, may be said to have rested, in order to give an opportunity of making expiation. But Christ Himself was clothed, not only with our flesh, but with human feelings. In Him, no doubt, those feelings were voluntary; for He did not fear out of constraint, but because He had, of His own accord, subjected Himself to fear. ... [W]hen we learn that He did not possess a hardness like stone or iron, we summon courage to follow Him. [Commentary on John]

AUGUST

AUGUST 13

Enduring the Cross

Blessed is the man whom you discipline, O LORD, and whom you teach out of your law.

PSALM 94:12

The Psalmist... comforts himself and others of the Lord's people with the truth that, though God might afflict them for a time, He is concerned with their true interests and safety. At no period of life is this a truth not important, given that we are called to lives of continued warfare.... We must remember the fact that, in calling us to be His people, He has separated us from the rest of the world to experience a blessed peace in the mutual cultivation of truth and righteousness. The Church is often cruelly oppressed by tyrants under the guise of the law.... Under such circumstances, our carnal judgment might conclude that if God were really concerned about our welfare, He would never allow these persons to perpetuate such wickedness. To prevent this, the Psalmist would have us distrust our own ideas of things, and experience the need for that wisdom which comes from above. I consider this passage to mean that it is only in the Lord's school we can ever learn to maintain composure of mind, and a posture of patient expectation and trust under the pressure of distress. The Psalmist declares that the wisdom which would bear us onward to the end, with an inward peace and courage under long-continued trouble, is not natural to any of us, but must come from God. Accordingly, he exclaims that those people are truly blessed whom God has habituated through His word to the endurance of the cross, and prevented from sinking under adversity by the secret supports and consolations of His Spirit. [Commentary on Psalms]

AUGUST 14

The Heavenly Reward

For you had compassion on those in prison, and you joyfully accepted the plundering of your property, since you knew that you yourselves had a better possession and an abiding one.

HEBREWS 10:34

No doubt, as men and women with feelings, the loss of their goods caused them grief; yet their sorrow was of such a kind that it did not prevent them from experiencing the joy of which the Apostle speaks. Since poverty is considered an evil, the plunder of their property in itself touched them with grief; but as they looked higher, they found a reason for joy, which relieved whatever grief they felt. Thus, it is necessary that our thoughts should be drawn away from the world, by looking at the heavenly reward. ... And no doubt we joyfully embrace what we are persuaded will result in our salvation; and this confidence the children of God no doubt have respecting the conflicts which they undertake for the glory of Christ. Hence carnal feelings never succeed in so overwhelming them with grief that they do not experience spiritual joy with their minds raised to heaven. ...

And indeed, wherever there is a lively perception of heavenly things, the world with all its temptations is not so relished that either poverty or shame can overwhelm our minds with grief. If then we wish to bear anything for Christ with patience and resolute minds, let us accustom ourselves to meditate frequently on that happiness, in comparison with which all the good things of the world are nothing but refuse. ... For unless a person is fully persuaded that the inheritance which God has promised to His children belongs to them, all their knowledge will be cold and useless. [Commentary on Hebrews]

AUGUST 15

Remaining at Our Posts

*In the LORD I take refuge; how can you say to my soul,
'Flee like a bird to your mountain ...'*
PSALM 11:1

[I]t may be asked, whether or not it would have been lawful
for [David] to flee; yes, we know that he was often forced to
retire into exile, and driven about from place to place, and
that he even sometimes hid himself in caves. I answer, it is
true he was unsettled like a poor fearful bird, which leaps
from branch to branch, and was forced to seek out different
bypaths, and to wander from place to place to avoid the snares
of his enemies; yet still his faith continued to be so steadfast
that he never alienated himself from the people of God. Others
accounted him a lost man, and one whose affairs were in a
hopeless condition, setting no more value upon him than if
he had been a rotten limb, yet he never separated himself from
the body of the Church. And, certainly these words, 'Flee like
a bird,' tended only to make him yield to utter despair. But it
would have been wrong for him to yield to these fears, and to
have betaken himself to flight, as if uncertain of what would
be the outcome. ... In short, although [David] had always
lived innocently as a true servant of God, yet these malicious
men would have doomed him to remain forever in a state
of exile from his native country. This verse teaches us that
however much the world may hate and persecute us, we ought
nevertheless to continue steadfast at our post ... and always to
continue firm and unwavering in the faith of our having been
called by God. [Commentary on Psalms]

AUGUST 16

The Church as Rock

'And I tell you, you are Peter, and on this rock I will build my church, and the gates of hell shall not prevail against it.'

MATTHEW 16:18

Hence it is evident how the name Peter comes to be applied both to Simon individually, and to other believers. It is because they are founded on the faith of Christ, and joined together, by a holy consent, into a spiritual building, that God 'will dwell in the midst of them' (Ezek. 43:7). For Christ, by announcing that this would be the common foundation of the whole Church, intended to associate with Peter all the godly that would ever exist in the world. ... Against all the power of Satan, the firmness of the Church will prove to be invincible, because the truth of God, on which the faith of the Church rests, will ever remain unshaken. And to this statement corresponds that saying of John, 'and this is the victory that has overcome the world – our faith' (1 John 5:4). It is a promise which eminently deserves our observation, that all who are united to Christ, and acknowledge Him to be Christ and Mediator, will remain to the end safe from danger; for what is said of the body of the Church belongs to each of its members, since they are one in Christ. Yet this passage also instructs us that, so long as the Church shall continue to be a pilgrim on the earth, she will never enjoy rest, but will be exposed to many attacks. ... [L] et us learn that this promise is, as it were, the sound of a trumpet, calling us to be always ready and prepared for battle. [Commentary on the Harmony of the Gospels]

AUGUST

AUGUST 17

Grief and Joy

Wretched man that I am! Who will deliver me from this body of death? Thanks be to God through Jesus Christ our Lord.

ROMANS 7:24-25

Paul teaches us that even the most perfect man or woman, as long as they dwell in the flesh, are exposed to misery, for they are still subject to death. Indeed, when they thoroughly examine themselves, they find their own [sinful] nature nothing but misery. Moreover, lest they should indulge their moral lethargy, Paul, by his own example, stimulates them to anxious groanings and urges them – as long as they sojourn on earth – to desire death as the only true remedy for their evils, which is the right reason to desire death. ... But it must be added that though the faithful fail to achieve God's standard, they are not yet carried away by an unbridled desire for death, but submit themselves to the will of God, to whom it is our duty both to live and die. ... Hence, saints do not overly fixate on the thoughts of their misery, but, being mindful of the grace received, they blend their grief with joy. ...

Paul then immediately adds this word of thanksgiving, lest anyone should think that in his complaint he perversely murmured against God. For we know how easy it is to slide into discontentment and impatience – even when experiencing legitimate grief. Though Paul then bewailed his situation, and longed for his departure, he yet confesses that he resigned himself to the good pleasure of God. For it is not appropriate for the saints, when examining their own defects, to forget what they have already received from God. ... Though they do not yet enjoy the promised glory of heaven, at the same time, being content with the measure they have obtained, they are never without reasons for joy. [Commentary on Romans]

AUGUST 18

Grief and Resurrection

But we do not want you to be uninformed, brothers, about those who are asleep, that you may not grieve as others do who have no hope.
1 THESSALONIANS 4:13

[I]t is inappropriate for those of us, who have been instructed as to the resurrection, to mourn otherwise than in moderation. ... Paul does not forbid us altogether to mourn but requires moderation in our mourning, for he says 'that you may not grieve as others do who have no hope.' He forbids the Thessalonians from grieving in the manner of unbelievers, who give full vent to their grief, because they look upon death as final destruction, and imagine that everything that is taken out of this world perishes. On the other hand, believers know that they leave this world so that they may at last be gathered into the kingdom of God – and thus they do not have the same grounds for grief. Hence, the knowledge of a resurrection is the means of moderating grief. Paul speaks of the dead as 'asleep,' in keeping with other Scripture passages – a term by which the bitterness of death is mitigated, for there is a great difference between sleep and destruction. It refers, however, not to the soul, but to the body, for the dead body lies in the tomb, as on a bed, until God raises them up. Those people, therefore, act foolishly who infer from this that souls sleep. ... Let, therefore, the grief of the pious be mixed with consolation, which may train them to be patient. The hope of a blessed resurrection, which is the mother of patience, will make this possible. [Commentary on 1 Thessalonians]

//
AUGUST 19

Nature's Testimony

'In past generations God … did not leave himself without witness, for he did good by giving you rain from heaven and fruitful seasons, satisfying your hearts with food and gladness.'

ACTS 14:16-17

God has, indeed, revealed Himself to all humanity by His word from the beginning. But Paul and Barnabas show that there was no age in which God did not bestow benefits, as a testimony that the world is governed by His government and commandment. … Nevertheless, they emphasize this principle, that in the order of nature there is a certain and clear manifestation of God, in that the earth is watered with rain; in that the heat of the sun comforts it; in that there comes such an abundance of fruit out of the earth every year – all of which provides a sure witness that there is some God who governs all things. … For why do the sun and stars shine in the heavens, save only that they may serve human beings? Why does the rain fall from heaven? Why does the earth bring forth her increase, save only that they may provide humans with food? Therefore, God has not set human beings upon the earth to be idle spectators of His work, as if they were at a theatre, but to exercise themselves in praising the liberality of God, while they enjoy the riches of heaven and earth. …

By the word 'gladness,' Paul and Barnabas mean that God gives more to humans, according to His infinite goodness, than necessity requires; as if one said that they have meat given to them not only to refresh their strength, but also to make their hearts merry. [Commentary on Acts]

AUGUST 20

The Christian's Blessed Hope

'In my Father's house are many rooms. If it were not so, would I have told you that I go to prepare a place for you?'

JOHN 14:2

By these words Christ intimates that the purpose of His departure is to prepare a place for His disciples. In a word, Christ did not ascend to heaven in a private capacity, to dwell there alone, but rather that it might be the common inheritance of all the godly, and that in this way the Head might be united to His members.

But a question arises, 'What was the condition of the fathers [of the Old Testament] after death, before Christ ascended to heaven?' For the conclusion usually drawn is that believing souls were shut up in an intermediate state or prison. ... But the answer is easy: This place is said to be prepared for the day of the resurrection; for by nature human beings are banished from the kingdom of God, but the Son, who is the only heir of heaven, took possession of it in their name, that through Him we may be permitted to enter; for in His person we already possess heaven by hope, as Paul informs us (Eph. 1:3). Still, we will not enjoy this great blessing, until He comes from heaven the second time. The condition of the fathers after death, therefore, is not distinguished from ours; because Christ has prepared both for them and for us a place into which He will receive us all at the last day. Before reconciliation had been made, believing souls were, as it were, placed on a watch-tower, looking for the promised redemption, and now they enjoy a blessed rest, until the redemption is finished. [Commentary on John]

AUGUST 21

Vanity of False Religions

For great is the LORD, and greatly to be praised; he is to be feared above all gods. For all the gods of the peoples are worthless idols, but the LORD made the heavens.

PSALM 96:4-5

We cannot but notice the confidence with which the Psalmist asserts the glory of the true God, in opposition to the universal opinion which humans might entertain. The people of God were at that time called to engage in a conflict of no small or common sort with the hosts and prodigious mass of superstitions which then filled the whole world. The true God might be said to be confined to an obscure corner of Judea, whereas Jupiter was the god received everywhere, and adored throughout the whole of Asia, Europe, and Africa. Every country had its own gods peculiar to itself, but these were not unknown in other regions, and it was the true God alone who was robbed of that glory which belonged to Him. All the world had conspired to believe a lie. Yet the Psalmist, sensible that the vain delusions of men and women could detract nothing from the glory of the one God, looks down with indifference upon the opinion and universal consensus of humankind. The inference is plain, that we must not conclude that the true religion must necessarily meet with the approval of the multitude, for ... true worship [is not] determined by human caprice. Regardless of how many people agree in error, we shall insist in accordance with the Holy Spirit that they cannot detract from God's glory; for humans are vain creatures and all that comes from them should be mistrusted. [Commentary on Psalms]

AUGUST 22

Following Christ's Example

For to this you have been called, because Christ also suffered for you, leaving you an example, so that you might follow in his steps. ... When he was reviled, he did not revile in return; when he suffered, he did not threaten ...

1 PETER 2:21, 23

It is necessary to know what in Christ should be our example. He walked on the sea, He cleansed the leprous, He raised the dead, He restored sight to the blind – to try to imitate Him in these things would be absurd. For when He gave these evidences of His power, it was not His object that we should imitate Him. When He fasted for forty days, this was not intended to be an example for us; rather, Christ had a very different purpose in mind. We ought, therefore, to exercise in this respect a right judgment ... when explaining the following passage, 'Learn from me, for I am gentle and lowly of heart' (Matt. 11:29). And the same thing may be learned from Peter's words here; for he marks the difference by saying that Christ's patience is what we ought to follow. This subject is handled in more detail by Paul in Romans 8:29, where he teaches us that all the children of God are foreordained to be made conformable to the image of Christ, in order that He might be the first-born among many brethren. Hence, that we may live with Him, we must previously die with Him. ...

Peter points out (in verse 23) what we are to imitate in Christ, namely, to calmly endure wrongs, and not to avenge them. For such is our disposition, that when we receive injuries, our minds immediately boil over with revengeful feelings; but Christ abstained from every kind of retaliation. [Commentary on 1 Peter]

AUGUST 23

God's Mercy

O Israel, hope in the Lord! For with the LORD there is steadfast love, and with him is plentiful redemption.

PSALM 130:7

It is to be noticed that, for the prophet, the foundation upon which the hope of all the godly rests is the mercy of God, the source from which redemption springs. In the first clause, he reminds them that although they bring with them no worth or merits of their own, it ought to be sufficient for them that God is merciful. This mutual relation between the faith of the Church and the free goodness of God is to be carefully noted, so that we may know that all those who depend upon their own merits – persuading themselves that God will be their rewarder – do not have their hope regulated according to the rule of Scripture. From this mercy, as from a fountain, the prophet derives redemption; for there is no other reason that moves God to reveal Himself as the redeemer of His people, except His mercy. He describes this redemption as 'plentiful,' so that the faithful, even when they are reduced to the last extremity, may sustain themselves by remembering that in God's hands are many and incredible means by which to save them. ... The true use of the present doctrine is, first, that even when faithful people are plunged into the deepest abyss, they should not doubt that their deliverance is in God's hand who (whenever it is necessary) is able to find a way, though it is hidden and unknown to us. And, secondly, that believers should hold it as certain that, as often as the Church is afflicted, God will reveal Himself as her deliverer. [Commentary on Psalms]

AUGUST 24

Born of God

Everyone who believes that Jesus is the Christ has been born of God, and everyone who loves the Father loves whoever has been born of him.

1 JOHN 5:1

The first truth is that all those born of God, believe that Jesus is the Christ. ... Jesus cannot be received as Christ, unless salvation is sought from Him, since for this purpose He was sent by the Father, and is daily offered to us.

Hence the Apostle declares that all those who really believe have been born of God; for faith is far above the reach of the human mind, so that we must be drawn to Christ by our heavenly Father; for none of us can ascend to Him by our own strength. And this is what the Apostle teaches us in his Gospel, when he says that those who believe in the name of the only-begotten, were not born of blood nor of the flesh (John 1:13). And Paul says that we are endued, not with the spirit of the world, but with the Spirit that is from God, that we may know the things given us by Him (1 Cor. 2:12). For no eye has seen, nor ear heard, nor the mind conceived the reward laid up for those who love God; but the Spirit alone penetrates into this mystery. And further, as Christ is given to us for sanctification, and brings with Him the Spirit of regeneration – in short, as He unites us to His own body – it is also another reason why no one can have faith unless they are born of God. [Commentary on 1 John]

AUGUST 25

Spirit of Regeneration

You, however, are not in the flesh but in the Spirit, if in fact the Spirit of God dwells in you. Anyone who does not have the Spirit of Christ does not belong to him.

ROMANS 8:9

The reign of the Spirit is the abolition of the flesh. Those in whom the Spirit does not reign, do not belong to Christ, for they are not Christians who serve the flesh. For those who separate Christ from His own Spirit make Him like a dead image or even a corpse. And we must always bear in mind what the Apostle intimates here, that the gracious remission of sins can never be separated from the Spirit of regeneration, for this would be as it were to tear Christ apart.

If this is true, it is strange that we are accused of arrogance by the enemies of the gospel, because we dare to claim that the Spirit of Christ dwells in us: we must either deny Christ, or confess that we become Christians through His Spirit. ... But let us observe here that the Spirit is, without any distinction, sometimes called the Spirit of God the Father, and sometimes the Spirit of Christ. He is called the latter not only because the Spirit's whole fullness was poured on Christ as our Mediator and Head, so that from Him a portion might descend on each of us, but also because He is equally the Spirit of the Father and of the Son, who have one essence, and the same eternal divinity. As, however, we do not have communion with God except through Christ, the Apostle wisely descends to Christ from the Father, who seems to be far off. [Commentary on Romans]

AUGUST 26

Life in Christ

Jesus said to [Thomas], 'I am the way, and the truth, and the life. No one comes to the Father except through me.'

JOHN 14:6

[Jesus] lays down three degrees, as if He had said that He is the beginning, the middle, and the end; and hence it follows that we ought to begin with Him, continue in Him, and end in Him. We certainly ought not to seek for higher wisdom than that which leads us to eternal life, and He testifies that this life is to be found in Him. Now the method of obtaining life is to become new creatures. He declares that we ought not to seek it anywhere else, and, at the same time, reminds us that He is 'the way' by which alone we can arrive at it. That He may not fail us in any respect, He stretches out the hand to those who are going astray; and stoops so low as to guide sucking infants. Presenting Himself as a leader, He does not leave His people in the middle of the course, but makes them partakers of the truth. At length He makes them enjoy the fruit of it, which is the most excellent and delightful thing that can be imagined. ...

The whole may be summed up in this way: If anyone turns aside from Christ, they will do nothing but go astray; if anyone refuses to rest on Him, they will feed elsewhere on nothing but wind and vanity; if anyone, not satisfied with Him alone, wishes to go farther, they will find death instead of life. [Commentary on John]

AUGUST 27

Earnest Prayer

Hear my prayer, O LORD; let my cry come to you! Do not hide your face from me in the day of my distress!

PSALM 102:1-2

In speaking in this fashion, the captive Jews bear testimony to the severe and excruciating distress which they endured, and to their ardent desire to obtain some relief. No person could utter these words with the mouth without profaning the name of God, unless they were, at the same time, motivated by a sincere and earnest affection of the heart. We ought to pay particular attention to the circumstances already observed, that we are thus stirred up by the Holy Spirit to the duty of prayer on behalf of the common welfare of the Church. While each person takes sufficient care of their own individual interests, there is scarcely one in a hundred who is appropriately impacted by the calamities of the Church. Hence, we need various prods, as even here the prophet seeks to do with his words, to correct our coldness and sloth. I admit that the heart ought to move and direct the tongue to prayer; but, as it often flags or performs its duty in a slow and sluggish manner, it requires to be aided by the tongue. There is a reciprocal influence. As the heart, on the one hand, ought to go before the words, and frame them, so the tongue, on the other hand, aids and remedies the coldness and apathy of the heart. True believers may indeed often pray not only earnestly but also fervently, while yet not a single word proceeds from their mouths. [Commentary on Psalms]

AUGUST 28

Imperfect Faith

And what more shall I say? For time would fail me to tell of Gideon, Barak, Samson, Jephthah, of David and Samuel and the prophets – who through faith conquered kingdoms, enforced justice, obtained promises, stopped the mouths of lions ...
                                        HEBREWS 11:32-33

It indeed seemed strange for Gideon, with three hundred men to attack an immense army of enemies, and shaking clay jars must have seemed like a sham alarm. Barak was far inferior to his enemies, and was guided only by the counsel of a woman. Samson was a mere farmer, and had never used any other arms than the implements of his farming; what could he do against such seasoned warriors, by whose power the whole nation had been subdued? What would not have initially condemned the rashness of Jephthah, who asserted that he was the avenger of a people already beyond hope? But as all these judges followed the guidance of God, and being energized by His promise, they undertook what was commanded of them. In so doing they have been honored [in chapter eleven] with the testimony of the Holy Spirit.

The Apostle then ascribes all that was praiseworthy in these men to faith, though not one of them had a faith that was perfect. [For example,] Gideon was slower to take up arms than he should have been; nor did he venture forth without some hesitation to commit himself to God. ... Thus, in all the saints, something reprehensible is always found; yet faith, though halting and imperfect, is still approved by God. There is therefore no reason why the faults we struggle with should break us down, or dishearten us, provided we by faith go on in the race of our calling. [Commentary on Hebrews]

AUGUST 29

God's Glory in the Church

Great is the LORD and greatly to be praised in the city of our God! His holy mountain, beautiful in elevation, is the joy of all the earth, Mount Zion, in the far north, the city of the great King.

PSALM 48:1-2

[The prophet] teaches in general that the city of Jerusalem was happy and prosperous, because God had been graciously pleased to take upon Himself the charge of defending and preserving it. In this way he separates and distinguishes the Church of God from all the rest of the world; and when God selects from amongst the whole human race a small number whom He embraces with His fatherly love, this is an invaluable blessing which He bestows upon them. His wonderful goodness and righteousness shine forth in the government of the whole world, so that there is no part of it void of His praise, but we are everywhere furnished with abundant matter for praising Him. Here, however, the inspired poet celebrates the glory of God which is manifested in the protection of the Church. ... But is He not also present in the whole world? Undoubtedly, He is. As I have said, there is not a corner so hidden, into which His wisdom, righteousness, and goodness, do not penetrate; but since it is His will that they should be manifested chiefly and in a particular manner in His Church, the prophet very properly sets before our eyes this mirror, in which God gives a clearer and more vivid representation of His character. ... The Psalmist next calls Mount Zion the 'joy of the whole earth' ... because from it salvation was to issue forth to the whole world. [Commentary on Psalms]

AUGUST 30

Royal Priesthood

But you are a chosen race, a royal priesthood, a holy nation, a people for his own possession, that you may proclaim the excellencies of him who called you ...
1 PETER 2:9

There is in the phrase 'royal priesthood' a striking inversion of the words Moses uses, for he speaks of 'a priestly kingdom' – but the same thing is meant. So, what Peter intends is this: 'Moses called your fathers a sacred kingdom, because the whole nation enjoyed as it were a royal liberty, and from their body were chosen the priest; both dignities were therefore joined together. But now you are royal priests, and, indeed, in a more excellent way, because you are – each one of you – consecrated in Christ, so that you may be members of His kingdom and partakers of His priesthood. Though, then, the fathers had something similar to what you have, yet you far excel them. For after the wall of partition has been pulled down by Christ, we are now gathered from every nation, and the Lord bestows these high titles on all whom He makes His people.'

With regard to these benefits, there is an additional contrast to be considered... For [God] sanctifies us, who are by nature polluted; He chose us, when He could find nothing in us but filth and vileness; He makes His special possession from worthless dregs; He confers the honor of the priesthood on the profane; He brings the vassals of Satan, of sin, and of death, to the enjoyment of royal liberty. ... This doctrine ought to be a subject of daily meditation, and it ought to be continually remembered by us, that all God's blessings with which He favors us are intended for this end, that His glory may be proclaimed by us. [Commentary on 1 Peter]

AUGUST 31

Spirit-Guided Prayer

Likewise, the Spirit helps us in our weakness. For we do not know what to pray for as we ought, but the Spirit himself intercedes for us with groanings too deep for words.

ROMANS 8:26

Although it does not appear that our prayers have been heard by God, yet Paul concludes that the presence of heavenly favor already shines forth in our desire for prayer; for no one can of themselves give birth to devout and godly aspirations. Unbelievers do indeed blab out their prayers, but they only trifle with God; for there is nothing in them that is sincere, or serious, or rightly formed. Hence the manner of praying in the right fashion must be suggested by the Spirit, and he calls those groanings 'too deep for words.' We break forth into these groanings by the impulse of the Spirit, because they far exceed the capability of our own minds. And the Spirit is said to 'intercede,' not because He really humbles Himself to pray or to groan, but because He stirs up in our hearts those desires which we ought to have; and He also affects our hearts in such a way that these desires by their intensity penetrate into heaven itself. And Paul has spoken in this way so that he might ascribe all of these prayers to the grace of the Spirit. We are indeed urged to knock; but no one, by themselves, can formulate one syllable, unless God Himself, by the secret impulse of His Spirit knocks at the door, and thus opens for Himself our hearts. ... This is a remarkable reason for strengthening our confidence, that we are heard by God when we pray through His Spirit, for He thoroughly knows our desires even as the thoughts of His own Spirit. [Commentary on Romans]

SEPTEMBER 1

The Saints Glorified

They will suffer the punishment of eternal destruction, away from the presence of the Lord and from the glory of his might, when he comes on that day to be glorified in his saints, and to be marveled at among all who have believed...

2 THESSALONIANS 1:9-10

As Paul has hitherto discussed the punishment of the wicked, he now returns to the pious, and says that Christ will come so that He may be glorified in them; that is, so that He may irradiate them with His glory, and they may be partakers of it. 'Christ will not have this glory for Himself individually, but it will be common to all the saints.' This is the crowning and choice consolation of the pious, that when the Son of God is manifested in the glory of His kingdom, He will gather them into the same fellowship with Himself. There is, however, an implied contrast between the present condition in which believers labor and groan, and that final restoration. For now they are exposed to the reproaches of the world, and are looked upon as vile and worthless; but then they will be precious, and full of dignity, when Christ will pour forth His glory upon them. The end of this is that the pious may, as it were, with closed eyes, pursue the brief journey of this earthly life, having their minds always intent upon the future manifestation of Christ's kingdom. For to what purpose does He make mention of Christ's coming in power, but in order that they may in hope leap forward to that blessed resurrection which is as yet hidden? [Commentary on 2 Thessalonians]

SEPTEMBER 2

First Commandment

And God spoke all these words, saying, 'I am the LORD your God, who brought you out of the land of Egypt, out of the house of slavery. You shall have no other gods before me.'

EXODUS 20:1-3

Part of this commandment is a sort of preface to the whole Law. For while He declares Himself the Lord our God, He implies that it is He who has the right to give commandments, and that His commandments are to be obeyed. ... At the same time, God recalls His benefit in order to prove our ungratefulness, unless we pay heed to His voice. For by that kindness He once set the Jewish people free from Egyptian bondage; by that same kindness He also frees all His servants from the everlasting 'Egypt' of believers, that is, from the power of sin.

His forbidding us to have other gods means that we are not to give to another than Himself what belongs to God. And He adds the phrase 'before me' in order to make clear that God wills Himself to be acknowledged not only by outward confession but also to be held in truth within the depths of the heart. Now these things belong to the one God and cannot be transferred to another without sacrilege; that we are to worship Him alone; we are to rely upon Him with complete faithfulness and hope; whatsoever is good and holy we are to recognize as received from Him; and we are to direct all praise for goodness and holiness to Him. [Calvin's First Catechism (1538), 11]

SEPTEMBER 3

Second Commandment

'You shall not make for yourself a carved image, or any likeness of anything that is heaven above, or that is in the earth beneath ... You shall not bow down to them or serve them.'

EXODUS 20:4-5

As in the previous commandment God declares Himself to be one, so now He states what He is like and how He is to be worshiped. Therefore, He forbids us to fashion any likeness of Him. In Deuteronomy 4 and in Isaiah the reason for this is given: that spirit and body are in no way alike. Accordingly, He forbids us to honor any image for the sake of religion. Let us therefore learn from this precept that the worship of God is spiritual, for as He is Spirit, so He bids us worship Him in spirit and in truth. Then He adds a dreadful threat, by which He suggests how gravely He is offended by the breaking of this commandment, 'I am the LORD GOD,' etc. It is as if He were saying that it is He alone to whom we should cleave, nor can He bear an equal. Also, He will be the vindicator of His own majesty and glory. If anyone transfers it to graven images or to other things, that vengeance is not to be a brief and simple one but one that is to extend to grandchildren and great-grandchildren, who will obviously be imitators of their fathers' impiety. Just as lasting also does He show mercy and kindness to be for long generations to those who love Him and keep His law. While He commends the wideness of His mercy to us, which He extends to a thousand generations, He has assigned only four generations to His vengeance. [Calvin's First Catechism (1538), 12]

SEPTEMBER 4

Third Commandment

'You shall not take the name of the LORD your God in vain, for the LORD will not hold him guiltless who takes his name in vain.'

DEUTERONOMY 5:11

The meaning of this is that God is indeed so to be feared and loved by us, that we should not for any reason misuse His most holy name. Rather, we should magnify Him above all else for His holiness, give the glory to Him in everything, whether favorable or adverse; we should wholeheartedly ask of Him all things which come to us from His hand, and give Him thanks. To sum up, let us carefully keep away from all arrogance and blasphemy, so as not to name Him by any other name, or speak other of Him than befits His lofty majesty. ... As far as pledges and oaths are concerned, we are not to call upon His holy name in any false way. For the eternal truth can be no more gravely dishonored than if it be cited as witness to falsehood. In short, we are not to use even a true oath rashly, unless God's glory or the need of our brothers and sisters demands it as necessary. Save for this cause, any kind of oath-swearing is forbidden. As Christ's words teach us, when He interprets this head of the law, it means that all our speech is, yes, yes; no, no; and what goes beyond this, testifies that it comes from the evil one (Matt. 5:37). ... Finally, to more effectively commend the excellent majesty of His name, the Lord has added the following words to this commandment: 'the LORD will not hold Him guiltless who takes His name in vain.' [Institutes (1536), 22]

SEPTEMBER 5

Divine Helpers

'And I will ask the Father, and he will give you another Helper, to be with you forever, even the Spirit of truth, whom the world cannot receive, because it neither sees him nor knows him.'

JOHN 14:16-17

'And He will give you another Comforter.' The word Comforter or Helper is here applied both to Christ and to the Spirit, and rightly so; for it is an office which belongs equally to both of them, to comfort and exhort us, and to guard us by their protection. Christ was the Protector of His disciples, so long as He dwelt in the world; and afterwards He committed them to the protection and guardianship of the Spirit. It may be asked, 'Are we not still under the protection of Christ?' The answer is easy. Christ is a continual Protector, but not in a visible way. So long as He dwelt in the world, He openly manifested Himself as their Protector; but now He guards us by His Spirit.

He calls the Spirit 'another Comforter' or 'Helper,' on account of the difference between the blessings which we obtain from both. The peculiar office of Christ was to appease the wrath of God by atoning for the sins of the world, to redeem men and women from death, to procure righteousness and life; and the peculiar office of the Spirit is to make us partakers not only of Christ Himself, but of all His blessings. [Commentary on John]

SEPTEMBER 6

God Unchanging

But you, O LORD, are enthroned forever; you are remembered throughout all generations.
PSALM 102:12

When the prophet, for his own encouragement, sets before himself the eternity of God, it seems at first sight to be a far-fetched consolation; for what benefit will we gain from the fact that God is immutable on His heavenly throne, when, at the same time, our frail and perishing condition does not permit us to continue unmoved for a single moment? And what is more, this knowledge of the blessed repose enjoyed by God enables us the better to perceive that our lives are a mere illusion. But the inspired writer … has no hesitation in representing all the godly – though they were languishing in a state of suffering and wretchedness – as partakers of this celestial glory in which God dwells. The word 'remembered' is also to be viewed in the same light. What advantage would we derive from this eternity and immutability of God's being, unless we had in our hearts the knowledge of Him, which, produced by His gracious covenant, begets in us the confidence arising from a mutual relationship between Him and us? The meaning then is this: 'We are like withered grass, we are decaying every moment, we are not far from death, indeed, we are, as it were, already dwelling in the grave. But since you, O GOD, have made a covenant with us, by which you have promised to protect and defend your people … instead of despairing, we must be of good courage; and although we may see only reasons for despair if we depend upon ourselves, we ought nevertheless to lift up our minds to the heavenly throne, from which you will in due time stretch forth your hand to help us.' [Commentary on Psalm]

SEPTEMBER 7

God's Secret Counsel

And [Paul and Silas] went through the region of Phrygia and Galatia, having been forbidden by the Holy Spirit to speak the word in Asia. And when ... they attempted to go into Bithynia, the Spirit of Jesus did not allow them.

ACTS 16:6-7

But here arises another hard question, why did the Lord forbid Paul to speak in Asia, and not allow him to go to Bithynia? For if we answer that those Gentiles were not worthy of the doctrine of salvation, we may again ask why Macedonia was more worthy? Those who desire to be too wise, assign the causes for this difference in human agents, that the Lord graciously bestows the gospel on everyone whom He sees inclined toward obedience of faith. But the Lord Himself says something far different, namely, that He appeared plainly to those who did not seek Him, and He spoke to those who did not ask of Him. For where does the ability to be taught and the mind to obey come from, except from His Spirit? Therefore, it is not due to merit that certain people are preferred over others, seeing that all men and women are naturally backward and stubborn toward faith. Therefore, there is nothing better [for us to do] than to leave to God the freedom to bestow and to deprive grace on whom He will. And surely as His eternal election is free, so His calling is also free and flows from it. ... Hence, let us know that the gospel springs forth and issues to us only from the fountain of mere grace. And yet, God does not lack good reasons why He offers His gospel to some and passes over others. But I say that that reason lies hidden in His secret counsel. [Commentary on Acts]

SEPTEMBER 8

God's Help, Our Infirmity

Whoever, therefore, eats the bread or drinks the cup of the Lord in an unworthy manner will be guilty concerning the body and blood of the Lord. 1 CORINTHIANS 11:27

No one should think of coming to this holy table carelessly and barging in like pigs that bury their snouts in the trough. Such a sacrilege will not go unpunished. But as often as the holy supper is prepared, we are reminded of our frailty and how God wants to provide for our weakness. Certainly, this happens when the gospel is daily preached to us; when we lift up our prayers and supplications; when we read in our homes; or when we hear talk related to our salvation. In such ways God always shows us that He supports us. Even so, the supper provides a special witness that our God, in the middle of our journey, helps us to continue to move forward and always hold on to Him. Let us note also that the supper is intended to correct and complete the things that are still lacking in us. It would be worthless if God simply began a work in us, unless He continued to extend His grace. We have a firm certainty of this fact in the supper. Woe then to us when we come and defile this holy table which has been given to support our salvation. Hence, when we commune at the table, let us take care to be well-grounded in faith, repentance, and love. And since we are fully aware of our weakness and frailty, and since we do not have all that our need requires, we should ask God to strengthen us, lead us forward, and increase our faith and the hope that we have in the heavenly life. [Sermons on Titus, CO 54:415-416]

SEPTEMBER 9

Fourth Commandment

Remember the Sabbath day, to keep it holy. Six days you shall labor, and do all your work, but the seventh day is a Sabbath to the LORD your God. EXODUS 20:8-10

We observe that there were three reasons for this commandment. For the Lord willed under the repose of the seventh day to represent spiritual rest to the people of Israel, by which believers ought to take holiday from their own work to let the Lord work in them. Secondly, He willed that a day be set to gather to hear the law and carry out the ceremonies. Thirdly, He determined that a day of rest be provided for servants and for those functioning under the authority of others in order that they might have some cessation from toil. As for the first reason, there is no doubt that it ceased in Christ. For He is truth at whose presence all figures disappear. He is the one at whose coming shadows are left behind. ... But since the latter two reasons ought not to be reckoned with the old shadows but fit all ages equally, after the Sabbath was abrogated, among us it still has this place: that on set days we gather together to hear the word, to break the mystical bread [and] to pray publicly. ... Therefore, as truth was conveyed to the Jews under a figure, so it is commended to us without shadows: first, that we might throughout life meditate on an everlasting Sabbath; secondly, that we may observe a lawfully constituted order for the hearing of the Word, the administration of the sacraments, and public prayers; thirdly, that we may not inhumanly oppress those who are subject to us. [Calvin's First Catechism (1538), 12-13]

SEPTEMBER 10

Fifth Commandment

Honor your father and your mother, that your days may be long in the land that the LORD your God is giving you.

EXODUS 20:12

By this commandment we are enjoined to piety toward parents and toward those who by the Lord's ordaining are in authority over us in the place of parents, such as magistrates. That is, we are to render to them the highest reverence, obedience, gratefulness, and whatever duties we are capable of. For it is the Lord's will that we grant mutual service to those who have brought us into this life. It makes no difference whether those to whom this honor is paid are worthy or unworthy. For of whatever sort they may be, they have been set over us as parents by the Lord, who has willed us to honor them. And this indeed is the first commandment with a promise, as Paul says, by which the Lord promises the blessing of the present life to His children who reverence with fitting observance their parents. At the same time, He hints that the most certain curse hangs over all disobedient and unyielding children. However, it should be noted in passing that we are bidden to obey our parents only in the Lord. Accordingly, we are not required to break the law of the Lord to please them. For in that case we are not to consider as parents but rather as strangers those who try to steal us away from obedience to our true Father. [Calvin's First Catechism (1538), 13-14]

SEPTEMBER 11

Sixth Commandment

You shall not murder. EXODUS 20:13

The purpose of this commandment is: the Lord has bound humanity together by a certain unity; hence, each person ought to concern themselves with the safety of all. To sum up, then, all violence, injury, and any harmful thing at all that may injure our neighbor's body are forbidden to us. We are accordingly commanded, if we find anything of use to us in saving our neighbors' lives, faithfully to employ it; if there is anything that makes for their peace, to see to it; if anything harmful, to ward it off; if they are in any danger, to lend a helping hand. If you recall that God is speaking here as Lawgiver, ponder at the same time that by this rule He wills to guide your soul. For it would be ridiculous that He who looks upon the thoughts of the heart and dwells especially upon them, should instruct only the body in true righteousness. Therefore, this law also forbids murder of the heart, and enjoins the inner intent to save a brother's life. The hand, indeed gives birth to murder, but the mind when infected with anger and hatred conceives it. …

If you perpetrate anything by deed, if you plot anything by attempt, if you wish or plan anything contrary to the safety of a neighbor, you are considered guilty of murder. Again, unless you endeavor to look out for their safety according to your ability and opportunity, you are violating the law with a similar heinousness. But if there is so much concern for the safety of their body, from this we may infer how much zeal and effort we owe the safety of the soul, which far excels the body in the Lord's sight. [Institutes (1559), II.viii.39-40]

SEPTEMBER 12

Remaining at Our Post

Jesus answered, 'You do not know what you are asking. Are you able to drink the cup that I am to drink?' [The sons of Zebedee] said to him, 'We are able.'

MATTHEW 20:22

To correct the ambition [of James and John] and to withdraw them from this wicked desire, Jesus holds out to them the cross, and all the difficulties which the children of God must endure. It's as if Jesus had said, 'Does your present warfare allow you so much leisure that you are now making arrangements for a triumphal procession?'… Our Lord enjoins His followers, indeed, to feel assured of victory, and to sing a triumphal song in the midst of death; for otherwise they would not have courage to fight valiantly. But it is one thing to advance courageously into battle, in reliance on the reward which God has promised to them, and to labor with their whole might for this object; and it is another thing to forget the contest, to turn aside from the enemy, to lose sight of dangers, and to rush forward to a triumph, for which they ought to wait until the proper time. Besides, this foolish speed, for the most part, draws men and women aside from their callings. … Most properly, therefore, does Christ command those who were puffed up with vain glory to keep at their post. The sum of the whole is this, that for none but those who have fought lawfully is the crown prepared; and especially, that none will be a partaker of the life and the kingdom of Christ who has not previously shared in His sufferings and death. [Commentary on the Harmony of the Gospels]

SEPTEMBER 13

Ministries of the Holy Spirit

*'But when the Helper [or Comforter] comes, whom I will
send to you from the Father, the Spirit of truth, who proceeds
from the Father, he will bear witness about me.'*

JOHN 15:26

Christ now, in opposition to the wicked fury of men and women,
produces the testimony of the Spirit; if their consciences rest on
this testimony, they will never be shaken. ... The Spirit is said
to testify to Christ, because He retains and fixes our faith on
Him alone, that we may not seek elsewhere any part of our
salvation. [Christ] also calls Him the Comforter [or Helper]
so that, relying on His protection, we may never be alarmed;
for by this title Christ intended to fortify our faith that it may
not yield to any temptations. When He calls Him 'the Spirit
of truth,' we must apply the term to the matter at hand ...
[for] when men and women do not have this witness, they are
carried about in various ways, and have no firm resting-place,
but, wherever He speaks, He delivers their minds from all
doubts and fears of being deceived.

When [Christ] says that 'He will send Him from the
Father,' and again, that 'He proceeds from the Father,' He
does so in order to increase the weight of His authority; for the
testimony of the Spirit would not be sufficient against attacks
so powerful, and against efforts so numerous and fierce, if we
were not convinced that He 'proceeds from God.' So then, it is
Christ who sends the Spirit, but it is from the heavenly glory,
that we may know that it is not a gift from human beings, but a
sure pledge of divine grace. [Commentary on John]

SEPTEMBER 14

God's Glorious Character

The LORD is merciful and gracious, slow to anger and abounding in steadfast love.
PSALM 103:8

David seems to allude here to the exclamation of Moses, recorded in Exodus 34:6, where the nature of God, revealed in a remarkable way, is more clearly described than in other passages. When Moses was allowed to take a closer view of the divine glory than was usually granted, he exclaimed upon viewing it, 'O God! merciful and gracious, forgiving iniquity, slow to anger, and abounding in goodness.' Thus, since he has summarized in that passage all that is important for us to know concerning the divine character, David happily applies these terms describing God to his purpose here. … Moreover, we must understand in general that the true knowledge of God corresponds to what faith discovers in the written Word; for it is not His will that we should search into His secret essence, except in so far as He makes Himself known to us, a point worthy of our special notice. … To whatever subjects men and women apply their minds, there is none from which they will derive greater benefit than from continual meditation on His wisdom, goodness, righteousness, and mercy; and especially the knowledge of His goodness is fitted both to build up our faith and to illustrate His praises. Accordingly, in Ephesians 3:18, Paul declares that our height, length, breadth, and depth consists in knowing the unspeakable riches of grace, which have been demonstrated to us in Christ. This is also the reason why David, copying Moses, magnifies the mercy of God using a variety of terms. [Commentary on Psalms]

SEPTEMBER 15

God for Us

What then shall we say to these things? If God is for us, who can be against us?

ROMANS 8:31

Paul urges the saints to lay ahold, above all things, of the fatherly love of God so that, relying on this shield, they may boldly triumph over all evils. For this is a brazen wall to us, that as long as God is propitious to us we shall be safe against all dangers....

This is the chief and only support that can sustain us in every temptation. For unless God is favorable toward us – even if all circumstances should smile on us – we shall achieve no sure confidence. On the other hand, God's favor alone is a sufficient comfort in every sorrow, a sufficient protection that is strong against all the storms of adversities. And on this subject there are many testimonies of Scripture, which show that when the saints rely on the power of God alone, they can boldly despise what is opposed to them in the world. 'Even though I walk through the valley of the shadow of death, I will fear no evil, for you are with me' (Ps. 23:4). 'In God I trust; what can man do to me?' (Ps. 56:11). 'I will not be afraid of many thousands of people who have set themselves against me all around' (Ps. 3:6). For there is no power either under or above the heavens which can resist the arm of God. Having Him then as our defender, we need fear no harm whatsoever. Hence, that person alone shows real confidence in God who, being satisfied with His protection, dreads nothing that might cause them to become dejected; certainly, believers are often shaken but are never completely cast down. [Commentary on Romans]

SEPTEMBER 16

Seventh Commandment

You shall not commit adultery.

EXODUS 20:14

[B]ecause God loves modesty and purity, all uncleanness must be far from us. ... We should not become defiled with any filth or lustful intemperance of the flesh. To this corresponds the affirmative commandment that we chastely and continently regulate all parts of our life. But He expressly forbids fornication, to which all lust tends. ...

Man has been created in this condition that he may not lead a solitary life, but may enjoy a helper joined to himself (Gen. 2:18). Then, by the curse of sin, he has been even more subjected to this necessity. Therefore, the Lord sufficiently provided for us in this matter when He established marriage, the fellowship of which, begun on His authority, He also sanctified by His blessing. From this it is clear that any other union apart from marriage is accursed in God's sight; and that the companionship of marriage has been ordained as a necessary remedy to keep us from plunging into unbridled lust. ...

If the Lord requires modesty of us, He condemns whatever opposes it. Consequently, if you aspire to obedience, let neither your heart burn with wicked lust within, nor your eyes wantonly run into corrupt desires, nor your body be decked with bawdy ornaments, nor your tongue seduce your mind to similar thoughts with filthy words, nor your appetite inflame it with intemperance. For all vices of this sort are like blemishes, which besmirch the purity of chastity. [Institutes (1559), II.viii.41, 44].

SEPTEMBER 17

Eighth Commandment

You shall not steal. EXODUS 20:15

The commandment means: Since God is to be feared and loved by us, we are not to snatch by fraud or seize by force what belongs to another. We are not to catch anyone unawares in bargaining or contracts, either by selling too expensively, or buying too cheaply from those who are ignorant of the prices of things. Nor are we to lay hands on another person's property by any sort of guile whatsoever. But, if there is in us any fear or love of God, we are rather to press with every effort to aid either friend or foe, as much as we can with advice and help, to hold onto their possessions, and we are rather to give up our own than take away anything from another. And not this alone, but if they are pressed by any material difficulty, we are to share their needs and relieve their poverty with our substance. [Institutes (1536), 26]

SEPTEMBER 18

Spirit and Truth

'But when the Helper [or Comforter] comes, whom I will send to you from the Father, the Spirit of truth, who proceeds from the Father, he will bear witness about me.'

JOHN 15:26

[W]hen the world rages on all sides, our only protection is that the truth of God, sealed by the Holy Spirit on our hearts, despises and defies all that is in the world; for if it were subject to the opinions of human beings, our faith would be overwhelmed a hundred times a day.

We ought, therefore, to observe carefully in what manner we ought to remain firm among so many storms. It is because 'we have received not the spirit of the world, but the Spirit who is from God, that we might understand the things freely given us by God' (1 Cor. 2:12). This single witness powerfully drives away, scatters, and overturns all that the world rears up to obscure or crush the truth of God. All who are endued with this Spirit are so far from being in danger of falling into despondency on account of the hatred or contempt of the world, that every one of them will obtain a glorious victory over the whole world. Yet we must beware of relying on the good opinion of other people; for so long as faith shall wander in this manner, or rather, as soon as it shall have gone out of the sanctuary of God, it will become involved in miserable uncertainty. It must, therefore, be brought back to the inward and secret testimony of the Spirit, which believers know, has been given to them from heaven. [Commentary on John]

SEPTEMBER 19

Invisible Yet Glorious

Bless the LORD, O my soul! O LORD my God, you are very great! You are clothed with splendor and majesty, covering yourself with light as with a garment ...

PSALM 104:1-2

After having exhorted himself to praise God [in Psalm 103], the Psalmist adds that there are abundant reasons for such an exercise. Thus, he indirectly condemns himself and others for ingratitude if the praises of God ... are buried in silence. In comparing the light with which God is clothed to a garment, he intimates that although God is invisible, yet His glory is conspicuous enough. With respect to His essence, God undoubtedly dwells in light that is inaccessible; but as He irradiates the whole world by His splendor, this is the garment in which He, who is hidden in Himself, appears in a manner visible to us. The knowledge of this truth is of the greatest importance. If anyone attempts to reach the infinite height to which God is exalted, although they fly above the clouds, they will certainly fail in the midst of their course. Those who seek to see God in His naked majesty are certainly very foolish. That we may enjoy the sight of Him, we must come forth to view Him with His clothing; that is to say, we must cast our eyes upon the very beautiful fabric of the world in which He wishes to be seen by us, and not be too curious and rash in searching into His secret essence. Now, since God presents Himself to us clothed with light, those who are looking for an excuse to live without the knowledge of Him, cannot justify their slothfulness by alleging that He is hidden in profound darkness. [Commentary on Psalms]

SEPTEMBER 20

Security for the Elect

'For false christs and false prophets will arise and perform great signs and wonders, so as to lead astray, if possible, even the elect.'

MATTHEW 24:24

Christ therefore exhorts and arouses His disciples to keep watch, and at the same time reminds them that there is no reason for being troubled at the strangeness of the sight, if they see many persons on every hand led away into error. While He excites them to watchfulness so that Satan may not overtake them in a state of laziness, He gives them abundant ground of confidence on which they may calmly rely, when He promises that they will be safe under the defense and protection of God against all the snares of Satan. And thus, however frail and slippery the condition of the godly may be, yet here is a firm footing on which they may stand; for it is not possible for them to fall away from salvation, to whom the Son of God is a faithful guardian. For they do not have sufficient energy to resist the attacks of Satan, except for the fact that they are the sheep of Christ, 'and no one will snatch them out of His hand' (John 10:28). It must therefore be observed that the permanency of our salvation does not depend on us, but on the secret election of God; for though our salvation is 'guarded through faith,' as Peter tells us (1 Pet. 1:5), yet we ought to ascend higher, and assure ourselves that we are in a safe condition, because the Father has given us to the Son, and the Son Himself declares that 'none of those who have been given to Him shall perish' (John 17:12). [Commentary on the Harmony of the Gospels]

SEPTEMBER 21

Love One Another

Above all, keep loving one another earnestly, since love covers a multitude of sins.
1 PETER 4:8

Peter commends charity or love as the first thing, for it is the bond of perfection. And he emphasizes that it is to be fervent, or intense, or vehement, which is the same thing; for whoever is immoderately fervent in self-love, loves others coldly. And he commends it on account of its fruit, because it buries innumerable sins...

Now the sentence is taken from Solomon, whose words are found in Proverbs 10:12: 'Hatred stirs up strife, but love covers all offenses.' What Solomon meant is sufficiently clear, for the two clauses contain things which are set in contrast the one with the other. For, as he states in the first clause that hatred is the reason why people vilify and defame one another, and spread reproachful and dishonorable words, so the opposite effect is ascribed to love, that is, the people who love one another, kindly and courteously forgive one another – hence, they willingly bury each other's vices and seek to preserve the honor of the other. Thus, Peter confirms his exhortation, that nothing is more necessary than to cherish mutual love. For who is there that doesn't have many faults? Therefore, all stand in need of forgiveness, and there is no one who does not wish to be forgiven.

This, then, is the singular benefit that love brings when it exists among us – innumerable evils are covered in oblivion. On the other hand, when people give loose reign to hatred, they are consumed by mutual biting and tearing of one another, as Paul says in Galatians 5:15. [Commentary on 1 Peter]

SEPTEMBER 22

Private Admonitions

'I did not shrink from declaring to you anything that was profitable, and teaching you in public and from house to house ...'

ACTS 20:20

Paul not only taught all men and women in the congregation, but also every one privately, as need required. For Christ has not appointed pastors upon this condition, that they only teach the Church in general in the open pulpit; but that they should take charge of every particular sheep, that they may bring back to the sheepfold those that wander and go astray, that they may strengthen those that are discouraged and weak, that they may cure the sick, that they may lift up and set on foot the feeble (Ezek. 34:4). For the general teaching of doctrine will oftentimes wax cold, unless it be strengthened with private admonitions. Hence, the negligence of those men is inexcusable who, having delivered one sermon (as if they had done their duty!) spend all the rest of their time in idleness, as if their voice was shut up within the church walls or their lips became dumb once they departed the church! Here disciples and students are also taught that if they will be numbered among Christ's flock, they must be attentive to their pastors whenever they come to them, and that they must not refuse private admonitions. For they are more like bears than sheep who refuse to gratefully heed the voice of their pastor unless he is in the pulpit; and cannot endure being admonished and reproved at home, indeed, fiercely resisting that necessary duty. [Commentary on Acts]

SEPTEMBER 23

Ninth Commandment

You shall not bear false witness against your neighbor.

EXODUS 20:16

[S]ince God (who is truth) abhors a lie we must practice truth without deceit toward one another. To sum up, then, let us not malign anyone with slanders or false charges, nor harm their substance by falsehood, in short, injure Him by unbridled evil-speaking and impudence. To this prohibition the command is linked that we should faithfully help everyone as much as we can in affirming the truth, in order to protect the integrity of their name and possessions. It seems that the Lord intended to express the meaning of this commandment in Exodus 23:1, in these words: 'You shall not spread a false report. You shall not join hands with a wicked man to be a malicious witness.'...

And yet it is shocking with what thoughtless unconcern we sin in this respect time and again! Those who do not markedly suffer from this disease are rare indeed. We delight in a certain poisoned sweetness, experienced in ferreting out and in disclosing the evils of others. And let us not think it an adequate excuse if in many instances we are not lying. For he who does not allow a brother's name to be sullied by falsehood also wishes it to be kept unblemished as far as truth permits. ... That God is concerned about it should be enough to prompt us to keep safe our neighbor's good name. Hence, evil-speaking is without a doubt universally condemned. [Institutes (1559), II.viii.48]

SEPTEMBER

SEPTEMBER 24

Tenth Commandment

You shall not covet your neighbor's house; you shall not covet your neighbor's wife, or his male servant, or his female servant, or his ox, or his donkey, or anything that is your neighbor's.

EXODUS 20:17

By this commandment the Lord imposes a bridle upon all our desires which outstrip the bounds of charity. For all that the other commandments forbid us to commit in action against the rule of love, this one prohibits from being conceived in the heart. Accordingly, by this commandment hatred, envy, and ill-will are condemned, just as much as murder was previously condemned. Lust and inner filth of heart, just as much as fornication, are forbidden. Where previously rapacity and cunning were restrained, here avarice is; where cursing, here spite is curbed.

We see how general the scope of this commandment is and how far and wide it extends. For God requires a wonderful affection and a love of the brethren of surpassing ardor, which He does not wish even by any desire to be aroused against a neighbor's possessions and advantage. This then is the sum of the commandment: we ought to be so minded as not to be tickled by any longing contrary to the law of love, and be prepared utterly freely to render to each what is their own. We must reckon as belonging to each person what we own then out of our duty. [Calvin's First Catechism (1538), 15]

SEPTEMBER 25

Love and Worship

And [Jesus] said to him, 'You shall love the Lord your God with all your heart and with all your soul and with all of your mind. This is the great and first commandment.'

MATTHEW 22:37-38

What follows is an abridgment of the Law, which is also found in the writings of Moses (Deut. 6:5). For, though the Law is divided into two tables, the first of which relates to the worship of God, and the second to charity, Moses properly and wisely draws up this summary, so that the Jews may perceive what is the will of God in each of the commandments. And although we ought to love God far more than human beings, yet God most properly requires love from us (instead of worship or honor), because in this way He declares that no other worship of Him is pleasing to Him than that which is voluntary; for no man or woman will actually obey God unless they love Him. But as the wicked and sinful inclinations of the flesh draw us aside from what is right, Moses shows that our life will not be regulated aright until the love of God fills all our senses. Let us therefore learn that the beginning of godliness is the love of God, because God disdains the forced service of humans, and chooses to be worshiped freely and willingly; and let us also learn that under the love of God is included the reference due Him. ... Lastly, we learn from this, that God does not rest satisfied with the outward appearances of works, but chiefly demands the inward feelings, that from a good root good fruits may grow. [Commentary on the Harmony of the Gospels]

SEPTEMBER 26

Prepared for Battle

'I have said all these things to you to keep you from falling away.'

JOHN 16:1

[Jesus] again states that none of those things which He has spoken are superfluous; for, since wars and contests await the disciples, it is necessary that they should be provided beforehand with the necessary weapons. Yet He also means that, if they meditate deeply on His teaching, they will be fully prepared for resistance. … [W]hat He then said to His disciples is also spoken to us. And, first, we ought to understand that Christ does not send His followers into combat unarmed; therefore, if anyone fails in this warfare, they have their own laziness to blame. And yet we ought not to wait till the struggle is actually commenced, but ought rather to endeavor to become well acquainted with these teachings of Christ, and commit them to memory, so that we may march into the field of battle, as soon as it is necessary; for we must not doubt that the victory is in our hands, so long as Christ's admonitions are deeply imprinted on our minds. For when He says 'to keep you from falling away,' He means that there is no danger, lest anything turn us aside from the right course. But how few there are that learn this doctrine in a proper manner, is evident from this fact, that they who think that they know these teachings by heart when they are beyond arrow-shot, are no sooner forced to enter into actual combat than they give way, as if they were utterly ignorant, and had never received any instruction. Let us therefore accustom ourselves to use this armor in such a manner that it may never drop out of our hands. [Commentary on John]

SEPTEMBER 27

Winds of Providence

He makes the clouds his chariot; he rides on the wings of the wind; he makes his messengers the winds, his ministers a flaming fire.

PSALM 104:3-4

[W]e do not need to pierce our way above the clouds to find God, since He meets us in the fabric of the world. ... What is meant by His 'riding on the wings of the wind' is rendered more obvious from the following verse, where it is said that the winds are His messengers. God rides on the clouds, and is carried upon the wings of the wind, inasmuch as He drives about the winds and clouds at His pleasure, and by sending them here and there as swiftly as He pleases, thereby showing the signs of His presence. By these words we are taught that the winds do not blow by chance, nor the lightning flashes by the impulse of fortune, but that God, in exercising His sovereign power, rules and controls all the agitations and disturbances of the atmosphere. From this doctrine we may reap a twofold benefit. In the first place, if at any time harmful winds arise, if the south wind corrupts the air, or if the north wind scorches the corn, and not only tears up trees by the roots, but overthrows houses, and if other winds destroy the fruits of the earth, we ought to tremble under these scourges of divine providence. In the second place, if, on the other hand, God moderates the excessive heat by a gentle cooling breeze, if He purifies the polluted atmosphere by the north wind, or if He moistens the parched ground by south winds; in this we ought to contemplate His goodness. [Commentary on Psalms]

SEPTEMBER 28

No Accusation

Who shall bring any charge against God's elect? It is God who justifies.

ROMANS 8:33

The first and chief consolation of the godly in the face of adversities, is to be fully persuaded of the fatherly kindness of God. For from this arises the certainty of their salvation and that calm quietness of the soul which sweetens the bitterness of adversities, or at least mitigates their sorrow. One can imagine hardly a more suitable encouragement for patience than this: the conviction that God is favorable toward us. And thus, Paul makes this confidence the main ground of that consolation, which makes it possible for the faithful to be strengthened against all evils. And since the salvation of a man or woman is first of all assailed by accusation, and then subverted by condemnation, Paul begins by averting the danger of accusation. There is indeed but one God, at whose tribunal we must stand; there is no room then for accusation when He justifies us. ...

It must be here observed that to be justified, according to Paul, is to be absolved by the sentence of God, and to be counted just; and this is not difficult to prove from the present passage in which Paul reasons by affirming one thing which nullifies its opposite; for to absolve and to regard persons as guilty are contrary things. Hence God will allow no accusation against us, because He has absolved us from all sins. The devil no doubt is an accuser of all the godly; the law of God itself and their own conscience convict them; but all these prevail nothing with the judge, who justifies them. Therefore, no adversary can shake or endanger their salvation. [Commentary on Romans]

SEPTEMBER 29

Work and Generosity

We hear that some among you walk in idleness, not busy at work, but busybodies. Now such persons we command and encourage in the Lord Jesus Christ to do their work quietly and to earn their own living.

2 Thessalonians 3:11-12

Paul corrects both faults mentioned above – a blustering restlessness and a retirement from useful employment. Accordingly, he exhorts the Thessalonians to remain quietly within the limits of their calling. ... For the truth is this: those people are most peaceable of all who busy themselves in legitimate employments, while those who have nothing to do give trouble both to themselves and to others. Moreover, he adds another precept – that they should 'work,' that is, that they should be intent upon their calling, and devote themselves to lawful and honorable employments. ... Hence, also, there follows this third command – that they should eat their own bread; by which he means that they should be satisfied with what belongs to them, that they may not be oppressive or unreasonable to others. 'Drink water,' says Solomon, 'from your own cistern, and let the streams flow down to neighbors' (Prov. 5:15). This is the first law of equity, that no one make use of what belongs to another, but only use what they can properly call their own. The second is that no one swallow up (like some abyss) what belongs to themselves, but that they be generous to their neighbors, so that by their abundance they may relieve the indigence of others. In the same way, the Apostle exhorts those who had been formerly idle 'to do their work,' not merely so that they may gain for themselves a livelihood, but so that they may also be helpful to the needs of their neighbor. [Commentary on 2 Thessalonians]

SEPTEMBER 30

Election and Free Grace

I am not praying for the world but for those whom you have given me, for they are yours.

JOHN 17:9

Hitherto Christ has brought forward what related to the disciples' favor with the Father. He now forms the prayer itself, in which He shows that He asks nothing but what is agreeable to the will of the Father, because He pleads with the Father on behalf of those only whom the Father Himself willingly loves. ...

[W]e learn from these words, that God chooses out of the world those whom He thinks fit to choose to be heirs of life, and that this distinction is not made according to human merits, but depends on [God's] mere good pleasure. ... Christ expressly declares that those who are given to Him belong to the Father; and it is certain that they are given so as to believe, and that faith flows from this act of giving. If the origin of faith is this act of giving, and if election comes before it in order and time, what remains but that we acknowledge that those whom God wishes to be saved out of the world are elected by free grace? Now, since Christ prays for the elect only, it is necessary for us to believe the doctrine of election, if we wish that He should plead with the Father for our salvation. A grievous injury, therefore, is inflicted on believers by those persons who endeavor to blot out the knowledge of election from the hearts of believers, because they deprive them of the pleading and intercession of the Son of God. [Commentary on John]

OCTOBER 1

Godly Temperance

You cause ... wine to gladden the heart of man, oil to make his face shine and bread to strengthen man's heart.

PSALM 104:15

In these words we are taught that God not only provides for people's necessity, and gives them as much as is sufficient for the ordinary purposes of life, but that in His goodness He deals still more bountifully with them by cheering their hearts with wine and oil. Nature would certainly be satisfied with water to drink; and therefore, the addition of wine is due to God's superabundant generosity. ...

But as there is nothing to which we are more prone than to abuse God's benefits by giving into excess, the more generous [God] is toward people, the more they ought to be careful not to pollute, by their intemperance, the abundance which is given to them. Paul therefore had good reasons for giving that prohibition in Romans 13:14: 'Make no provision for the flesh, to gratify its desires.' For there will be no limits if we give full scope to our fleshly desires. As God generously provides for us, so He has appointed a law of temperance, that each person may voluntarily restrain themselves in their abundance. ... The proper rule with respect to the use of bodily sustenance, then, is to partake of it so that it may sustain us, but not oppress us. The mutual sharing of those things necessary for bodily support, which God has commanded of us, is a very good check to our intemperance; for the wealthy are favored with their abundance ... so that they might relieve the needs of their brothers and sisters. [Commentary on Psalms]

OCTOBER 2

True Confession

Deliver me from all my transgressions. Do not make me the scorn of the fool!

PSALM 39:8

In this verse the Psalmist still continues his godly and holy prayer. He is now no longer carried away by the violence of his grief to murmur against God, but, humbly acknowledging himself guilty before God, he has recourse to His mercy. In asking to be delivered from his transgressions, he ascribes the praise of righteousness to God, while he charges upon himself the blame of all the misery which he endures; and he blames himself not only on account of one sin, but acknowledges that he is justly guilty of manifold transgressions. By this rule we must be guided if we would wish to obtain any alleviation of our miseries; for, until the very source of our sins has been dried up, they will never cease to follow one another in rapid succession. David unquestionably wished an alleviation of his miseries, but, as he expected that, as soon as he should be reconciled to God, the chastisement of his sins would also cease, he only here asks that his sins may be forgiven him. We are thus taught by the example of David, not merely to seek deliverance from the miseries which afflict and trouble us, but to trace them to their cause and source, entreating God that He would not lay our sins to our charge, but blot out our guilt. [Commentary on Psalms]

OCTOBER 3

Invincible Faith

Some were tortured, refusing to accept release, so that they might rise again to a better life. Others suffered mocking and flogging, and even chains and imprisonment.

HEBREWS 11:35-36

The author already mentioned instances in which God has rewarded the faith of His servants; he now refers to those saints, who, reduced to extreme miseries, struggled by faith so as to persevere invincible even to death. ... These [latter examples] seem to have been treated very differently than the former ones, and yet faith ruled in both and was powerful in both. Nay, rather, in the latter example God's power shone forth in a much clearer light. For the victory of faith appears more splendid in the contempt of death than if life were extended to five generations. Faith is more gloriously evidenced, and worthy of higher praise, when insults, poverty, and extreme troubles are borne with resignation and firmness, than when people experience a miraculous recovery from sickness, or any other benefit from God.

In summary, then, the endurance of the saints, which shone forth in all ages, was the work of faith; for our weakness is such that we are not capable of overcoming evils, unless faith sustains us. Thus, we learn from this that all who really trust in God are endued with sufficient power to resist Satan in whatever way he may attack them, and especially that patience in enduring evils shall never be lacking in us, if we possess faith. Hence, we are proved guilty of unbelief when we faint under persecution and the cross. For the nature of faith is the same now as in the days of the holy fathers whom the author here mentions. If then we imitate their faith, we will never faithlessly break down through laziness or weakness. [Commentary on Hebrews]

OCTOBER 4

Living for Christ

Or do you not know that your body is the temple of the Holy Spirit within you, whom you have from God? You are not your own, for you were bought with a price. So glorify God in your body.

1 CORINTHIANS 6:19-20

Now the great thing is this: we are consecrated and dedicated to God in order that we may thereafter think, speak, meditate, and do, nothing except to His glory. For a sacred thing may not be applied to profane uses without marked injury to Him. ... We are not our own: let not our reason nor our will, therefore, sway our plans and deeds. We are not our own: let us therefore not set it as our goal to seek what is expedient for us according to the flesh. We are not our own: in so far as we can, let us therefore forget ourselves and all that is ours. Conversely, we are God's: let us therefore live for Him and die for Him. We are God's: let His wisdom and will therefore rule all our actions. We are God's: let all the parts of our life accordingly strive toward Him as our only lawful goal. O, how much has the man or woman profited who, having seen that they are not their own, have taken away dominion and rule from their own reason that they may yield it to God! For, just as consulting our self-interest is the pestilence that most effectively leads to our destruction, so the sole haven of salvation is to be wise in nothing and to will nothing through ourselves but to follow the leading of the Lord alone. [Institutes (1559), III.vii.1]

OCTOBER 5

No Condemnation

Who is to condemn? Christ Jesus is the one who died – more than that, who was raised – who is at the right hand of God, who indeed is interceding for us. ROMANS 8:34

Christ is the one who, having once for all suffered the punishment due to us, thereby declared that He undertook our cause, in order to deliver us. ... He has not only died, but also came forth, by a resurrection, as the conqueror of death, and triumphed over all its power. Paul adds still more – that Christ now sits at the right hand of the Father; by which is meant that He possesses dominion over heaven and earth, and full power and rule over all things (as he states in Eph. 1:20). Paul also teaches us that Christ is seated so that He may be a perpetual advocate and intercessor in securing our salvation. It thus follows that when someone seeks to condemn us, they not only attempt to render void the death of Christ, but also contend with that unequalled power with which the Father has honored Christ – a power that also confers on Him supreme authority. This great ground of assurance, which triumphs over the devil, death, sin, and the gates of hell, ought to lodge deep in the hearts of all godly people; for our faith is nothing, unless we experience assurance that Christ is ours, and that the Father is favorable toward us in Christ. ...

Even though, from His elevated throne, Christ holds all things in subjection under His feet, yet Paul represents Him as a Mediator, whose presence would be strange for us to fear, since He not only kindly invites us to Himself, but also appears as an intercessor for us before the Father. [Commentary on Romans]

OCTOBER 6

The Diligent Pastor

'Pay careful attention to yourselves and to all the flock, in which the Holy Spirit has made you overseers, to care for the church of God, which he obtained with his own blood.'

ACTS 20:28

Paul now applies his speech to [the Ephesian elders], and with many reasons shows that they must watch diligently, and that no one can be too careful as necessity requires. The first reason is because they are bound to the flock over which they have been appointed. The second, because they were called to this ministry not by mortal man, but by the Holy Spirit. The third, because it is no small honor to govern the Church of God. The fourth, because the Lord has declared by clear testimony the great importance He ascribes to the Church, seeing that He has redeemed it by His blood. Regarding the first, Paul not only commands them to take heed to the flock, but first to themselves. For those who neglect their own salvation will never care for the salvation of others. And those who show no desire for godliness will be unsuccessful in pricking others to pursue it. Indeed, that man will not show concern for his flock who ignores himself, seeing that he too is part of the flock. Therefore, so that the elders may attend to the flock committed to their care, Paul commands and warns each of them to keep themselves in the fear of God. ... For Paul reasons from their calling, that the elders are required to be diligent in the Church of God, over which they have leadership. It's as if he were saying, that they cannot do whatever they would like to do ... but they are publicly bound to the well-being of their flock. [Commentary on Acts]

OCTOBER 7

Spiritual Combat

I do not ask that you take them out of the world, but that you keep them from the evil one.
JOHN 17:15

[Christ] shows in what the safety of believers consists; not that they are free from every annoyance and live in luxury and at their ease, but that, in the midst of dangers, they continue to be safe through the assistance of God. For He does not admonish the Father of what is proper to be done, but rather makes provision for their weakness, that, by the method which He prescribes, they may restrain their desires, which are apt to go beyond all bounds. In short, He promises to His disciples the grace of the Father; not to relieve them from all anxiety and toil, but to furnish them with invincible strength against their enemies, and not to allow them to be overwhelmed by the heavy burden of spiritual battles which they will have to endure. If, therefore, we wish to be kept according to the rule which Christ has laid down, we must not desire exemption from evils, or pray to God to remove us immediately into a state of blessed rest, but must rest satisfied with the certain assurance of victory, and, in the meantime, resist courageously all the evils, from which Christ prayed to His Father that we might have a happy outcome. In short, God does not take His people out of the world, because He does not wish them to be effeminate and slothful; but He delivers them from evil, that they may not be overwhelmed; for He wishes them to fight, but does not allow them to be mortally wounded. [Commentary on John]

OCTOBER 8

God's Deliverance

Some sat in darkness and in the shadow of death, prisoners in affliction and in irons, for they had rebelled against the words of God, and spurned the counsel of the Most High.

PSALM 107:10-11

The Spirit of God mentions here another kind of danger through which God clearly demonstrates His power and grace in protecting and delivering men and women. The world ... calls these circumstances the sport of fortune, and hardly one person in a hundred can be found who ascribes them to the superintending providence of God. Here He expects of us a different kind of practical wisdom, namely, that we ought to meditate on His judgments in the time of adversity, and on His goodness when He delivers us from it. For surely it is not by mere chance when people fall into the hands of enemies or robbers; neither is it by chance that they are rescued from them. But this is what we must constantly keep in mind, that all afflictions are God's disciplining rod, and that therefore there is no remedy for them except in His grace. If a person falls into the hands of robbers or pirates, and they are not instantly murdered, ... the deliverance of such a person is a striking proof of God's grace, which shines all the more brightly in proportion to the small number of people who make their escape. Thus, when a great number of people perish, this circumstance should in no way diminish praises of God. On this account the prophet charges all those with ingratitude who, after they have been wonderfully rescued, very soon lose sight of the deliverance bestowed on them. [Commentary on Psalms]

OCTOBER 9

The Believer's Hope

But I am like a green olive tree in the house of God. I trust in the steadfast love of God forever and ever.

PSALM 52:8

[H]ere let us engrave the useful lesson upon our hearts, that we should consider it the great goal of our existence to be found numbered among the worshipers of God; and that we should take advantage of the inestimable privilege of the gathered assemblies of the Church, which are necessary helps to our weakness and a means of mutual edification and encouragement. By these, along with our common sacraments, the Lord, who is one God, and who intended that we should be one in Him, is training us up together in the hope of eternal life, and in the united celebration of His holy name. Let us learn with David to prefer a place in the house of God to all the deceptive vanities of this world. He adds the reasons why he should be like the green olive tree – because he hoped in the goodness of God. ... And in this he points to the contrast between himself and his enemies. They may flourish for a time, spread their branches far and wide, and shoot themselves up to a gigantic size, but will quickly wither away, because they have no root in the goodness of God; whereas [David] was certain to derive from this divine source ever renewed supplies of sap and strength. ... [Here we see] the great distinction between the genuine children of God and those who are hypocrites. They are to be found together in the Church, ... but the one abides forever in a steadfast and well-founded hope, while the other is driven away in the vanity of its false confidences. [Commentary on Psalms]

OCTOBER 10

Redemption Is Near

'Now when these things begin to take place, straighten up and raise your heads, because your redemption is drawing near.'

LUKE 21:28

Luke expresses more clearly the consolation by which Christ animates the minds of His followers. ... For it was necessary to contrast the joy of the godly with the general sorrow and distress of the world, and to point out the difference between them and the reprobate, that they might not view with horror the coming of Christ. We know that Scripture, when it speaks not only of the last judgment, but of all the judgments which God executes every day, describes them in a variety of ways, depending on whether the discourse is addressed to believers or to unbelievers. ... Christ therefore shows that, at His coming, the light of joy will arise on His disciples, that they may rejoice in the approaching salvation, while the wicked are overwhelmed with terror. Accordingly, Paul distinguishes them by this mark, that they 'wait for the revealing of our Lord Jesus Christ' (1 Cor. 1:7) for that which is their crown, and perfect happiness, and solace, is delayed till that day (2 Tim. 4:8). ... Let our ears therefore be awake for the sound of the angel's trumpet, which will then sound, not only to strike the reprobate with the dread of death, but to arouse the elect to a second life; that is, to call to the enjoyment of life those whom the Lord now quickens by the voice of His gospel; for it is a sign of infidelity to be afraid when the Son of God comes in person for our salvation. [Commentary on the Harmony of the Gospels]

OCTOBER 11

Expiation for Sin

He himself bore our sins in his body on the tree, that we might die to sin and live to righteousness. By his wounds you have been healed.

1 PETER 2:24

There are three things to be noticed in this passage. The first is that Christ by His death has given us an example of patience; the second, that by His death He restored us to life; it hence follows, that we are so bound to Him, that we ought cheerfully to follow His example. In the third place, He refers to the general purpose of His death, that we, being dead to sins, ought to live to righteousness. ...

Peter, therefore, expresses well the truth that Christ's death was a sacrifice for the expiation of our sins; for being fixed to the cross and offering Himself as a victim for us, He took on Himself our sin and our punishment. Isaiah, from whom Peter has taken the substance of his doctrine, employs various forms of expression, [stating] that He was smitten by God's hand for our sins, that He was wounded for our iniquities, that He was afflicted and broken for our sake, that the chastisement of our peace was laid on Him. But Peter intended to set forth the same thing by the words of this verse, even that we are reconciled to God on this condition, because Christ made Himself before His tribunal a pledge and as one guilty for us, that He might suffer the punishment that we deserved. [Commentary on 1 Peter]

OCTOBER 12

Labyrinth of Predestination

*What shall we say then? Is there injustice on God's part?
By no means! For he says to Moses, 'I will have mercy on
whom I have mercy, and I will have compassion on whom
I have compassion.'*

ROMANS 9:14-15

The predestination of God is indeed in reality a labyrinth, from
which the human mind can by no means extricate itself. But
so unreasonable is the curiosity of men and women, that the
more perilous the study of a subject may be, the more boldly
they proceed. Thus, when predestination is discussed, because
they cannot restrain themselves within appropriate limits,
they immediately through their rashness plunge themselves (as
it were) into the depth of the sea. What remedy then is there
for the godly man or woman? Must they avoid every thought
of predestination? By no means! For as the Holy Spirit has
taught us nothing but what is necessary for us to know, so
the knowledge of this [doctrine] would no doubt be useful,
provided it be confined to the word of God. Let this then be
our sacred rule, that we seek to know nothing concerning
predestination except what Scripture teaches us. ...

In order to remove the difficulty [of God's apparent
unrighteousness], Paul divides his subject into two parts. In the
former he speaks of the elect, and in the latter of the reprobate.
In the former he would have us contemplate the mercy of God,
and in the latter to acknowledge God's righteous judgment.
Paul's first reply is that the thought that there is injustice with
God deserves to be abhorred. Thereafter, he shows that with
regard to the elect and reprobate, there can be no injustice.
[Commentary on Romans]

OCTOBER 13

God's Incomprehensible Wisdom

*To the King of the ages, immortal, invisible, the only God,
be honor and glory forever and ever. Amen.*

1 TIMOTHY 1:17

Paul's amazing vehemence at length breaks out into this exclamation; because he could not find the words to express his gratitude. Indeed, sudden outbursts of this kind occur primarily when we are constrained to break off a discourse because we have been overpowered by the vastness of the subject. And is there anything more astonishing than Paul's conversion? Yet, at the same time, by his example he reminds all of us that we ought never to think of the grace manifested in God's calling without being carried to lofty adoration.

'Eternal, invisible, only wise.' This sublime praise of the grace which God has bestowed on Him swallows up the memory of His former life. For how great and deep is the glory of God! Those attributes which Paul ascribes to God, though they belong to Him always, are admirably adapted to the present occasion. The apostle calls Him the King of the ages, for He's not liable to any change; Invisible, because He dwells in light that is inaccessible (1 Tim. 6:16); and lastly, the Only Wise God, because He renders foolish, and condemns as vanity, all human wisdom. The whole agrees with that conclusion at which he arrives: 'Oh, the depth of the riches and wisdom and knowledge of God! How unsearchable are His judgments and how inscrutable His ways!' (Rom. 11:33). Paul means that we should behold the infinite and incomprehensible wisdom of God with such reverence that, if His works surpass our senses, we should still be restrained by wonder. [Commentary on 1 Timothy]

OCTOBER 14

Christ's Prayer for Believers

'I do not ask for these only, but also for those who will believe in me through their word.'
JOHN 17:20

[Christ] now gives a wider range to His prayer, which hitherto had included the apostles alone; for He extends it to all the disciples of the gospel ... to the end of the world. This is assuredly a remarkable ground of confidence; for if we believe in Christ through the doctrine of the gospel, we ought to entertain no doubt that we are already gathered with the apostles into His faithful protection, so that not one of us shall perish. This prayer of Christ is a safe harbor, and whoever retreats into it is safe from all danger of shipwreck; for it is as if Christ had solemnly sworn that He will devote His care and diligence to our salvation. ...

[T]herefore, whenever Satan attacks us, let us learn to meet him with this shield, that it is with good reason that the Son of God united us with the apostles, so that the salvation of all was bound up, as it were, in the same bundle. There is nothing, therefore, that ought more powerfully to excite us to embrace the gospel; for as it is an inestimable blessing that we are presented to God by the hand of Christ, to be preserved from destruction, so we ought justly to love it, and to care for it above all things else. ... Let the world condemn us a thousand times, this alone ought to satisfy us, that Christ acknowledges us to be His heritage, and pleads with the Father for us. [Commentary on John]

OCTOBER 15

Praying and Cursing

When he is tried, let him come forth guilty; let his prayer be counted as sin! May his days be few; may another take his office! May his children be fatherless and his wife a widow!

PSALM 109:7-9

Regarding the imprecations contained in this psalm, it is important to keep in mind … that when David forms such curses, or expresses his desires for them, he is not moved by any immoderate carnal disposition, nor is he motivated by zeal without knowledge, nor is he influenced by any private personal considerations. These three matters must be carefully considered, for in proportion to the amount of self-love that a man or woman possesses, to that degree they are so enamored by their own interests that they rush headlong into revenge. Hence it happens that the more people are devoted to selfishness, the more they are immoderately addicted to the advancement of their own individual interests. This desire for the promotion of one's personal interests gives birth to another type of vice. For no one desires vengeance on their enemies because such a thing would be right and equitable, but because it is the means to gratify their own spiteful tendency. Some, indeed, make a pretext of righteousness and equity in the matter, but the spirit of hatred, with which they are inflamed, erases every trace of justice, and blinds their minds. …

[L]et believers be on their guard, lest they should betray too much haste in their prayers, and let them rather leave room for the grace of God to manifest itself in their behalf, because it may turn out that the man or woman, who today bears toward us a deadly hatred, may by tomorrow through God's grace become our friend. [Commentary on Psalms]

OCTOBER 16

Ministry of Hospitality

Do not neglect to show hospitality to strangers, for thereby some have entertained angels unawares.
HEBREWS 13:2

This ministry of compassion has nearly ceased to be correctly observed in human society, for the ancient hospitality – which was celebrated in the histories – is unknown to us and inns now supply the place where foreigners find accommodation. But the author here is speaking not so much about the practice of hospitality that the wealthy once practiced; rather, he is commending that hospitality be shown to the miserable and the needy, since at that time there were many fugitives who left their homes for the name of Christ.

And so as to commend this duty all the more, he adds that angels had sometimes been entertained by those who thought that they received only fellow human beings. I do not doubt that he is making reference to Abraham and Lot; for having been in the habit of showing hospitality, they entertained angels without knowing and thinking about it, and thus their houses were in no small way honored. And doubtless God proved that hospitality was especially acceptable to Him, when He rendered such a reward to Abraham and Lot (cf. Gen. 18–19). Were someone to object and say that this happened only rarely, the obvious answer is this: not mere angels are received, but we receive Christ Himself when we receive the poor in His name. [Commentary on Hebrews]

OCTOBER 17

God's Timely Deliverance

So also the chief priests, with the scribes and elders, mocked him saying... 'He trusts in God; let God deliver him now, if he desires him.'

MATTHEW 27:41-43

Since God watches over the safety of His people, and not only grants them seasonable aid, but even anticipates their needs (as Scripture everywhere teaches us), He appears not to love those whom He does not assist. Satan, therefore, attempts to drive us to despair by this logic, that it is in vain for us to feel assured of the love of God, when we do not clearly perceive His aid. ... We ought, therefore, to reject as false this argument, that God does not love those whom He appears for a time to forsake; and, indeed, nothing is more unreasonable than to limit His love to any point of time. God has, indeed, promised that He will be our Deliverer; but if He sometimes winks at our calamities, we ought patiently to endure the delay. It is, therefore, contrary to the nature of faith, that the word now should be insisted on by those whom God is training by the cross and by adversity to obedience, and whom He entreats to pray and to call on His name; for these are rather the testimonies of His fatherly love, as the apostle tells us (Heb. 12:6). But there was this peculiarity in Christ, that, though He was the well-beloved Son, yet He was not delivered from death until He had endured the punishment which we deserved; because that was the price by which our salvation was purchased. [Commentary on the Harmony of the Gospels]

OCTOBER 18

Preaching and Faith

So, faith comes from hearing, and hearing through the word of Christ.

ROMANS 10:17

This is a remarkable passage with regard to the efficacy of preaching; for Paul testifies that by it faith is produced. He had indeed previously declared that, in and of itself, preaching is of no avail; but when it pleases the Lord to work, it becomes the instrument of His power. And indeed the human voice can by no means penetrate into the soul; and mortal human beings would be too much exalted, were they said to have the power to regenerate us. So too, the light of faith is something more sublime than what can be conveyed by humans. But all these things are no hindrances to God, who works effectually through the voice of a man so as to create faith in us through his ministry. It must be further noticed that faith is grounded on nothing else but the truth of God. For Paul does not teach us that faith springs from any other kind of doctrine, but he expressly restricts it to the word of God; and this restriction would have been improper if faith could rest on human decrees. Away then with all the devices of men and women when we speak of the certainty of faith. ... And more detestable still is that blasphemy, that the truth of the word remains suspended until the authority of the Church establishes it. [Commentary on Romans]

OCTOBER 19

Repentance and Faith

'I did not shrink back from declaring to you anything that was profitable, ... testifying both to Jews and to Greeks of repentance toward God and of faith in our Lord Jesus Christ.'

ACTS 20:20-21

We must first note the distinction between faith and repentance, which some people falsely and unskillfully confuse, saying that repentance is a part of faith. I grant, indeed, that they cannot be separated; because God illuminates no one with the Spirit of faith whom He does not also regenerate into newness of life. Yet the two must be distinguished, as Paul does in this passage. For repentance is a turning to God, when we resolve in all our life to obey Him; but faith is a receiving of the grace offered us in Christ. For all religion leads to this end, that, embracing holiness and righteousness, we serve the Lord purely; also, that we seek no part of our salvation anywhere else except in His hands, and that we seek salvation in Christ alone. Therefore, the doctrine of repentance contains the rule of the good life; it requires the denial of ourselves, the mortifying of our flesh, and meditating on the heavenly life. But because we are all naturally corrupt, strangers from righteousness, and turned away from God Himself ... the means to obtain free reconciliation as newness of life must be set before us. Therefore, unless faith is added, it is vain to speak about repentance; indeed, those teachers of repentance who, neglecting faith, stand only upon human resolve, and precepts of good works, differ not at all – or very little – from profane philosophers. ... [Thus,] we see now how repentance and faith are so linked together that they cannot be separated. [Commentary on Acts]

OCTOBER 20

Wisdom of the Cross

So, they took Jesus, and he went out, bearing his own cross, to the place called Golgotha. There they crucified him...

JOHN 19:16-18

We ought always to remember, that the wicked executioners of Christ did nothing but what had been determined by the hand and purpose of God; for God did not surrender His Son to their lawless passions, but determined that, according to His own will and good pleasure, He should be offered as a sacrifice. ... [In the cross] we observe the dreadful weight of God's wrath against sin, and, on the other hand, His infinite goodness toward us. In no other way could our guilt be removed than by the Son of God becoming a curse for us. We see Him driven out into an accursed place, as if He had been defiled by a mass of all sorts of crimes, that there He might appear to be accursed before God and humanity. Assuredly we are prodigiously stupid if we do not plainly see in this mirror with what abhorrence God regards sin; and we are harder than stones, if we do not tremble at such a judgment as this. When, on the other hand, God declares that our salvation was so dear to Him, that He did not spare His only-begotten Son, what abundant goodness and astonishing grace do we here behold? Whoever, then, takes a right view of the causes of the death of Christ, together with the advantage which it yields to us, will not, like the Greeks, regard the doctrine of the cross as foolishness, nor, like the Jews, regard it as an offense (1 Cor. 1:23), but rather as a priceless token and pledge of the power, wisdom, righteousness, and goodness of God. [Commentary on John]

OCTOBER 21

God's Rich Blessings

His offspring will be mighty in the land; the generation of the upright will be blessed. Wealth and riches are in his house, and his righteousness endures forever.

PSALM 112:2-3

Sometimes it happens that a good man is childless; and barrenness itself is considered a curse of God. Again, many of God's servants are oppressed by poverty and want, and are weighed down under the burden of sickness, and harassed and perplexed with various calamities. It is therefore necessary to keep this general principle in view, that God sometimes bestows bounty upon His children more abundantly, and, at other times, more sparingly, according to what He sees as most advantageous to them. Moreover, He sometimes conceals the tokens of His kindness, apparently as if He had no concern for His people at all. Still, amidst this perplexity, it is clear that these words were not uttered in vain, that 'the generation of the upright will be blessed.' God very frequently explodes the vain hopes of ungodly men and women whose only concern is to possess power in this world and raise their children to positions of wealth and honor. On the other hand, as the faithful remain satisfied with bringing up their children in the fear of God, and are contented to live frugally, God exalts them to honor, as if with an outstretched hand. ... This, in fact, constitutes the true and proper difference between the godly and ungodly: though the latter may, for a time, hoard up great wealth, yet all that they have may, as the prophet Haggai says, suddenly vanish away at the blast of the Almighty (Hag. 1:9). ... But for the faithful their integrity is the best and surest preserver of God's blessings. [Commentary on Psalms]

OCTOBER 22

Under God's Wings

He will cover you with his pinions, and under his wings you will find refuge; his faithfulness is a shield and buckler.

PSALM 91:4

This figure, which is employed in other parts of Scripture, is one that beautifully expresses the unique and tender care with which God watches over our safety. When we consider the majesty of God, there is nothing which would suggest an analogy such as is here drawn between Him and the hen or other birds, who spread their wings over their young ones to cherish and protect them. But, in accommodation to our weakness, He does not hesitate to descend, as it were, from the heavenly glory which belongs to Him, and to encourage us to approach Him under so humble an analogy. Since He condescends in such a gracious manner to our weakness, surely there is nothing to prevent us from coming to Him with the greatest freedom.

By the statement 'His faithfulness is a shield and buckler,' we must understand God's faithfulness never to desert His people in the time of their need; still we cannot doubt that He had in His eye the divine promises, for it is only by looking to these that anyone can venture to cast themselves upon the protection of God. ... Formerly, under the comparison of a 'fortress' [in verse 2], he had taught that by trusting in God we shall enjoy safety and security; now he compares God to a 'shield,' intimating that He will come between us and all our enemies to preserve us from their attacks. [Commentary on Psalms]

OCTOBER 23

Christ's Second Coming

'But concerning that day and hour no one knows, not even the angels of heaven, nor the Son, but the Father only.'

MATTHEW 24:36

By this sentence, Christ intended to hold the minds of believers in suspense, that they might not, by a false imagination, fix any time for the final redemption. We know how fickle our minds are, and how much we are tickled by a vain curiosity to know more than is proper. Christ likewise perceived that the disciples were pushing forward with excessive haste to enjoy a triumph. He therefore wishes the day of His coming to be the object of such anticipation and desire, that none shall dare to inquire when it will happen. In short, He wishes His disciples to walk in the light of faith to such a degree, that while they are uncertain as to the time, they may patiently wait for the revelation of Him. We ought therefore to be on our guard, lest our anxiety about the time be carried farther than the Lord allows; for the chief part of our wisdom lies in confining ourselves soberly within the limits of God's word. So that men and women may not feel uneasy as not knowing that day, Christ represents angels as their associates in this matter; for it would be a proof of excessive pride and wicked covetousness, to desire that we who creep on the earth should know more than is permitted to the angels in heaven. ... And surely, that person must be singularly mad who would hesitate to submit to the ignorance that even the Son of God Himself did not hesitate to endure on our account. [Commentary on the Harmony of the Gospels]

OCTOBER 24

Rejoicing in Christ's Suffering

But rejoice insofar as you share Christ's sufferings, that you may also rejoice and be glad when his glory is revealed.

1 Peter 4:13

Peter proves that the cross is useful to us with two arguments: that God thus tests our faith, and that we become partakers with Christ. In the first place, let us remember that the trial of our faith is most necessary, and that we ought thus willingly to obey God who provides for our salvation. However, the chief consolation is derived from a fellowship with Christ. Hence, Peter not only forbids us to think it strange [when we suffer], but also bids us to rejoice. It is, indeed, a cause of joy, when God tries our faith by persecution; but the other joy far surpasses it, that is, when the Son of God grants to us the same course of life with Himself, that He might allow us to enjoy with Him blessed participation in heavenly glory. …

Here, then, is the whole consolation of the godly, that they are associates with Christ, that hereafter they may be partakers of His glory; for we are always to bear in mind this transition from the cross to the resurrection. But as this world is like a labyrinth, in which no end of evils appears, Peter refers to the future revelation of Christ's glory, as though he had said, that the day of its revelation is not to be overlooked, but ought to be expected. Now he mentions a twofold joy, one which we now enjoy in hope, and the other the full fruition which the coming of Christ will bring to us; for the first is mingled with grief and sorrow, the second is connected to exultation. [Commentary on 1 Peter]

OCTOBER 25

Godly Sympathy

Rejoice with those who rejoice, weep with those who weep.

ROMANS 12:15

A general truth [is here] laid out – that the faithful are to regard each other with mutual affection and consider the condition of others as their own. Paul first specifies two particular things: that they are to 'rejoice with the joyful' and to 'weep with the weeping.' For such is the nature of true love, that one prefers to weep with his brother or sister, rather than to look at a distance on their grief, and to live in pleasure or ease. What is meant then is this, that we, as much as possible, ought to sympathize with one another, and that, whatever our lot may be, each should transfer to themselves the feelings of others, whether of grief in adversity, or of joy in prosperity. And, doubtless, not to regard with joy the happiness of a brother or sister is envy; and not to grieve for their misfortune is inhumanity. Let there be such a sympathy among us as may at the same time adapt us to all kinds of feelings. [Commentary on Romans]

OCTOBER 26

Praying for Magistrates

First of all, then, I urge that supplications, prayers, intercessions, and thanksgivings be made for all people, for kings and all who are in high positions, that we may live a peaceful and quiet life, godly and dignified in every way.

1 TIMOTHY 2:1-2

Paul explicitly mentions kings and other magistrates, because, more than all others, they might be hated by Christians. All the magistrates who existed at that time were so many sworn enemies of Christ; and therefore, this thought might occur to them, that they should not pray for those who devoted all their power and all their wealth to fight against the kingdom of Christ, the advance of which is most desirable. The Apostle meets this difficulty, and expressly commands Christians to pray for them also. And, indeed, the depravity of men and women is not a reason why God's ordinances should not be loved. Accordingly, seeing that God appointed magistrates and princes for the preservation of humanity, however much they fall short of the divine appointment, still we must not on that account cease to love what belongs to God, and to desire that it may remain in force. That is the reason why believers, in whatever country they live, must not only obey the laws and the government of magistrates, but likewise in their prayers petition God for their salvation. Jeremiah said to the Israelites, 'Pray for the peace of Babylon, for in its welfare you will find your welfare' (Jer. 29:7). The universal doctrine is this, that we should desire the continuance and peaceful condition of those governments which have been appointed by God. [Commentary on 1 Timothy]

OCTOBER 27

Faithful in Old Age

'[W]hen you were young, you used to dress yourself and walk wherever you wanted, but when you are old, you will stretch out your hands, and another will dress you and carry you where you do not want to go.'

JOHN 21:18

After having exhorted Peter to 'feed his sheep,' Christ likewise arms him to maintain the warfare which was approaching. Thus, He demands from him not only faithfulness and diligence, but invincible courage in the midst of dangers, and firmness in bearing the cross. ...

Old age appears to be set apart for tranquility and repose; and, accordingly, old men are usually discharged from public employments, and soldiers are discharged from service. Peter might, therefore, have promised himself at that age a peaceful life. Christ declares, on the other hand, that the order of nature will be inverted, so that he who had lived at his ease when he was young will be governed by the will of another when he is old, and will even endure violent subjection.

In Peter we have a striking mirror of our ordinary condition. Many have an easy and agreeable life before Christ calls them; but as soon as they have made profession of His name, and have been received as His disciples ... they are led to distressing struggles, to a troublesome life, to great dangers, and sometimes to death itself. This condition, though hard, must be patiently endured. Yet the Lord moderates the cross by which He is pleased to try His servants, so that He spares them a little while, until their strength has come to maturity; for He knows well their weaknesses, and He does not pressure them beyond its measure. [Commentary on John]

OCTOBER 28

Antidote for Anxiety

His is not afraid of bad news; his heart is firm, trusting in the LORD.

PSALM 112:7

[U]nlike unbelievers who tremble at even the slightest rumor, the righteous calmly and peacefully entrust themselves to God's fatherly care, amidst all the evil reports that may reach them. Why is it that unbelievers are in constant agitation, imagining that they are the sport of fortune on earth, while God remains at ease in heaven? No wonder, then, that the rustling of a fallen leaf troubles and alarms them. The faithful are freed from such uneasiness, because they neither pay attention to rumors, nor does the fear of them prevent them from constantly calling out to God. The children of God may also manifest symptoms of fear at the prospect of impending dangers; for if they were entirely unconcerned about calamities, such indifference would be the result of apathy rather than confidence in God. But even if [believers] cannot lay aside all fear and anxiety, yet, acknowledging God as the guardian of their life … they entrust themselves to His preserving care and cheerfully resign themselves to His purposes. This is that magnanimity of the righteous which (as the prophet notes) allows them to disregard those rumors of evil that strike others with alarm. They are also wise to rely upon God for support; because, surrounded on all sides by innumerable deaths, we would sink into despair were we not buoyed by the confidence that we are secure under God's protection. Hence, the prophet here describes a genuine stability which consists in resting with unshaken confidence in God. [Commentary on Psalms]

OCTOBER 29

The Blessed Life

Blessed are those whose way is blameless, who walk in the law of the LORD! Blessed are those who keep his testimonies, who seek him with their whole heart.
PSALM 119:1-2

All men and women naturally aspire to happiness, but instead of searching for it in the right path, they intentionally prefer wandering up and down through the endless bypaths, to their ruin and destruction. The Holy Spirit rightly condemns this apathy and blindness. ...

If people follow their own temperament and caprice, they are certain to go astray; and even if they should enjoy the applause of the whole world, they will only weary themselves with their vanity. But it may be asked, whether the prophet here excludes from the hope of happiness all who do not worship God perfectly? Were this his meaning, it would follow that none except angels would be happy, seeing that the perfect observance of the law will be found in no place on earth. The answer is easy: When righteousness is required of the children of God, they do not lose the gracious forgiveness of their sins, in which their salvation alone consists. Thus, while the servants of God are happy, they still need to take refuge in His mercy, because their uprightness is not complete. In this manner they are said to be truly happy who faithfully observe the law of God – who thus fulfill that which is declared in Psalm 32:2: 'Blessed is the man against whom the LORD counts no iniquity.'... Moreover, by these words, he tells us that God is by no means satisfied with mere outward service, for He demands the sincere and honest affection of the heart. [Commentary on Psalms]

OCTOBER 30

Christian Charity

'For I was hungry and you gave me food, I was thirsty and you gave me drink, I was a stranger and you welcomed me, I was naked and you clothed me, I was sick and you visited me, I was in prison and you came to me.'

MATTHEW 25:35-36

Christ does not here specify everything that belongs to a pious and holy life, but only, by way of example, refers to some of the duties of charity, by which we give evidence that we fear God. For though the worship of God is more important than charity toward others, and though, in a similar manner, faith and supplication are more valuable than alms, yet Christ had good reasons for bringing forward those evidences of true righteousness which are more obvious. If a man or woman were to take no thought about God, and were only to be generous toward other people, such compassion would be of no use to them for appeasing God, who had all the while been defrauded by his right. Accordingly, Christ does not make the chief part of righteousness to consist in alms, but ... shows what it is to live a holy and righteous life; as unquestionably believers not only profess with the mouth, but prove by actual actions, that they serve God. ... But while Christ, in recommending to us the exercise of charity, does not exclude those duties which belong to the worship of God, He reminds His disciples that it will be an authentic evidence of a holy life if they practice charity, in a manner agreeable to the words of the prophet, 'I choose mercy, and not sacrifice' (Hosea 6:6). [Commentary on the Harmony of the Gospels]

OCTOBER 31

God's Justification of Sinners

[B]y his knowledge shall the righteous one, my servant, make many to be accounted righteous, and he shall bear their iniquities.

ISAIAH 53:11

Men and women are not only taught righteousness in the school of Christ, but are actually justified. And this is the difference between the righteousness of faith and the righteousness of the Law. For although the Law shows what it is to be righteous, yet Paul affirms that it is impossible that righteousness should be obtained by it – and experience proves the same thing. For the Law is a mirror in which we behold our own unrighteousness. Now, the doctrine which Christ teaches, as it relates to obtaining righteousness, is nothing other than the 'knowledge of Him,' and this is faith, when we embrace the benefit of His death and fully rely on Him. ... We must therefore seek another way of righteousness [other than the Law], namely, in Christ, whom the Law also pointed out as its end (Rom. 10:3). The righteousness of the Law was of this nature: 'The one who does them shall live by them' (Lev. 18:5; Gal. 3:12). But nobody has done them, and therefore another righteousness is necessary, which Paul proves by a quotation from Moses himself, 'But the word is near you ... that is, the word of faith that we proclaim' (Rom. 10:8; Deut. 30:14). By this doctrine, therefore, we are justified; not by the bare and simple doctrine, but inasmuch as it exhibits the benefits of the death of Christ, by which atonement is made for our sins, and we are reconciled to God (Rom. 5:10). For, if we embrace this benefit by faith, we are reckoned righteous before God. [Commentary on Isaiah]

NOVEMBER 1

Put On Christ

But put on the Lord Jesus Christ, and make no provision for the flesh, to gratify its desires.
ROMANS 13:14

This metaphor is commonly used in Scripture with respect to what tends to adorn or to deform a man or woman. Both of these can be seen in a person's clothing: for a filthy and torn garment dishonors a person; but what is becoming and clean speaks well of a person. Now, in this passage, to 'put on Christ' means to be on every side fortified by the power of His Spirit, and thereby prepared to discharge all the duties of holiness. For thus is the image of God renewed in us, which is the only true ornament of the soul. For Paul had in view the end of our calling, inasmuch as God, by adopting us, unites us to the body of His only-begotten Son, and for this purpose: that we, renouncing our former life, may become new men and women in Him. On this account he says also, in another passage, that we put on Christ in baptism (Gal. 3:27).

As long as we carry about us our flesh, we cannot cast away every care for it; for though our fellowship is in heaven, yet we sojourn on earth. The things then which belong to the body must be taken care of, but not otherwise than as they are helps to us in our pilgrimage, and not that they make us to forget our country. ... Paul has therefore laid down this rule, that we are to provide for the needs of our flesh, but not to indulge its lusts. It is in this way that we shall use this world without abusing it. [Commentary on Romans]

NOVEMBER 2

God's Sure Promises

The following night the Lord stood by [Paul] and said,
'Take courage, for as you have testified to the facts about me
in Jerusalem, so you must testify also in Rome.'

ACTS 23:11

The Lord does not promise to deliver Paul. Nor does he indicate that he shall have a joyful end. He only says that those troubles and afflictions, which already sorely oppressed him, would long continue. But by this we better discern how important this confidence is, that the Lord looks upon us in our miseries, even if in the meantime He does not stretch forth His hand to help us. Therefore, let us learn, even in the most extreme afflictions, to establish ourselves upon the word of God alone; and let us never faint so long as He revives us with the testimony of His fatherly love. And since oracles are no longer sent from heaven, nor does the Lord Himself appear in visions, we must meditate upon His innumerable promises, whereby He testifies that He will continually be close to us. If it is expedient for an angel to come down to us, the Lord will not deny even this kind of confirmation. Nevertheless, we must give this honor to the word, that being content with it alone, we wait patiently for that help which it promises us. ... And even as the Lord impresses those promises upon our hearts and often repeats them, let us diligently exercise our faith in the continual remembrance of them. For if it was necessary for Paul to reinforce his faith with new helps, how many more helps will be necessary for us! [Commentary on Acts]

NOVEMBER 3

Faith and Predestination

'For this is the will of my Father, that everyone who looks on the Son and believes in him should have eternal life, and I will raise him up on the last day.'
JOHN 6:40

The election of God is in itself hidden and secret; the Lord manifests it by calling, that is, when He bestows on us this blessing of calling us. Those people are insane, therefore, who seek to discern their own salvation or that of others in the whirlpool of predestination, not keeping the way of salvation which is exhibited to them. Nay more, by this foolish speculation they endeavor to overturn the force and effect of predestination; for if God has elected us so that we might believe, take away faith, and election will be imperfect. But we have no right to break through the order and succession of the beginning and the end, since God, by His purpose, has decreed and determined that it shall be unbroken. Besides, as the election of God, by an indissoluble bond, draws His calling along with it, so when God has effectually called us to faith in Christ, let this have as much weight with us as if He had engravened His seal to ratify His decree concerning our salvation. For the testimony of the Holy Spirit is nothing else than the sealing of our adoption (Rom. 8:15). For everyone, therefore, their faith is a sufficient attestation of the eternal predestination of God, so that it would be a shocking sacrilege to carry the inquiry further; for that person offers an aggravated insult to the Holy Spirit, who refuses to assent to His simple testimony. [Commentary on John]

NOVEMBER 4

True Source of Happiness

Blessed are the people to whom such blessings fall! Blessed are the people whose God is the LORD! PSALM 144:15

[David] thus concludes that God's favor had been sufficiently shown and manifested to his people. Should someone object that to base human happiness on transitory benefits betrays a gross and worldly spirit, I would say in reply that we must read the two things in connection: that those people are happy who recognize God's favor in the abundance they enjoy and who perceive and are persuaded from these transitory blessings God's fatherly love to aspire after the true inheritance. There is nothing inappropriate in calling those people happy whom God blesses in this world, provided they do not show themselves blinded from improving and using these mercies, or foolishly and apathetically overlooking the author of them. God's providence whereby He does not allow us to lack any of the means of life is surely a striking illustration of His love. What could be more desirable than to be the objects of God's care, especially if we sufficiently understand that the generosity with which He supports us comes because He is our Father? For everything should be viewed with a reference to this point. It would be better to perish immediately from poverty than to have a mere brute satisfaction, and forget the main thing of all, that those people alone are happy whom God has chosen for His people. ... [W]hile God in giving us meat and drink permits us to enjoy a certain measure of happiness, it does not follow that those believers are miserable who struggle through life in want and poverty, for God can counterbalance this poverty with better consolations. [Commentary on Psalms]

NOVEMBER 5

Loving God

I love you, O LORD, my strength. The LORD is my rock and my fortress and my deliverer, my God, my rock, in whom I take refuge, my shield, and the horn of my salvation, my stronghold.

PSALM 18:1-2

It is to be observed that love for God is here laid down as constituting the principal part of true godliness; for there is no better way of serving God than to love Him. No doubt, the service which we owe Him is better expressed by the word 'reverence,' so that His majesty might prominently stand forth to our view in its infinite greatness. But as He requires nothing so expressly as to possess all the affections of our hearts ... so there is no sacrifice which He values more than when we are tightly bound to Him by the chain of a free and spontaneous love; and, on the other hand, there is nothing in which His glory shines forth more conspicuously than in His free and sovereign goodness. Moses, therefore, when he meant to give a summary of the law, says 'And now, Israel, what does the LORD your God require of you, but to fear the LORD your God ... [and] to love Him' (Deut. 10:12). In speaking this way, David, at the same time, intended to show that his thoughts and affections were not so intently fixed upon the benefits of God as to be ungrateful to Him who was the author of them – a sin which has been too common in all ages. ... David, to prevent himself from falling into such ingratitude, in these words makes a solemn vow, 'Lord, as you are my strength, I will continue united and devoted to you by unfeigned love.' [Commentary on Psalms]

NOVEMBER 6

Godly Leaders

Obey your leaders and submit to them, for they are keeping watch over your souls, as those who will have to give an account. Let them do this with joy and not with groaning, for that would be of no advantage to you.

HEBREWS 13:17

The author here is speaking of pastors and other rulers of the Church, for there were then no Christian magistrates; and what follows, 'for they keep watch over your souls,' properly belongs to spiritual government. He commands first obedience, and then honor be rendered to them. These two things are necessarily required, so that people might have confidence in their pastors and also reverence for them. But it ought at the same time to be noticed that the Apostle speaks only of those who faithfully performed their office; for those who have nothing but the title, indeed, those who use the title of pastors for the purpose of destroying the Church, deserve little reverence and still less confidence. ...

The author further reminds us of the weighty concerns that pastors employ on our behalf; for, if the salvation of our souls is precious to us, then pastors ought by no means to be deemed of little importance by those whose advantage they serve. He also bids us to be teachable and ready to obey, so that what pastors do as a result of the demands of their office, they may do willingly and with joy. For if their minds are restrained by grief or weariness – even if they are sincere and faithful – they will yet become disheartened and careless, for their energy will fail at the same time with their cheerfulness. [Commentary on Hebrews]

NOVEMBER 7

Christian Combat

Be sober-minded; be watchful. Your adversary the devil prowls around like a roaring lion, seeking someone to devour. Resist him, firm in your faith ...
1 PETER 5:8-9

Peter says that we must carry on a warfare in this world; and he reminds us that we have to deal with no common enemy, but one who, like a lion, runs here and there, ready to devour. He thus concludes that we ought carefully to watch. Paul stimulates us with the same argument in Ephesians 6, where he says that we have a contest not with flesh and blood, but with spiritual wickedness, etc. But we too often turn peace into idleness, and hence it happens that the enemy then circumvents and overwhelms us; for, as though placed beyond the reach of danger, we indulge ourselves according to the will of the flesh.

He compares the devil to a lion, as though he had said, that he is a savage wild beast. He says that he 'prowls around' to devour, in order to rouse us to wariness. He calls him the 'adversary' of the godly, that they might know that they worship and profess faith in Christ on this condition, that they are to have continual war with the devil, for he who fights with the head does not spare the members. 'Resist him.' ... [The Apostle] shows that the outcome of the war will be prosperous, if we indeed fight under the banner of Christ; for whosoever comes to this contest equipped with faith, he declares that he will certainly be a conqueror. [Commentary on 1 Peter]

NOVEMBER 8

Dying in the Lord

For if we live, we live to the Lord, and if we die, we die to the Lord. So then, whether we live or whether we die, we are the Lord's.

ROMANS 14:8

[This passage teaches] that we conform to God's will and pleasure, and design all things for His glory. Nor are we only to live to the Lord, but also to die; that is, our death as well as our life is to be referred to His will. Paul adds the best of reasons, for whether we live or die 'we are the Lord's,' and hence it follows that He has full authority over our life and our death.

The application of this doctrine opens into a wide field. God thus claims authority over life and death, that every person should bear their own condition as a yoke laid on them; for it is only right that He should assign to everyone their station and course of life. And thus, we are not only forbidden rashly to attempt this or that without God's command, but we are also commanded to be patient in the face of all troubles and losses. ... [W]e are also taught here the rule by which we are to live and to die, so that if God extends our life in continual sorrows and miseries, even so we are not to seek to depart before our time. But if He should suddenly call us hence in the flower of our age, we ought ever to be ready for our departure. [Commentary on Romans]

NOVEMBER 9

Persecution

Indeed, all who desire to live a godly life in Christ Jesus will be persecuted...
2 TIMOTHY 3:12

By this general statement, therefore, Paul classes himself with the children of God, and, at the same time, exhorts all the children of God to prepare for enduring persecutions; for, if this condition is laid down, 'all who desire to live a godly life in Christ,' those who wish to be exempt from persecutions must necessarily renounce Christ. We shall in vain endeavor to detach Christ from His cross; for it may be said to be natural that the world should hate Christ even in His members. Now hatred is accompanied by cruelty, and from this arises persecutions. In short, let us know that we are Christians on this condition, that we shall be liable to many tribulations and various contests. But it is asked, must all Christians be martyrs? for it is evident that there have been many godly persons who have never suffered banishment, or imprisonment, or flight, or any kind of persecutions. I reply that it is not always in one way that Satan persecutes the servants of Christ. But yet it is absolutely unavoidable that all of them shall have the world for their enemy in some form or other, so that their faith may be tried and their steadfastness proved; for Satan, who is the continual enemy of Christ, will never allow anyone to be at peace during their whole lives; and there will always be wicked people that are thorns in our sides. ... Accordingly, although they are not exposed to the same assaults, and do not engage in the same battles, yet Christians have a warfare in common, and shall never be entirely at peace and exempt from persecutions. [Commentary on 2 Timothy]

NOVEMBER 10

Fulfill Your Calling

When Peter saw [John], he said to Jesus, 'Lord, what about this man?' Jesus said to him, 'If it is my will that he remain until I come, what is that to you. You follow me!'

JOHN 21:21-22

We have in Peter an instance of curiosity, which is not only superfluous, but even hurtful, when we are drawn aside from our duty by looking at others; for it is almost natural for us to examine the way in which other people live, instead of examining our own, and to attempt to find in them idle excuses. ... Scarcely one person in a hundred considers the import of those words of Paul, 'each will have to bear his own load' (Gal. 6:5). In the person of [Peter], therefore, there is a general reproof of all who look around themselves in every direction, to see how other people act, and pay no attention to the duties which God has enjoined on themselves. ...

Out of ten persons it may happen that God shall choose one man or woman, that He may try them with heavy calamities or by vast labors, and that He shall permit the other nine to remain at ease, or, at least, shall try them lightly. Besides, God does not treat all in the same manner, but makes trial of every one as He thinks fit. As there are various kinds of Christian warfare, let every person learn to keep their own station, and let us not make inquiries like busybodies about this or that person, when the heavenly Captain addresses each of us, to whose authority we ought to be so submissive as to forget everything else. [Commentary on John]

NOVEMBER 11

Spirit's Illumination

Open my eyes, that I may behold wondrous things out of your law.

PSALM 119:18

Having acknowledged that the power to keep the law is imparted to men and women by God, [the Psalmist] adds that everyone is born blind until God also enlightens the eyes of their understanding. Admitting that God gives light to us by His word, the prophet here means that we are blind amidst the clearest light, until He removes the veil from our eyes. When [the Psalm writer] confesses that his eyes are veiled and shut – which renders him unable to discern the light of heavenly doctrine, until God, by the invisible grace of His Spirit, opens them – he speaks as if he were deploring his own blindness, along with that of the whole human race. But while God claims this power for Himself, He tells us that this remedy is at hand, provided we do not, by trusting in our own wisdom, reject the gracious illumination offered to us. Let us also learn that we do not receive the illumination of the Spirit of God so that we might condemn the external word and take pleasure only in secret inspirations, like so many fanatics, who do not think that they are 'spiritual' unless they reject the word of God and substitute in its place their own wild speculations. The prophet's goal is very different, which is to inform us that our illumination is to enable us to discern the light of life that God manifests by His word. [Commentary on Psalms]

NOVEMBER 12

Trusting in God's Strength

Some trust in chariots and some in horses, but we trust in the name of the LORD our God.
PSALM 20:7

[In this passage] there is a comparison between the people of God and all the rest of the world. We see how natural it is for almost all men and women to be the more courageous and confident the more they possess riches, power, and military forces. The people of God, therefore, here protest that they do not place their hope in their military strength and weapons of war (as men usually do), but only in the aid of God. As the Holy Spirit here contrasts the assistance of God to human strength, it ought to be particularly noticed that whenever our minds come to be occupied with carnal confidence, they fall at the same time into a forgetfulness of God. It is impossible for those, who promise themselves victory by trusting in their own strength, to have their eyes turned toward God. The inspired writer, therefore, uses the word 'remember' to show that when the saints entrust themselves to God, they must cast off everything that would hinder them from placing an exclusive trust in Him. This remembrance of God serves two important purposes for the faithful. In the first place, however much power and resources they may possess, it nevertheless protects them from all vain confidence, so that they do not expect any success except from the pure grace of God. In the second place, if they are bereft and utterly destitute of human support, it nevertheless so strengthens and encourages them that they call upon God both with confidence and constancy. [Commentary on Psalms]

NOVEMBER 13

Christ the True Teacher

[Peter] was still speaking when, behold, a bright cloud overshadowed them, and a voice from the cloud said, 'This is my beloved Son, with whom I am well pleased; listen to him.'

MATTHEW 17:5

The Father calls Him 'my beloved Son, in whom I am well pleased,' and thus declares Him to be the Mediator, by whom He reconciles the world to Himself. When He enjoins us to 'listen to Him,' He appoints Him to be the supreme and only teacher of His Church. ...

For, though Christ came to maintain the authority of the Law and the Prophets (Matt. 5:17), yet He holds the highest rank, so that, by the brightness of His gospel, He causes those sparks which shone in the Old Testament to disappear. He is the Sun of righteousness, whose arrival brought the full light of day. And this is the reason why the Apostle says that 'at many times and in many ways, God spoke to our fathers by the prophets, but in these last days He has spoken to us by His Son' (Heb. 1:1-2). In short, Christ is as truly heard at the present day in the Law and in the Prophets as in His Gospel; so that in Him dwells the authority of a Master, which He claims for Himself alone, saying 'you have one teacher' (Matt. 23:8). But His authority is not fully acknowledged, unless all the tongues of men and women are silent. If we would submit to His doctrine, all that has been invented by humans must be thrown down and destroyed. ... [N]o one can be regarded a faithful teacher of the Church, unless they are themselves a disciple of Christ, and bring others to be taught by Him. [Commentary on the Harmony of the Gospels]

NOVEMBER 14

Spiritual Combat

For everyone who has been born of God overcomes the world. And this is the victory that has overcome the world – our faith.

1 JOHN 5:4

This passage is remarkable, for though Satan continually repeats his dreadful and horrible attacks, yet the Spirit of God, declaring that we are beyond reach of danger, removes fear, and animates us to fight with courage. And his use of the past tense gives more emphasis than had he used the present or future tenses; for he says 'has overcome the world,' in order that we might feel certain, as though the enemy had already been put to flight. It is, indeed, true that our warfare continues through life, that our conflicts are daily, indeed, that new and various battles are stirred up by the enemy against us on every side. But since God does not arm us only for one day, and as faith is not of one day, but is the perpetual work of the Holy Spirit, we are already partakers of victory, as though we had already conquered. ...

The term 'world' has here a wide meaning, for it includes whatever is adverse to the Spirit of God; thus, the corruption of our nature is a part of the world; all lusts, all the crafts of Satan, in short, whatever leads us away from God. Having such a force to contend with, we have an immense war to wage, and we should have been already conquered a hundred times daily, had not God promised us the victory. But God encourages us to fight by promising us the victory. But as this promise secures to us perpetually the invincible power of God, so, on the other hand, it annihilates all human strength. [Commentary on 1 John]

NOVEMBER 15

Baptized into Moses

For I do not want you to be unaware, brothers, that our fathers were all under the cloud, and all passed through the sea, and all were baptized into Moses in the cloud and in the sea, and all ate the same spiritual food, and all drank the same spiritual drink.

1 CORINTHIANS 10:1-4

As Paul, in speaking of the passage of the Israelites across the Red Sea, allegorically represents the drowning of Pharaoh as the mode of deliverance by water (1 Cor. 10:1), so we may be permitted to say that in baptism our Pharaoh is drowned, our old man is crucified, our members are mortified, we are buried with Christ, and removed from the captivity of the devil and the power of death – but removed only into the desert, a land arid and poor, unless the Lord rain manna from heaven, and cause water to gush forth from the rock. For our soul, like that land without water, lacks all things, till He, by the grace of His Spirit, rains upon it. We afterwards pass into the land of promise, under the guidance of Joshua the son of Nun, into a land flowing with milk and honey; that is the grace of God frees us from the body of death, by our Lord Jesus Christ. ... After we take up our residence in the land, we feed abundantly. White robes and rest are given us. But Jerusalem, the capital and seat of the kingdom, has not yet been erected; nor yet does Solomon, the Prince of Peace, hold the scepter and rule over all. ... But when the heavenly Jerusalem shall have risen up in its glory, and Christ, the true Solomon, the Prince of Peace, shall be seated aloft on his tribunal, the true Israelite will reign with their King. [Psychopannychia, CTS 3:467]

NOVEMBER 16

Devil's Defeat

Since therefore the children share in flesh and blood, he himself likewise partook of the same things, that through death he might destroy the one who has the power of death, that is, the devil.

HEBREWS 2:14

This passage deserves special notice for it not only confirms the reality of the human nature of Christ, but also shows the benefits which flow to us from it. 'The Son of God became man,' he says, 'that he might partake of the same condition and nature with us.' What could be said more fitted to confirm our faith? Here His infinite love toward us appears; but its overflowing appears in this – that He put on our nature that He might thus make Himself capable of dying, for as God He could not undergo death. And though he only refers briefly to the benefits of His death, yet there is in this brevity of words a singularly striking and powerful lesson, that He has so delivered us from the tyranny of the devil, that we are rendered safe, and that He has so redeemed us from death that it is no longer to be dreaded.

But given that all words are important, they must be examined a little more carefully. First, the destruction of the devil, which he mentions, conveys this: that he cannot prevail against us. For though the devil still lives, and constantly attempts our ruin, yet all his power to hurt us is destroyed or restrained. It is a great consolation to know that we have to deal with an enemy who cannot prevail against us. [Commentary on Hebrews]

NOVEMBER 17

Word and Spirit

Keep steady my steps according to your promise, and let no iniquity get dominion over me.

PSALM 119:133

Here two points are particularly deserving of our notice. First, that God deals bountifully with men and women, when He invites them to Himself by His word and doctrine; and secondly, that all this remains lifeless and unprofitable, until He governs by His Spirit those whom He has already taught by His word. As the Psalmist desires not simply to have his steps directed, but to have them directed to God's word, we may learn that he did not hunt after secret revelations, and disregard the word, as many fanatics do, but connected the external doctrine with the inward grace of the Holy Spirit; and herein consists the maturity of the faithful, in that God engraves on their hearts what He shows them to be right by His word. ... In vain does divine truth sound in our ears, if the Spirit of God does not effectually pierce into our hearts. The Prophet confesses that it is to no purpose for him to read or hear the law of God unless his life is regulated by the secret influence of the Holy Spirit, who enables him to walk in that righteousness that the law commands. ... The freedom of the godly consists solely in this – that they are governed by the Spirit of God, and thus are preserved from succumbing to wickedness, although harassed with hard and painful conflicts. [Commentary on Psalms]

NOVEMBER 18

True Worship

Sing aloud to God our strength; shout for joy to the God of Jacob!

PSALM 81:1

It is probable that this Psalm was appointed to be sung on the festival days on which the Jews kept their solemn assemblies. In the introduction, there is set forth the order of worship which God had enjoined, They were not to stand deaf and dumb at the tabernacle; for the service of God does not consist in idleness, nor in cold and empty ceremonies; but they were, by such exercises as here prescribed, to cherish among themselves the unity of faith; to make an open profession of their piety; to stir up themselves to continual progress in godliness; to endeavor to join, with one accord, in praising God; and, in short, to continue steadfast in the sacred covenant by which God had adopted them to Himself. ... [W]henever true believers assemble together in the present day, their goal should [also] be to remember the benefits which they have received from God – to make progress in the knowledge of His word – and to testify the oneness of their faith. Men and women only mock God by presenting to Him vain and unprofitable ceremonies, unless the doctrine of faith goes before, stirring them up to call upon God; and unless, also, the memory of God's benefits furnish reasons for praise. ... Accordingly, the faithful are here not only commanded to come together to the tabernacle, but are also ... to remember anew the free and gracious covenant that God has made with them so as to increase their faith and piety. And, thus, the benefits that they have received from Him may be celebrated, and their hearts thereby moved to thanksgiving. [Commentary on Psalms]

NOVEMBER 19

God's Incredible Grace

One of the criminals who were hanged railed [against Jesus], saying, 'Are you not the Christ? Save yourself and us!' But the other rebuked him, saying, 'Do you not fear God, since you are under the same sentence of condemnation?'

LUKE 23:39-40

In this wicked man a striking mirror of the unexpected and incredible grace of God is held out to us, not only in his being suddenly changed into a new man, when he was near death, and drawn from hell itself to heaven, but likewise in having obtained in a moment the forgiveness of all the sins in which he had been plunged through his whole life, and in having been thus admitted to heaven before the apostles and first-fruits of the new Church. First, then, a remarkable instance of the grace of God shines in the conversion of that man. For it was not by the natural movement of the flesh that he laid aside his fierce cruelty and proud contempt of God, so as to repent immediately, but he was subdued by the hand of God. ... [W]ho would ever have thought that a robber, in the very throes of death, would become not only a devout worshiper of God, but a distinguished teacher of faith and piety to the whole world, so that we too must receive from his mouth the rule of a true and proper confession? ... [The criminal] added a second proof, by humbling himself in open acknowledgment of his crimes, and ascribing to Christ the praise due to His righteousness. Thirdly, he displayed astonishing faith by committing himself and his salvation to the protection of Christ, while he saw Him hanging on the cross and near death. [Commentary on the Harmony of the Gospels]

NOVEMBER 20

United to Christ

[F]or in Christ Jesus you are all sons of God, through faith. For as many of you as were baptized into Christ have put on Christ.

GALATIANS 3:26-27

We must now examine this question. How do we receive those benefits which the Father bestowed on His only-begotten Son – not for Christ's own private use, but that He might enrich poor and needy people? First, we must understand that as long as Christ remains outside of us, and we are separated from Him, all that He has suffered and done for the salvation of the human race remains useless and of no value for us. Therefore, to share with us what He has received from the Father, He had to become ours and to dwell within us. For this reason, He is called 'our Head' (Eph. 4:15), and 'the firstborn among many brethren' (Rom. 8:29). We also, in turn, are said to be 'engrafted into Him' (Rom. 11:17), and to 'put on Christ' (Gal. 3:27); for, as I have said, all that He possesses is nothing to us until we grow into one body with Him. It is true that we obtain this by faith. Yet since we see that not all indiscriminately embrace that communion with Christ which is offered through the gospel, reason itself teaches us to climb higher and to examine into the secret energy of the Spirit, by which we come to enjoy Christ and all His benefits. ... To sum up, the Holy Spirit is the bond by which Christ effectually unites us to Himself. [Institutes (1559), III.i.1]

NOVEMBER 21

Seeking God

And the world is passing away along with its desires, but whoever does the will of God abides forever.

1 JOHN 2:17

As there is nothing in the world that is not fading — and, as it were, in a moment — John thus concludes that those who seek their happiness from it make a wretched and miserable provision for themselves, especially when God calls us to the ineffable glory of eternal life. It's as if he had said: 'The true happiness which God offers to His children is eternal; it is then a shameful thing for us to be entangled with the world, which with all its benefits will soon vanish away.' I take 'desires' here to signify what is desired or coveted, or what captivates the desires of men and women. The meaning is that what people deem to be most precious in the world and especially desirable, is nothing but a shadowy phantom.

By saying that they who do the will of God shall abide forever, or perpetually, John means that those people who seek God shall be perpetually blessed. Were anyone to object and say that no one does what God commands, the obvious answer is that what is spoken of here is not the perfect keeping of the law, but the obedience of faith, which, however imperfect it may be, is yet approved by God. The will of God is first made known to us in the law; but since no one satisfies the law no happiness can be hoped from it. But Christ comes to meet those who despair with new aid, who not only regenerates us by His Spirit that we may obey God, but assures also that our efforts, such as they are, will obtain the praise of perfect righteousness. [Commentary on 1 John]

NOVEMBER 22

Miseries of Life

For we know that if the tent that is our earthly home is destroyed, we have a building from God, a house not made with hands, eternal in the heavens.

2 CORINTHIANS 5:1

Paul has in mind to correct within us the impatience, dread, and disgust of the cross, contempt for humble things, and in short, arrogance and effeminacy. These things cannot happen unless we raise up our minds to heaven through contempt of this world. Now he advances two arguments. On the one hand, he shows the miserable condition of men and women in this life. Then he shows the supreme and perfect blessedness that awaits believers in heaven after death. For what is it that keeps people so bound to a perverse attachment to this life, except that they deceive themselves with false imaginings – thinking that they are happy living here? On the other hand, it is not enough to recognize the miseries of this life unless we become aware of the happiness and glory of the future life.

This is common to good and bad people alike – that both desire to live. This also is common to both – that, when they consider how many and how great are the miseries they encounter they often groan, often deplore their condition, and desire a remedy for their evils. (There is this difference, however: that unbelievers are aware of no adversities except those of the body, while godly people are more deeply affected by various spiritual distresses.) However, as all people naturally view death with horror, unbelievers never willingly leave this life, except when they throw it off in disgust or despair. Believers, on the other hand, depart willingly, because they have a better hope set before them beyond this world. [Commentary on 2 Corinthians]

NOVEMBER 23

Good Character

[F]or we aim at what is honorable not only in the Lord's sight but also in the sight of man.

2 CORINTHIANS 8:21

Paul declares that he is not merely concerned to have a good conscience in the sight of God, but also to have a good character among men and women. … Here, however, we must consider what Paul means by this. Certainly, nothing is worse than ambition, which corrupts the best things in the world, disfigures, I say, the most respectable things and renders the sacrifices of the sweetest smell an offensive odor before the Lord. That is why this passage is slippery, and people must be careful lest they pretend to desire a good reputation along with Paul, when they are (in fact) very far from Paul's devotion. For, Paul here was concerned to live honorably before men and women so that no one might stumble by his example, but rather all might be edified. Hence, we must take care not to seek a good name for our own benefit if we desire to be like him. 'The one who is unconcerned about their reputation is cruel,' Augustine states, 'because it is no less necessary to have a good conscience before our neighbor as before God.' This is true, provided you consider the welfare of your brothers and sisters with a view toward the glory of God, and in the meantime are prepared to endure abuse and disgrace in place of praise, if the Lord should so will it. Let the Christian man or woman, however, always take care to frame their lives for the edification of their neighbors, and pay diligent attention so that the ministers of Satan have no pretext for reviling them. [Commentary on 2 Corinthians]

NOVEMBER 24

God's Divine Counsel

Now the son of Paul's sister heard of their ambush, so he went and entered the barracks and told Paul. Paul called one of the centurions and said, 'Take this young man to the tribune, for he has something to tell him.'

ACTS 23:16-17

We see in this passage how the Lord frustrates the purposes of the ungodly. He permitted them to attempt many things, and He endured their wicked endeavors, but at length He shows, just in the nick of time, that He frustrates from heaven whatsoever the wicked attempt on the earth. 'No wisdom,' said Solomon, 'no counsel can avail against the Lord' (Prov. 21:30). ... This is set before our eyes for consideration in this present history, as in a mirror. The matter was almost determined that Paul on the next day should come out and be murdered as an avowed victim. But the Lord shows that his life is most safely kept, so that whatever people plot is in vain. As for us, let us not fear, for God's providence (displayed in this account) extends even to defending us, because this promise continues to be certain, 'Not a hair on your head will perish' (Luke 21:18). Moreover, it is worth noting that He works sometimes by unexpected means to save those who are His own, so as to better exercise our faith. Who would have thought that a boy would have disclosed the fact that [Paul's enemies] were laying a trap for him – a conspiracy that they thought was known to no one but themselves? Therefore, let us learn to lean upon and establish ourselves upon the Lord, even when we see no way to save ourselves, for He will find a path even through situations that seem impassible. [Commentary on Acts]

NOVEMBER 25

Contentment in Ministry

For I have no one like [Timothy], who will be genuinely concerned for your welfare.   PHILIPPIANS 2:20

From this it appears how great a hindrance it is for Christ's ministers to seek their own interests. Nor is there any weight in the excuses: 'I harm no one' – 'I must also be concerned for my own wellbeing' – 'I am not so devoid of feeling as not to be motivated toward my own advantage.' For you must give up your own right if you would discharge your duty, and concern for your own interest must not be put in preference to Christ's glory, or even placed on a level with it. Wherever Christ calls you, you must go promptly, leaving aside all other things. Your calling ought to be regarded by you in such a way that you will turn away all your powers of perception from everything that would impede you. It might be in your power to live elsewhere in greater wealth, but God has bound you to the church, which gives you only a very moderate support. You might have greater honor in other places, but God has assigned you a situation, in which you live in a humble style. You might elsewhere have a healthier sky, or a more delightful region, but it is here that your station is appointed. You might wish to be assigned to a more humane people; you feel offended with their ingratitude, lack of culture, or pride – in short, you have no sympathy with the disposition or the manners of the nation in which you find yourself. You must struggle with yourself, and battle opposing inclinations so as to find contentment with the place that is appointed for you. For you are not free or at your own disposal. In sum, forget yourself, if you would serve God. [Commentary on Philippians]

NOVEMBER 26

Principle of Prayer

O my God, I cry by day, but you do not answer, and by night, but I find no rest.

PSALM 22:2

In this verse, the Psalmist expresses the long duration of his affliction, which increased his anxiety and weariness. It was a temptation even still more grievous, that his crying seemed only to be wasted effort; for, as calling upon God is our only means of relief in the face of calamities, if we derive no advantage from our prayers, what other remedy remains for us? David, therefore, complains that God is in a manner deaf to his prayers. When he says in the second clause, 'but I find no rest,' the meaning is that he experiences no comfort or consolation – nothing that could bring tranquility to his troubled mind. As long as afflictions pressed upon him, his mind was so anxious that he was constrained to cry out. Here we observe the constancy of faith, in that the long duration of calamities could neither overthrow it, nor interrupt its exercise. Thus, the true rule of praying is this, that those who seem to have beaten the air to no purpose, or to have wasted their effort in praying for a long time, should not on that account give up or desist from that duty. Meanwhile, there is this advantage which God in His fatherly kindness grants to His people, that if, at any time, their desires and expectations have been disappointed, they may make known to God their perplexities and distresses, and unburden them, as it were, into His bosom. [Commentary on Psalms]

NOVEMBER 27

Sacrifice of Praise

Through him then let us continually offer up a sacrifice of praise to God, that is, the fruit of lips that acknowledge his name.

HEBREWS 13:15

Here a question arises, whether any sacrifices remained for Christians to perform. ... The apostle ... says that another kind of sacrifice remains for us which no less pleases God, namely the offering of the 'bulls of our lips,' as the prophet Hosea says (14:2). Now the fact that the sacrifice of praise is not only equally pleasing to God, but more so than all those external sacrifices under the Law, is clear from Psalm 50; for God there repudiates all these as things worth nothing, and bids the sacrifice of praise be offered to Him. Hence, we see that it is the highest worship of God, rightly preferred to all other exercises, when we acknowledge God's goodness by thanksgiving; yes indeed, this is the ceremony of sacrificing which God commends to us now. It is clear that under this one part is included prayer in its entirety, for we cannot give thanks to Him except when we are heard by Him; and no one obtains anything except the one who prays. ...

But as it was the Apostle's purpose to teach us the legitimate way of worshiping God under the New Testament, so along the way he reminds us that God cannot be truly invoked by us and His name glorified, except through Christ the Mediator. For it is He alone who sanctifies our lips, which are otherwise unclean, to sing the praises of God. And it is He who opens a way for our prayers, who in short performs the office of a priest, presenting Himself before God in our name. [Commentary on Hebrews]

NOVEMBER 28

Enjoying God's Gifts

And God saw everything that he had made, and behold, it was very good.
GENESIS 1:31

Let this be our principle: that the use of God's good gifts is not wrongly directed when it is referred to that purpose for which the Author Himself created and destined them for us, since He created them for good, not for our ruin. ... Now if we ponder to what end God created food, we shall find that He meant not only to provide for necessity but also for delight and good cheer. Thus, the purpose of clothing, apart from necessity, was attractiveness and decency. In grasses, trees, and fruits, apart from their various uses, there is beauty of appearance and pleasantness of odor. For if this were not true, the prophet would not have reckoned them among the benefits of God, that 'wine to gladden the heart of man, [and] oil to make his face shine' (Ps. 104:15). Scripture would not have reminded us repeatedly, on commending His kindness, that He gave all such things to human beings. ... Has the Lord clothed the flowers with the great beauty that greets our eyes, the sweetness of smell that is wafted upon our nostrils, and yet will it be unlawful for our eyes to be affected by that beauty, or our sense of smell by the sweetness of that odor? What? Did He not distinguish colors as to make some more lovely than others? What? Did He not endow gold and silver, ivory and marble, with a loveliness that renders them more precious than other metals or stones? Did He not, in short, render many things attractive to us, apart from their necessary use? [Institutes (1559), III.x.2]

NOVEMBER 29

Knowledge and Obedience

And by this we know that we have come to know him, if we keep his commandments.

1 JOHN 2:3

John first reminds us that the knowledge of God, derived from the gospel, is not ineffectual, but that obedience proceeds from it. He then shows what God especially requires from us, what is the chief thing in life, namely to love God. The Scripture does not without reason repeat everywhere that which we read here about a living knowledge of God; for nothing is more common in the world than to turn religious doctrine into frigid speculations. ...

John then takes this principle as granted, that the knowledge of God is efficacious. He thus concludes that those people who do not keep God's precepts or commandments do not know Him. ... How then is it possible for you to know God, and to be moved by no feeling? Nor does it indeed proceed only from God's nature, that to know Him is to immediately love Him; but the Spirit also, who illuminates our minds, inspires our hearts with a feeling that conforms to our knowledge. At the same time the knowledge of God leads us to fear Him and to love Him. For we cannot know Him as Lord and Father, as He shows Himself, without being dutiful children and obedient servants. In short, the doctrine of the gospel is a lively mirror in which we contemplate the image of God, and are transformed into the same, as Paul teaches us in 2 Corinthians 3:18. Where, therefore, there is no pure conscience, nothing can be there but an empty phantom of knowledge. [Commentary on 1 John]

NOVEMBER 30

Spiritual Warfare

For though we walk in the flesh, we are not waging war according to the flesh. For the weapons of our warfare are not of the flesh but have divine power to destroy strongholds.

2 CORINTHIANS 10:3-4

The warfare corresponds with the kinds of weapons. Paul boasts that he is furnished with spiritual weapons. Accordingly, the warfare is spiritual. Hence, it follows by way of opposites, that this warfare is not according to the flesh. In comparing the ministry of the gospel to warfare, Paul uses a most appropriate analogy. The life of a Christian, it is true, is a perpetual warfare, for whoever gives themselves to the service of God will have no truce from Satan at any time, but will be harassed with unceasing concerns. It is the responsibility, however, of ministers of the word and pastors to be standard bearers, going before the others; and, certainly, there are none that Satan harasses more, that are more severely assaulted, or that sustain more numerous or more dreadful attacks. Those are mistaken, therefore, who gird themselves for the discharge of this office, and are not at the same time furnished with courage and bravery for the battle. ... For we must take this into account, that gospel is like a fire, by which the fury of Satan is enkindled. ... But by what weapon is he to be repelled? It is only by spiritual weapons that he can be repelled. Whoever, therefore, is not armed with the influence of the Holy Spirit – however much they may boast that they are a minister of Christ – will prove that not to be the case. [Commentary on 2 Corinthians]

DECEMBER 1

Wonderful Counselor

For to us a son is born, to us a son is given; and the government shall be on his shoulder, and his name shall be called Wonderful Counselor, Mighty God, Everlasting Father, Prince of Peace.

ISAIAH 9:6

It ought to be observed that these titles are not foreign to the subject, but are adapted to the case in hand, for the Prophet describes what Christ will show Himself to be toward believers. He does not speak of Christ's mysterious essence, but applauds His excellencies, which we perceive and experience by faith. ... By the first title [i.e. Wonderful] Isaiah arouses the minds of the godly to earnest attention, that they may expect from Christ something more excellent than what they see in the ordinary course of God's works. It's as if he had said that 'in Christ are hidden all the treasures of wisdom and knowledge' (Col. 2:3). And, indeed, the redemption which He has brought surpasses even the creation of the world. It amounts to this that the grace of God, which will be exhibited in Christ, exceeds all miracles. ... [Isaiah adds the title] 'Counselor.' The reason for this second title is that the Redeemer will come endowed with absolute wisdom ... Because He proceeds from the bosom of the Father (John 1:18), Christ is in every respect the highest and most perfect teacher. In like manner, we are not permitted to get wisdom from anywhere except His gospel, and this contributes also to the praise of the gospel, for it contains the perfect wisdom of God, as Paul frequently shows (Eph. 1:17; Col. 1:9). All that is necessary for salvation is opened up by Christ in such a manner ... that He addresses the disciples no longer as servants but as friends (John 15:14, 15). [Commentary on Isaiah]

DECEMBER 2

Harvest of Joy

Those who sow in tears shall reap with shouts of joy!

PSALM 126:5

When led into captivity, the Jews were doubtless no less sorrowful than a person who in the time of scarcity, casts precious seed into the ground. But afterwards, a joyful harvest followed, when they were delivered; for the Lord restored them to gladness, as in the case of a most bountiful harvest. ... This doctrine extends still further [to us]. Our life is, in other parts of Scripture, compared to the seedtime, and since we must frequently sow in tears, it is necessary for us to raise our minds to the hope of the harvest lest sorrow should weaken or slacken our diligence. Let us remember that all the Jews who were carried into Babylon did not sow; for many of them had hardened themselves against God and the prophets and despised all threats, and thus had lost all hope of returning [from exile]. Those in whom such despair brooded were consumed in their miseries; but those who were sustained by the promise of God, cherished in their hearts the hope of harvest, although in a time of extreme scarcity they cast their seed into the ground as if on a whim. In order then that joy may follow our present sorrow, let us learn to apply our minds to the contemplation of the conclusion that God promises. Thus ... all true believers can claim the benefits of this prophecy, that God not only will wipe away tears from their eyes, but that He will also infuse into their hearts inconceivable joy. [Commentary on Psalms]

DECEMBER 3

The Hope of Resurrection

... waiting for our blessed hope, the appearing of the glory of our great God and Savior Jesus Christ.
TITUS 2:13

Let us, however, consider this settled: that no one has made progress in the school of Christ who does not joyfully await the day of death and final resurrection. Paul too distinguishes all believers by this mark, and Scripture habitually recalls us to it whenever it would set forth proof of perfect happiness. 'Rejoice,' says the Lord, 'and raise your heads, because your redemption is drawing near' (Luke 21:28). ... Let us not hesitate to await the Lord's coming, not only with longing, but also with groaning and sighs, as the happiest thing of all. He will come to us as Redeemer, and rescuing us from this boundless abyss of all evils and miseries, He will lead us into that blessed inheritance of His life and glory. ... For before their eyes the Lord on that day will receive His faithful people into the peace of His Kingdom, 'will wipe away every tear from their eyes' (Rev. 7:17), will clothe them with 'a robe of glory ... and rejoicing,' will feed them with unspeakable sweetness of His delights, will elevate them to His sublime fellowship – in sum, will stoop to make them sharers in His happiness. ... This truly is our sole comfort. If it is taken away, either our minds must become despondent or, to our destruction, be captivated with the empty solace of this world. ... To conclude in a word: if believers' eyes are turned to the power of the resurrection, in their hearts the cross of Christ will at last triumph over the devil, flesh, sin, and the wicked. [Institutes (1559), III.ix.5-6]

DECEMBER 4

Unanswered Prayer

Three times I pleaded with the Lord about this, that [the thorn] should leave me. But he said to me, 'My grace is sufficient for you, for my power is made perfect in weakness.'

2 CORINTHIANS 12:8-9

Now it may seem to follow from this that Paul in no way prayed in faith, unless we want to consider all God's promises null and void. For we read everywhere in Scripture that whatever we ask for in faith will be given to us. Yet Paul prays, and does not receive. I answer: as there are different ways of asking, so there are differing ways of receiving. We ask in simple terms for those things for which we have an explicit promise, such as the perfecting of the kingdom of God and the hallowing of His name, the remission of our sins, and whatever works toward our salvation. But when we assume that the kingdom of God can, or rather must, be advanced in this or that particular way … we are often mistaken in our opinion. In a similar fashion, we often fall into error as to what tends toward our salvation. Therefore, we ask confidently and without exception for those prior things, while it is not left to us to prescribe the means. … Now Paul was not so ignorant as not to know this. Hence, as to the object of his praying, there is no doubt that he was heard, even if he experienced a refusal as to its exact form. From this we are admonished not to become despondent as if praying were wasted effort when God does not satisfy or comply with our wishes. But let us be satisfied with His grace, that is, that we are not being forsaken by Him. [Commentary on 2 Corinthians]

DECEMBER 5

God Knows Our Afflictions

You have kept count of my tossings; put my tears in your bottle. Are they not in your book?

PSALM 56:8

These words run in the form of an abrupt prayer. ... [David's] years had been spent in the anxieties and dangers of such a perplexing pilgrimage. Accordingly, he prays that God might put his tears into His bottle. It was usual to preserve wine and oil in bottles; so that these words amount to a request that God would not allow his tears to fall to the ground, but keep them with care as a precious deposit. The prayers of David, as appears from the passage before us, proceeded from faith in the providence of God, who watches our every step, and by whom (to use an expression of Christ) 'even the hairs of [our] head are all numbered' (Matt. 10:30). Unless persuaded in our mind that God takes special notice of each affliction that we endure, it is impossible we can ever attain such confidence as to pray that God would put our tears into His bottle, so that He might look at them and be moved by them to intervene on our behalf. ... [David] animates his hope by the consideration that all his tears were written in the book of God, and would therefore certainly be remembered. And we may surely believe that if God bestows honor upon the tears of His saints, He must number every drop of their blood which is shed. Tyrants may burn their flesh and their bones, but the blood continues to cry aloud for vengeance; and intervening ages can never erase what has been written in the register of God's remembrance. [Commentary on Psalms]

DECEMBER 6

Armed and Alert

But since we belong to the day, let us be sober, having put on the breastplate of faith and love, and for a helmet the hope of salvation.
1 THESSALONIANS 5:8

So that he might more effectively shake us out of our slumber, Paul calls us to arms to show that there is no time for sleep. It is true that he does not make use of the word 'war'; but when he arms us with a breastplate and a helmet, he is admonishing us to be engaged in warfare. Whoever, therefore, is afraid of being surprised by the enemy, must keep awake and be constantly on watch. As Paul has already exhorted [the Thessalonians] to vigilance, on the ground that the doctrine of the gospel is like the light of day so he now stirs us up by another argument – that we must wage war with our enemy. From this it follows that idleness is an extremely hazardous thing. For we see that soldiers, though in other situations they may be intemperate, when the enemy is near – out of fear of destruction – they refrain from gluttony and all bodily delights and are diligently on watch so as to be on their guard. ... Therefore, Paul's meaning is that the life of Christians is like a perpetual warfare, inasmuch as Satan does not cease to trouble and molest them. He would have us, therefore, be diligently prepared and on the alert for resistance. ... He does not, however, enumerate all the parts of the armor, but simply makes mention of two, the breastplate and the helmet. Even so, he omits nothing of what belongs to spiritual armor, for the man or woman that is provided with faith, love, and hope, will be found in no way unarmed. [Commentary on 1 Thessalonians]

DECEMBER 7

Sympathy and Humility

For we ourselves were once foolish, disobedient, led astray, slaves to various passions and pleasures, passing our days in malice and envy, hated by others and hating one another.

TITUS 3:3

Paul states that there are two things that need to be understood. The first is, that [Christians] who have now been enlightened by the Lord (having been humbled by the memory of their former ignorance), should not exalt themselves proudly over others, or treat them with greater harshness and severity than that which, they think, ought to have been exercised toward themselves, when they were what those are now. The second is that, based on their personal experience, they should consider that those who today are strangers may tomorrow be received into the Church, and, having been led to amendment of their sinful practices, may become partakers of the gifts of God, of which they are now destitute. There is a bright mirror of both in believers, who 'at one time were darkness, but now are light in the Lord' (Eph. 5:8). The knowledge of their former condition should therefore dispose them to sympathy for others. On the other hand, the grace of God, which they now enjoy, is a proof that others may be brought to salvation. Thus, we see that we must be humbled before God in order that we may be gentle toward fellow Christians; for pride is always cruel and disdainful of others. In another passage (Gal. 6:1), where Paul exhorts us to mildness, he advises everyone to remember their own weakness. Here he goes farther, for he bids us to remember those vices from which we have been delivered, so that we may not criticize too harshly those vices which still dwell in other people. [Commentary on Titus]

DECEMBER 8

Contentment

O LORD, my heart is not lifted up; my eyes are not raised too high; I do not occupy myself with things too great and too marvelous for me.

PSALM 131:1

In this passage [David] teaches us a very useful lesson, and one by which we should be ruled in life – to be contented with the lot which God has marked out for us, to consider what He calls us to do, and not aim at fashioning our own lot – to be moderate in our desires, to avoid entering upon rash projects, and to confine ourselves cheerfully to our own sphere, rather than attempting great things. He denies that his 'heart had been lifted up,' for this is the true cause of all unwarranted rashness and presumption in conduct. Is it not pride that leads men and women, under the instigation of their passions, to dare such presumptuous undertakings, to hurry on recklessly in their plans, and throw the whole world into confusion? If this loftiness of spirit were checked, the consequence would be that all men and women would become more moderate in their conduct. His 'eyes' were not lifted up; there was no symptom of pride in his looks or gestures, as elsewhere we find proud looks condemned (Ps. 18:28). Something more than this, however, may be intended. For while [David] put a restraint upon the rising ambition in his heart, he was careful not to allow his eyes to provide assistance to his heart in coveting after greatness. All his senses, in short, as well as his heart, were subjected to the restraints of humility. [Commentary on Psalms]

DECEMBER 9

Songs of Creation

Let the heavens be glad, and let the earth rejoice; let the sea roar, and all that fills it; let the field exult, and everything in it! Then shall all the trees of the forest sing for joy before the LORD ...

PSALM 96:11-13

With the view of giving us a more exalted conception of the display of God's goodness in condescending to take all men and women under His government, the Psalmist calls upon the irrational things themselves, the trees, the earth, the seas, and the heavens, to join in the general joy. Nor are we to understand that by 'the heavens,' he means the angels, and by 'the earth' human beings; for he calls even upon the dumb fishes of the deep to shout for joy. The language must therefore be hyperbolical, designed to express the desirableness and blessedness of being brought unto the faith of God. At the same time, it shows us that God does not reign with terror, or as a tyrant, but that His power is exercised sweetly, and so as to spread joy amongst His subjects. The wicked may tremble when His kingdom is introduced, but the establishment of it is only the cause of their fear indirectly. We should notice also that the hyperbole here employed does not lack a certain foundation of a more literal kind. As all elements in the creation groan and agonize together with us, according to Paul's statement (Rom. 8:22), they may reasonably rejoice in the restoration of all things according to their earnest desire. ... From the close of the psalm we learn that it is impossible to experience the slightest measure of true joy, as long as we have not seen the face of God. [Commentary on Psalms]

DECEMBER 10

Christ the Foundation

Jesus Christ is the same yesterday and today and forever.

HEBREWS 13:8

The only way by which we can persevere in the right faith is to hold to the foundation, and not in the smallest degree to depart from it. For those who do not hold to Christ know nothing but mere vanity, though they may comprehend heaven and earth; for in Christ are included all the treasures of celestial wisdom. This then is a remarkable passage, from which we learn that there is no other way of being truly wise than by fixing all our thoughts on Christ alone.

Now as he is dealing with the Jews, the author teaches them that Christ had always had the same sovereignty which He holds at this day: 'the same yesterday and today and forever.' By these words he intimates that Christ, who was then made known in the world, had reigned from the beginning of the world and that it is not possible to advance farther when we come to him. 'Yesterday,' then, includes the entire time of the Old Testament; and so that no one might expect a sudden change for a short time, as the promulgation of the gospel had only recently occurred, he declares that Christ had been recently revealed for this very purpose, that the knowledge of Him might continue the same forever. Hence, it appears that the apostle here is not speaking of the eternal existence of Christ, but of that knowledge of Him which was possessed by godly people in all ages, and was the perpetual foundation of the Church. [Commentary on Hebrews]

DECEMBER 11

Zechariah's Doubt

*And Zechariah said to the angel, 'How shall I know this?
For I am an old man, and my wife is advanced in years.'*

LUKE 1:18

The reason why Zechariah doubted [that his wife Elizabeth would have a child] was that, considering the ordinary course of nature, he ascribed less than he should have to the power of God. ... At the same time, we ought to know that Zechariah was not so unbelieving as to turn aside entirely from the faith; for there is a general faith which embraces the promise of eternal salvation and the testimony of a free adoption. On the other hand, when God has once received us into favor, He gives us many special promises – that He will feed us, will deliver us from dangers, will vindicate our reputation, will protect our life – and so there is a special faith which answers particularly to each of these promises. Thus, it will sometime happen that some people who trust in God for the pardon of their sins, and for salvation, will waver on some point – will be too much alarmed by the dread of death, too worried about daily food, or too anxious about their plans. Such was the unbelief of Zechariah, for while he held the root and foundation of faith, he hesitated only on one point, whether God would give him a son. Let us know, therefore, that those who are perplexed or disturbed by weakness on some particular occasion do not entirely depart or fall off from the faith, and that, though the branches of faith are agitated by various storms, it does not give way at the root. [Commentary on the Harmony of the Evangelists]

DECEMBER 12

The Angel's Announcement

[An] angel of the Lord appeared to him in a dream, saying,
'Joseph, son of David, do not fear to take Mary as your wife,
for that which is conceived in her is from the Holy Spirit.
She will bear a son, and you shall call his name Jesus, for he
will save his people from their sins.'

MATTHEW 1:20-21

The first truth taught us by these words is that those whom Christ is sent to save are in themselves lost. ... The angel declares that we have perished, and are overwhelmed by an awful condemnation, because we stand excluded from life by our sins. Thus, we obtain a view of our corruption and depravity; for if anyone lived a perfectly holy life, they might do without Christ as redeemer. But each and every person needs His grace. ... Hence, too, we learn in what way or manner Christ saves: He delivers us from sins. This deliverance consists of two parts. Having made a complete atonement, He brings us a free pardon, which delivers us from condemnation to death and reconciles us to God. Again, by the sanctifying power of the Spirit, He frees us from the tyranny of Satan, that we may 'live to righteousness' (1 Pet. 2:24). Christ is not truly acknowledged as a Savior until, on the one hand, we learn to receive a free pardon of our sins, and know that we are accounted righteous before God ... and on the other hand, we ask from Him the Spirit of righteousness and holiness, having no confidence whatsoever in our own works or power. [Commentary on the Harmony of Confessions]

DECEMBER 13

Christ's Eternal Kingdom

Of the increase of his government and of peace there will be no end, on the throne of David and over his kingdom, to establish it and to uphold it with justice and righteousness from this time forth and forever more.

ISAIAH 9:7

[Isaiah] begins to explain and confirm what he had formerly said that Christ is the Prince of Peace, by saying that his government is extended to every age, and is perpetual; that there will be no end to the government of peace. This was also repeated by Daniel, who predicts that his 'kingdom shall be an everlasting kingdom' (Dan. 7:27). [The angel] Gabriel also alluded to it when he carried the message to the virgin ... 'He will reign,' he says, 'over the house of Jacob forever, and of his kingdom there shall be no end' (Luke 1:33). ... How fickle and changeable all the kingdoms under heaven are, we learn from history and from daily examples. ... Though the kingdom of Christ is in such a condition that it appears as if it were about to perish at any moment, yet God not only protects and defends it, but also extends its boundaries far and wide, and He preserves and carries it forward in uninterrupted progression to eternity. We ought firmly to believe this, that the frequency of those shocks by which the Church is shaken may not weaken our faith, when we learn that, amidst the mad outcry and violent attacks of enemies, the kingdom of Christ stands firm through the invincible power of God, so that, though the whole world should oppose and resist, it will remain through all ages. [Commentary on Isaiah]

DECEMBER 14

Christ's Good Confession

I charge you in the presence of God, who gives life to all things, and of Christ Jesus, who in his testimony before Pontius Pilate made the good confession ...

1 TIMOTHY 6:13

What Paul now adds about Christ contains a remarkable confirmation; for we are taught that we are not in the school of Plato, to learn philosophy from him, and to hear him discoursing in the shade about idle disputes; but that the doctrine which Timothy professes was ratified by the death of the Son of God. Christ made His confession before Pilate, not in a multitude of words, but in reality; that is, by undergoing a voluntary death. For, although Christ chose to be silent before Pilate, rather than speak in His own defense, because He had come before Him already devoted to a certain condemnation, yet in His silence there was a defense of His doctrine no less magnificent than if He had defended Himself with a loud voice. He ratified it by His blood, and by the sacrifice of His death, better than He could have ratified it by His voice. This confession the Apostle calls 'good.' For Socrates also died; and yet his death was not a satisfactory proof of the doctrine which he held. But when we hear that the blood of the Son of God was shed, that is an authentic seal which removes all doubt. Accordingly, whenever our hearts waver, let us remember that we should always go to the death of Christ for confirmation. What cowardice would there be in deserting such a leader going before us to show us the way! [Commentary on 1 Timothy]

DECEMBER 15

Prince of Peace

For to us a child is born, to us a son is given; and the government shall be on his shoulder, and his name shall be called Wonderful Counselor, Mighty God, Everlasting Father, Prince of Peace.

ISAIAH 9:6

This is the last title, and the prophet Isaiah declares by it that the coming of Christ will be the cause of full and perfect happiness, or, at least, of calm and blessed safety. In the Hebrew language the word peace often signifies prosperity, for of all blessings not one is better or more desirable than peace. The general meaning is, that all who submit to the dominion of Christ will lead a quiet and blessed life in obedience to Him. Hence it follows that life, without this King, is restless and miserable. But we must also take into consideration the nature of this peace. It is the same with that of the kingdom, for it resides chiefly in our consciences; otherwise, we must be engaged in unceasing conflicts and liable to daily attacks. Not only, therefore, does He promise outward peace, but that peace by which we return to a state of favor with God, we who were formerly His enemies. 'Since we have been justified by faith,' says Paul, 'we have peace with God' (Rom. 5:1). … Now, when Christ will have brought composure to our minds, the same spiritual peace will hold the highest place in our hearts, so that we will patiently endure every kind of adversity, and from the same fountain will likewise flow outward prosperity, which is nothing other than the effect of the blessing of God. [Commentary on Isaiah]

DECEMBER 16

Root of Jesse

His offspring shall endure forever, his throne as long as the sun before me. Like the moon it shall be established forever, a faithful witness in the skies. PSALM 89:36-37

There now follows the promise that the right of sovereignty shall always remain with the posterity of David. These two things – his offspring and his throne – are conjoined; and by these words the everlasting duration of the kingdom is promised, so that it should never pass to those who were of a strange and different race. The sun and the moon are produced as witnesses; for although they are creatures subject to corruption, they yet possess more stability than the earth or air. The elements, as we see, are subject to continual changes. As the whole of this lower world is subject to unceasing agitation and change, there is presented to us a more solid state of things in the sun and moon, that the kingdom of David might not be evaluated according to the common order of nature. Since, however, this royal throne was shaken in the time of king Rehoboam ... and was afterwards broken down and overthrown, it follows that this prophecy cannot be limited to David. For although at length the outward majesty of this kingdom was put to an end without hope of being re-established, the sun did not cease to shine by day, nor the moon by night. Accordingly, until we come to Christ, God might seem to be unfaithful to His promises. But in the branch which sprung from the root of Jesse (Isa. 11:1), these words were fulfilled in their fullest sense. [Commentary on Psalms]

DECEMBER 17

Mary's Song

And Mary said, 'My soul magnifies the Lord, and my spirit rejoices in God my Savior, for he has looked on the humble estate of his servant. For behold, from now on all generations will call me blessed...'
LUKE 1:46-48

By calling herself 'humble,' Mary rejects all merit, and ascribes to the undeserved goodness of God every reason for boasting. ... And this was not the loud cry of pretended humility, but the plain and honest statement of that conviction that was graven on her mind; for, in the eyes of the world, she was of no importance, and her estimation of herself was nothing more. ...

Now observe that Mary makes her happiness to consist in nothing else than in what she acknowledges to have been given to her by God, and what she mentions as the gift of grace. 'I shall be called blessed,' she says, 'through all ages.' Was it because she sought this praise by her own power or effort? On the contrary, she makes mention of nothing but the work of God.

Hence, we see how greatly [the followers of the pope] differ from her, who idly adorn her with their empty devices and consider as almost worthless the benefits she received from God. They heap up an abundance of magnificent and presumptuous titles, such as 'Queen of Heaven, Star of Salvation, Gate of Life, Sweetness, Hope, and Salvation.' ... None of these modes of expression have come from the Lord! All are rejected by the holy virgin in a single word, when she makes her whole glory consist in acts of the divine kindness. ... [I]t was her duty to praise the name of God alone, who 'had done great things.' [Commentary on the Harmony of Confessions]

DECEMBER 18

Zechariah's Song

'Blessed be the Lord God of Israel, for he has visited and redeemed his people and has raised up a horn of salvation for us in the house of his servant David ... that we should be saved from our enemies and from the hand of all who hate us.'

LUKE 1:68-71

Zechariah explains more clearly the power and office of Christ. And certainly, it would be of little to no advantage to learn that Christ was given to us, unless we also know what He bestows [on His people]. For this reason, he states more fully the purpose for which the horn of salvation was raised up: that believers may obtain salvation from their enemies. Unquestionably, Zechariah was well aware that the principal war of the Church of God is not with flesh and blood, but with Satan and all his weapons, by which he labors to accomplish our everlasting ruin. Though the Church is also attacked by outward foes, and is delivered from them by Christ, yet, as the kingdom of Christ is spiritual, it is chiefly to Satan, the prince of this world, along with his legions, that the present discourse relates. ... This passage reminds us that as long as the Church continues her pilgrimage in the world, she lives amongst her enemies, and would be exposed to their violence, if Christ were not always at hand to grant assistance. But such is the inestimable grace of Christ that, though we are surrounded on every side by our enemies, we enjoy a sure and undoubted salvation. ... No machinations or power, no wiles, no attacks will prevent our being delivered from them and saved 'by the Lord with everlasting salvation' (Isa. 45:17). [Commentary on the Harmony of Confessions]

DECEMBER 19

Bethlehem

In those days a decree went out from Caesar Augustus that all the world should be registered.... And Joseph also went up ... the city of David, which is called Bethlehem.

LUKE 2:1, 4

Luke relates how it happened that Christ was born in the city of Bethlehem .... If [Mary and Joseph] had intentionally and purposefully changed their residence so that Mary might bring forth her child in Bethlehem, we would then have focused only on the decisions made by human beings. But as they have no other design than to obey the edict of Augustus, we readily acknowledge that they were led like blind persons by the hand of God, to the place where Christ must be born. This may appear to be accidental as everything else that does not proceed from direct human intention – which irreligious people ascribe to fortune. ... [But] we must remember also the prediction that was uttered by the prophet so many centuries before (Micah 5:2). A comparison will clearly show it to have been accomplished by the wonderful providence of God, that a registration was then enacted by Augustus Caesar, and that Joseph and Mary set out from home, so as to arrive in Bethlehem at that very point of time. Thus, we see that the holy servants of God, even though they wander from their plans, unconscious where they are going, still keep to the right path, because God directs their steps. Nor is the providence of God less wonderful in employing the mandate of a tyrant to draw Mary from her home so that the prophecy may be fulfilled. God had marked out by His prophet ... the place where He determined that His Son should be born. [Commentary on the Harmony of the Gospels]

DECEMBER 20

Excellencies of Christ

For to us a child is born, to us a son is given; and the government shall be on his shoulder, and his name shall be called Wonderful Counselor, Mighty God, Everlasting Father, Prince of Peace.

ISAIAH 9:6

Now to apply this for our instruction, whenever any distrust arises, and all means of escape are taken away from us – in short, whenever it appears to us that everything is in a ruinous condition – let us recall to our remembrance that Christ is called wonderful, because He has inconceivable ways of assisting us and because His power is far beyond what we are able to conceive. When we need strength, let us remember that He is mighty and strong. When new terrors spring up suddenly every moment, and when deaths threaten us from various quarters, let us rely on that eternity by which He is of good reason called the Father, and by the same comfort let us learn to sooth all temporal distresses. When we are inwardly tossed by various storms, and when Satan attempts to disturb our consciences, let us remember that Christ is the Prince of Peace, and that it is easy for Him to quickly allay all our uneasy feelings. In this way, these titles will confirm us more and more in the faith of Christ, and fortify us against Satan and against hell itself. [Commentary on Isaiah]

DECEMBER 21

Love of Christ

... so that Christ may dwell in your hearts through faith – that you, being rooted and grounded in love, may have strength to comprehend with all the saints what is the breadth and length and height and depth, and to know the love of Christ ...

EPHESIANS 3:17-19

Those who know the love of Christ fully and perfectly are in every respect wise. It is as if Paul had said: 'In every direction that men and women may look, they will find nothing in the doctrine of salvation that does not bear some relation to this subject.' The love of Christ contains within itself the whole of wisdom, so that the words may be interpreted like this: 'that you may be able to comprehend the love of Christ, which is the length and breadth, and depth, and height, that is, the complete perfection of all wisdom.' The metaphor is borrowed from mathematics, taking the parts as expressive of the whole. Almost everyone is infected with the disease of desiring to obtain useless knowledge. It is of great importance that we should be told what is necessary for us to know, and what the Lord desires us to contemplate, above and below, on the right hand and on the left, before and behind. The love of Christ is held out to us as the subject which ought to occupy our daily and nightly meditations, and in which we ought to be entirely immersed. Those who are in possession of this alone have enough. Beyond it, there is nothing solid, nothing useful – in short, nothing that is proper and sound. Though you survey the heaven and earth and sea, you will never go beyond this without overstepping the lawful boundary of wisdom. [Commentary on Ephesians]

DECEMBER 22

Mighty God

For to us a son is born, to us a son is given; and the government shall be on his shoulder, and his name shall be called Wonderful Counselor, Mighty God, Everlasting Father, Prince of Peace.

ISAIAH 9;6

The Hebrew word *El* is one of the names for God, though it is derived from the word *strength*, so that it is sometimes used as an attribute [for God]. But here it is evidently a proper name, because Isaiah ... adds to it the adjective *gibbōr*, which means *strong*. And indeed if Christ had not been God, it would have been unlawful to worship him; for it is written 'Cursed is the man who trusts in man' (Jer. 17:5). ... Christ is therefore called Mighty God for the same reason that he was formerly called Immanuel (Isa. 7:14). For if we find in Christ nothing but the flesh and nature of man, our boasting will be foolish and vain, and our hope will rest on an uncertain and insecure foundation; but if he shows himself to be to us God and the Mighty God, we may now rely on him for safety. With good reason does Isaiah call him strong or mighty, because our contest is with the devil, death, and sin (Eph. 6:12), enemies too powerful and strong, by whom we would be immediately vanquished, if the strength of Christ had not rendered us invincible. Thus, we learn from this title that there is in Christ abundance of protection for defending our salvation, so that we desire nothing beyond Him. For He is *God*, who is pleased to show Himself *strong* on our behalf. This application may be regarded as the key to this and similar passages, leading us to distinguish between Christ's mysterious essence and the power by which He has revealed Himself to us. [Commentary on Isaiah]

DECEMBER 23

Restoration of Creation

'The wolf and the lamb shall graze together; the lion shall eat straw like the ox, and dust shall be the serpent's food. They shall not hurt or destroy in all my holy mountain,' says the LORD.

ISAIAH 65:25

This passage means that everything shall be fully restored, when Christ shall reign. And here it appears as if there were an implied comparison between Adam and Christ. We know that all the afflictions of the present life flowed from the sin of the first man and woman; for, at that time we were deprived of the dominion and sovereignty which God had given them over animals of every kind, all of which at first undoubtedly bowed cheerfully to their dominion, and were obedient to their will. But now, most of [these animals] rise up against humans and even wage mutual warfare against each other. Thus, when wolves, bears, lions, and other savage animals of that kind, harm humans and … this ought to be imputed to human sinfulness, because their disobedience overthrew the right order of things. But since it is the office of Christ to bring everything back to its right condition and order, that is the reason why He declares that the confusion or ruin that now exists in human affairs shall be removed by the coming of Christ. For at that time, corruption having been taken away, the world shall return to its first origin. … [At that time], the lion shall eat harmlessly, and shall no longer seek his prey. The serpent, satisfied with his dust, shall wrap himself in it, and shall no longer hurt by his venomous bite. In a word all that is disordered or confused shall be restored to its proper order. [Commentary on Isaiah]

DECEMBER 24

Shepherds

And in the same region there were shepherds out in the field, keeping watch over their flocks by night. LUKE 2:8

It would have been to no purpose that Christ was born in Bethlehem, if it had not been made known to the world. But the method of doing so, which is described by Luke, appears to human perspective very unsuitable. First, Christ is revealed but to a few witnesses, and that amidst the darkness of night. Again, though God had at His command many honorable and distinguished witnesses, He passed by them and chose shepherds, persons of humble rank and of no account among other people. Here the reason and wisdom of the flesh proves to be foolishness; and we must acknowledge that 'the foolishness of God' (1 Cor. 1:25) excels all the wisdom that exists, or appears to exist in the world. But this too was part of Christ's emptying of Himself (Phil. 2:7), not that any part of Christ's glory should be taken away by it, but that it should lie hidden for a time. Again, as Paul reminds us, the gospel is humble according to the flesh so that our 'faith should stand' in the power of the Spirit, not in 'plausible words of human wisdom,' or in any worldly splendor (2 Cor. 2:4-5). Thus, this inestimable treasure has been deposited by God, from the beginning, 'in jars of clay' (2 Cor. 4:7) so that He might more fully test the obedience of our faith. If then we desire to come to Christ, let us not be ashamed to follow those whom the Lord, in order to cast down the pride of the world, has taken from among the dung of cattle to be our instructors. [Commentary on the Harmony of the Gospels]

DECEMBER 25

True Joy

And the angel said to [the shepherds], 'Fear not, for behold, I bring you good news of great joy that will be for all the people. For unto you is born this day in the city of David a Savior, who is Christ the Lord.'
LUKE 2:10-11

The angel opens his discourse by saying that he announces great joy, that a Savior is born. These words show us, first, that until men and women have peace with God, and are reconciled to Him through the grace of Christ, all the joy that they experience is deceitful and of short duration. Ungodly people frequently indulge in frantic and intoxicating mirth; but if there is no one to make peace between them and God, the hidden stings of conscience must produce fearful torment. Besides, to whatever extent they may flatter themselves in luxurious indulgence, their own lusts serve to torment them. The beginnings of authentic joy is to perceive the fatherly love of God toward us, which alone gives tranquility to our minds. And this 'joy,' in which (Paul tells us) the kingdom of God consists, is 'in the Holy Spirit' (Rom. 14:17). By calling it a 'great joy,' the author shows us, not only that we ought to rejoice above all things in the salvation brought us by Christ, but that this blessing is so great and boundless that it fully compensates for all the pains, distresses, and anxieties of the present life. Let us learn to be so delighted with Christ alone, that the perception of His grace may overcome, and at length remove from us all the distresses of the flesh. [Commentary on the Harmony of the Gospels]

DECEMBER 26

True Peace

And suddenly there was with the angel a multitude of the heavenly host praising God and saying, 'Glory to God in the highest, and on earth peace among those with whom he is pleased!'

LUKE 2:13-14

We must now see what the angels mean by the word 'peace.' They certainly do not speak of an outward peace cultivated by men and women with each other; but they say that the earth is at peace when human beings have been reconciled to God, and enjoy an inward tranquility in their own spirits. We know that we are born 'children of wrath' (Eph. 2:3) and are by nature enemies to God; and must be distressed by fearful dread as long as we feel that God is angry with us. ... We obtain peace with God when He begins to be gracious to us, by taking away our guilt and not imputing to us our trespasses (2 Cor. 5:19), and when we, relying on His fatherly love, address Him with full confidence, and boldly praise Him for the salvation which He has promised to us. ... [O]ur present reality shows that nothing is fuller of trouble than our worldly condition ... yet the angels expressly say that there is 'peace on earth.' This is intended to inform us that, as long as we trust in the grace of Christ, no troubles can arise that will prevent us from enjoying composure and serenity of mind. Let us then remember that faith is seated amidst the storms of temptations, amidst various dangers, amidst violent attacks, amidst contests and fears, so that our faith may not fail or be shaken by any kind of opposition. [Commentary on the Harmony of the Gospels]

DECEMBER 27

Wise Men

Now after Jesus was born in Bethlehem of Judea in the days of Herod the king, behold, wise men from the east came to Jerusalem.

MATTHEW 2:1

This is a very remarkable narrative. God brought wise men from Chaldea, to come to the land of Judea for the purpose of adoring Christ in the stable where He lay, amidst the tokens, not of honor, but of contempt. It was truly God's wonderful purpose that caused the entrance of His Son into the world to be attended by deep humility, and yet bestowed upon Him illustrious ornaments of commendation ... so that our faith might be supplied with everything necessary to prove His divine majesty.

Here we find exhibited a beautiful example of real harmony amidst apparent contradiction. A star from heaven announces that he is a king, to whom a manger, intended for cattle, serves for a throne, because he is refused admittance among the lowest of the people. His majesty shines in the East, while in Judea it is so far from being acknowledged, that it is visited by many marks of dishonor. Why is this? The heavenly Father chose to appoint the star and the wise men as our guides to lead directly to His Son, while He stripped Him of all earthly splendor, for the purpose of informing us that His kingdom is spiritual. This history conveys profitable instructions for us, not only because God brought the wise men to His Son, as the first-fruits of the Gentiles, but also because He appointed the kingdom of His Son to receive their commendation... [Commentary on the Harmony of the Gospels]

DECEMBER 28

Flight to Egypt

Now when they had departed, behold, an angel of the Lord appeared to Joseph in a dream and said, 'Rise, take the child and his mother, and flee to Egypt, and remain there until I tell you, for Herod is about to search for the child, to destroy him.'

MATTHEW 2:13

[T]he angel orders [Joseph] to defend the life of the child by flight and exile. ... We are taught here that God has more than one way of preserving His people. Sometimes He makes astonishing displays of His power; while at other times He employs dark coverings or shadows, from which feeble rays of it escape. This wonderful method of preserving the Son of God under the cross teaches us that people act improperly who prescribe to God a fixed plan of action. Let us permit Him to advance our salvation by a diversity of methods; and let us not refuse to be humbled, that He may more abundantly display His glory. Above all, let us never avoid the cross, by which the Son of God Himself was trained from His earliest infancy. This flight is a part of the foolishness of the cross, but it surpasses all the wisdom of the world. That He may appear at His own time as the Savior of Judea, He is forced to flee from it, and is nourished by Egypt, from which nothing but what was destructive to the Church of God had ever proceeded. Who would not have regarded with amazement such an unexpected work of God? [Commentary on the Harmony of the Gospels]

DECEMBER 29

A World That Rages

The kings of the earth set themselves, and the rulers take counsel together, against the LORD and against his Anointed saying, 'Let us burst their bonds apart and cast away their cords from us.'

PSALM 2:2-3

A twofold consolation may be drawn from this passage. First, as often as the world rages, in order to disturb and put an end to the prosperity of Christ's kingdom, we have only to remember that all of this fulfills of what was long ago predicted, and no changes that can happen will greatly disturb us. Yes, rather it will be highly profitable for us to compare those things which the apostles experienced with what we witness at the present time. Of itself the kingdom of Christ is peaceable, and from it true peace issues forth to the world; but through the wickedness and malice of human beings, [Christ's kingdom] never rises from obscurity into open view without people stirring up disturbances. Nor is it at all strange, or unusual, if the world begins to rage as soon as a throne is erected for Christ. The other consolation which follows is, that when the ungodly have mustered their forces, and when ... they not only pour forth their proud blasphemies, but furiously assault heaven itself, we may safely laugh them to scorn, relying on this one consideration, that He whom they are attacking is the God who is in heaven. When we see Christ almost completely overwhelmed by the number and strength of His enemies, let us remember that they are making war against God over whom they shall not prevail. [Commentary on Psalms]

DECEMBER 30

Sabbath Rest

So then, there remains a Sabbath rest for the people of God, for whoever has entered God's rest has also rested from his works as God did from his.
HEBREWS 4:9-10

This is a definition of that perpetual Sabbath in which there is the highest happiness, where there will be a likeness between human beings and God, to whom they will be united. For whatever the philosophers may have ever said of the chief good, it was nothing but cold and vain, for they limited humans only to themselves, while it is necessary for us to go out of ourselves to find happiness. The chief good of men and women is nothing else but union with God; this is achieved when we are formed according to Him as our example.

Now the Apostle teaches us that this confirmation takes place when we rest from our works. Hence, it follows that men and women experience happiness by self-denial. For what else does it mean to cease from our works than to mortify our flesh – when we renounce ourselves that we may live to God. For here we must always begin, when we speak of a godly and holy life, that men and women ... should allow God to live in them, that they should abstain from their own works, so as to give room for God to work. Indeed, we must confess that our life is rightly formed only when it becomes subject to God. But, due to our inbred corruption, this never happens until we rest from our works. ... Even so, though the completion of this rest cannot be achieved in this life, yet we ought ever to strive for it. Thus, believers enter the Sabbath only on this condition – that by running they may continually go forward. [Commentary on Hebrews]

DECEMBER 31

Running to the End

Therefore, since we are surrounded by so great a cloud of witnesses, let us also lay aside every weight, and sin which clings so closely, and let us run with endurance the race that is set before us.

HEBREWS 12:1

As the author compares [the Christian life] to a race, he bids us to be rightly equipped; for nothing slows us down more than to be encumbered with burdens. Now there are various burdens which delay and impede our spiritual course, such as the love of this present life, the pleasures of the world, the lusts of the flesh, worldly cares, riches also and honors, and other things of this kind. Whoever, then, would run in the course prescribed by Christ, must first disentangle themselves from all these impediments. ...

The meaning of what is said then is this: that we are engaged in a contest, even a most celebrated race; that many witnesses stand around us; that the Son of God is the umpire who invites and exhorts us to secure the prize; and that therefore it would be most disgraceful for us to grow weary or inactive in the midst of our race. And at the same time, that the holy men and women whom he mentioned previously, are not only witnesses, but have been fellow participants in the same race, who have shown us the way beforehand. ... Christ is not only the umpire, but also extends His hand to us, and supplies us with strength and energy; in short, He prepares and fits us to enter on our course, and by His power leads us on to the end of the race. [Commentary on Hebrews]

HERITAGE

Daily Readings

The Puritans

Edited by
Randall J. Pederson

Daily Readings–the Puritans

RANDALL J. PEDERSON

As you draw daily from the wisdom of the Puritans, you will find renewed joy for your daily service. This beautifully presented gift edition has 12 months of readings from Richard Baxter; John Bunyan; Stephen Charnock; Jonathan Edwards; John Flavel; William Gurnall; William Guthrie; Matthew Mead; John Owen; Samuel Rutherford; Thomas Watson; Thomas Vincent.

ISBN: 978-1-8455-0978-1

Daily Readings

George Whitefield

Edited by
Randall J. Pederson

Daily Readings–George Whitefield

RANDALL J. PEDERSON

The first devotional compiled solely from Whitefield's works and provides an excellent introduction to the spirituality of this eighteenth century evangelical. In this carefully edited edition, Randall Pederson has chosen passages based upon George Whitefield's letters and sermons that will encourage, inspire and challenge the reader each day. Bible passages are based upon the ESV.

ISBN: 978-1-8455-0580-6

Daily Readings

Matthew Henry

Edited by
Randall J.
Pederson

Daily Readings–Matthew Henry

RANDALL J. PEDERSON

This beautifully present gift edition is a new selection of Matthew Henry's writings that will nourish your spiritual life. Matthew Henry is one of the best known of our spiritual ancestors. His commentary on the whole Bible is still a staple book for those seeking understanding of God's word to the world. In this carefully edited edition, Randall Pederson has chosen passages that will encourage, inspire and challenge the reader each day. Bible passages are based upon the English Standard Version of the Bible.

ISBN: 978-1-8455-0509-7

Christian Focus Publications

Our mission statement
Staying Faithful

In dependence upon God we seek to impact the world through literature faithful to His infallible Word, the Bible. Our aim is to ensure that the Lord Jesus Christ is presented as the only hope to obtain forgiveness of sin, live a useful life and look forward to heaven with Him.

Our Books are published in four imprints:

⟨OX CHRISTIAN FOCUS

Popular works including biographies, commentaries, basic doctrine and Christian living.

⟨OX MENTOR

Books written at a level suitable for Bible College and seminary students, pastors, and other serious readers. The imprint includes commentaries, doctrinal studies, examination of current issues and church history.

⟨OX CHRISTIAN HERITAGE

Books representing some of the best material from the rich heritage of the church.

⟨OX CF4KIDS

Children's books for quality Bible teaching and for all age groups: Sunday school curriculum, puzzle and activity books; personal and family devotional titles, biographies and inspirational stories – because you are never too young to know Jesus!

Christian Focus Publications Ltd,
Geanies House, Fearn, Ross-shire,
IV20 1TW, Scotland, United Kingdom.
www.christianfocus.com